DATE DUE

AN ILLUSTRATED HISTORY OF THE Horror Film

by Carlos Clarens

CAPRICORN BOOKS NEW YORK

Copyright © 1967 by Carlos Clarens

All rights reserved. This book, or parts thereof, must not be reproduced in any form without permission. Published simultaneously in the Dominion of Canada by Longmans Canada Limited, Toronto.

Library of Congress Catalog Card Number: 67–10951

Fifth Impression

SBN: 399-50111-8

CAPRICORN BOOKS EDITION 1968

The stills illustrating this volume were issued by the original producing companies at the time of the films' release and belong to the author's collection.

PRINTED IN THE UNITED STATES OF AMERICA

Of the many people who contributed to making this book a reality, I must single out for special acknowledgment my mentors here and abroad, William K. Everson and Henri Langlois who *showed* me most of the films I mention; and Edward Connor, William C. Kenly, and Gerald McDonald who *told* me about those I never saw. To them all, my deepest gratitude.

This book is for Helen Weintraub.

56941

CONTENTS

Foreword xi

1. THE WIZARD OF MONTREUIL
   Paris, 1895–1913 1

2. DOUBLES, DEMONS, AND THE DEVIL HIMSELF
   Germany, 1913–1932 9

3. A SILENT CONSPIRACY OF TERROR
   America, 1900–1928 37

4. CHILDREN OF THE NIGHT
   Hollywood, 1928–1947 59

5. THE DEAD NEXT DOOR 105

6. HORROR, THE SOUL OF THE PLOT 111

7. "KEEP WATCHING THE SKY!" 118

8. HORROR AROUND THE WORLD 138

9. NO END TITLE 161

APPENDIX: Cast and Credits of Relevant Films Mentioned in the Text 173

Index 243

"The bogey of violence is particularly horrifying and intolerable to us when we meet it in cold-blood. The arts, however, avoid its brutal impact by their appeal to the emotions, they warm us to its presence, turning terror into enjoyment and cruelty into compassion. We participate in the act of violence without suffering its evil consequences. Art, in fact, allows us, as in certain rituals, to satisfy our Olympian yearning to stimulate the forces of nature. Its non-violent power has a therapeutic and catalystic influence."

Roland Penrose reviewing
Violence in Contemporary Art.

FOREWORD

It would seem logical to suppose that troubled art is born out of troubled times. But it would be wrong to be that simple or systematic about it. What period of history has sailed in, preordained and self-acknowledged a golden age? Edgar Allan Poe existed in a momentary byway of relative peace and security in a new country full of hope, yet his work is limned by the same dark phantoms that haunt E. T. A. Hoffmann's, a writer who lived when Europe was an open field trampled by the Napoleonic Wars. The landscape of the mind does not always correspond to external circumstance. Rather, there seems to be inside us a constant, ever-present yearning for the fantastic, for the darkly mysterious, for the choked terror of the dark. This demand is orthodoxly satisfied by religion or, surreptitiously, by superstition. Unfortunately, the enemies of the surviving religions have not survived with them: in recent times, witches and demons have lost their hold on us. Everything horrible has been swallowed up by the unconscious—that swamp of self-dread from which there emerge many ambiguous manifestations of itself. And these are the black arts of the day.

Those superficial moralists who deplore the tendencies of certain movies to alarm them and in the same breath pretend that film is art would do better to realize that always alongside the art that pleases, "the art of seduction," springs the art of terror. Often we find pleasure in nonpleasurable forms. Next to smiling terracotta couples reclining on top of their Etruscan tombs, to whispering angels with gold-leafed wings, to "The Rape of the Lock" and *The Marriage of Figaro* there have always arisen hair-blanching depictions of the damned, of Saturn devouring his own children, the temptations of St. Anthony, *Wozzeck,* and Man the Wastrel lost to gorgons, dragons, destiny, and death. Moreover, art works that stir the black grue in human experience have a steady unvarying coherence in their emblems and embodiments, while the style patterns of perfect, healthy, happy beauty fluctuate as rapidly as fashion itself and contradict one another's ideal forms according to period and culture. Satan is immutable, it would seem, whether ancestral dark angel or devil in the flesh. Who imagines him today are not the doctors of demonology but the psychiatrist, the anthropologist, the sociologist. To them, horror movies might be seen as a historical imperative, if not an aesthetic necessity. There are myths in these films, ancient and modern, that are as relevant to modern living as the myths of right-thinking, of comfort, and of middle-class patience to be found in family dramas, biblical spectacles, or the Western. There is an ambivalence in human nature familiar to all between love/admiration/ideals and resentments/revulsion/revolt. Often, these are in severe combat when we are forced to cheer on, and at the same time be terrified by, the monsters and fiends of horror films.

Unlike the Western, the horror film has not attracted sufficient critical attention. And yet the latter offers a variety of emotion and a degree of involvement that the former, with its Manichaean simplifications, usually lacks. In dramatizing horror, hero versus villain frequently becomes the villain-as-hero, and the liberty to effect this gives the horror film an edge on "nicer" kinds of movies. We are meant to be frightened by the horror film, and fear, no matter how diluted or sublimated, is still a powerful instrument and the most intense reaction to an experience, aesthetic or otherwise. What seems to put the reviewers off horror films, what prevents them from surrendering their critical resistance, is the frequent—and necessary—depiction of the fantastic. But do we dismiss a painting by Fra Angelico or Max Ernst because we don't, simply won't, believe in angels and sphinxes? Is it indispensable that one be a Christian to read Saint John in Patmos?

I do not believe, as most critics seem to, that people go to horror movies exclusively to be scared. This was conclusively proved, I believe, when the classic American horror films of the thirties began to appear on television almost a decade ago. Things that had made us shiver thirty years ago had lost their power to horrify; yet they now emerged as myths, more powerful than ever before and, indeed, the present popular revival of horror in the various media stems from that time. A supremely violent age like ours calls for unprecedented violence in its aesthetic manifestations: hence the appearance of the Happening, the most characteristic spectacle of the times, with its ritualized violence and forceful, sometimes forced, involvement of the audience. Comic strips have also grown progressively more ferocious. And somewhere between the two-dimensional world of the printed page and the total involvement of the Happening (or other extended kinetic experiences) lies the horror film.

Horror movies have been called all kinds of names, running from incitement to crime to the psychotherapy of the masses. Those that condemn horror movies, along with comic strips and literary thrillers of the more violent type, cogitate under the assumption that consumers of these products are irrevocably bound to commit murder and mayhem. (Heaven knows, the studios would pay a lovely sum to anyone who could establish a direct link between one of their films and an act of violence.) Horror movie fans, like readers of James Bond novels or collectors of *Fantastic Comics,* do not wallow in morbidity because they want to go out and mug, maim, or spill blood, but quite the opposite, because they will not attain such extreme behavior, since they have realized, if any have, their power to exorcize, to sublimate. The flowering of the fantastic in the last century, the period that produced William Blake, Odilon Redon, Gustave Moreau, Gustave Doré, and Robert Louis Stevenson, accompanied the most remarkable strides in the field of science. The more rationalistic a time becomes the more it needs the escape valve of the fantastic. This delicate balance is even more obvious today when the demand for the fantastic (and the horrific) has reached a never before attained height, coinciding with the peak period of scientific technological development. Fantastic art, of which horror films and science fiction are the popular champions, makes us realize that man carries in himself an instinct for destruction, but also the will to curb this instinct.

Whether horror films set out to scare us or elevate what scares us to the status of myths, the movies follow popular taste or at least try to, inasmuch as they are the products of an industry, and are bound to reflect something of the collective unconscious of their audience. It may commonly be that the artistic best does not always coincide with the mythologically most tangible: a film may hit a very definite chord in the public mind and still not be distinguished on any other terms. This could go some distance toward explaining the lack of critical attention or contempt of the critics for the horror film. Also, horror, aesthetic or otherwise, under cool recollection, is depressingly unhorrifying.

In France, most of the movies discussed in this book fall under the rather vague (for Anglo-Saxons) heading of *le fantastique*. Besides horror films, *le fantastique* includes such titles as *Alice in Wonderland* and *The Wizard of Oz,* while excluding the more earthbound thrillers that carry no supernatural implications. I am aware of the shortcomings of "horror films" as a designation—the term unavoidably carries its connotation of repulsion and disgust—but it is the one sanctioned by usage and the best available in English. Yet, in writing about horror films, I have occasionally included for illustrative purposes a fantastic movie that contains little or no horror. I have not singled out, however, serials such as Feuillade's *Les Vampires* or Universal's *Flash Gordon,* although their mention crops up in the text several times. Despite the fact that it contains some delightful moments of near-fantasy, *Les Vampires* is unshakably (and in spite of its masked hoods and hooded vamps) on the side of light: its essence is poetry and movement and one would look in vain for the dark undertow of, say, the Fritz Lang serials, which are included. As for *Flash Gordon,* it is pure prewar science fiction, utterly devoid of anxiety, a superior adventure romance. But my respect for the serial excludes its inclusion here as a mere appendage to the horror film.

As far as the quality of experience, or re-experience, is concerned, television by its very nature seems to operate directly in opposition to the effect intended by horror films, which require as indispensable the personal compact between spectator and the unraveling action in the preternatural darkness of the theater. (This is also something of a ritual.) It is asking a lot to expect to be moved or shocked in one's own home, where the cognizance that one can escape to the next room instantly dissolves tension. The theater spectator has but two choices: either he watches the movie (and thus sits there and takes it) or else he gets up and goes (or falls asleep which is another way of walking out on a movie). This rapport between spectator and spectacle is nonexistent in viewing television and, not gainsaying the relative excellence of *The Outer Limits, The Eleventh Hour,* or *The Twilight Zone,* for this reason the mapping of that already considerable territory belongs elsewhere.

Film is an immensely rich, free-flowing, and disorganized medium. Our period is one of systematic classification and not unappropriately, this chronicle closes with *Alphaville.* As we tend to pigeonhole the enormous mass of film laid at our disposal through seventy years of industry, we apply to movies the strict rules and superficial restrictions of genre headings, when horror films (and Westerns) at their best obey no rules and transcend the limitations we impose on them. Let me be the first to realize that such a staggering number of movies can wreak havoc on any serious attempt at theorizing. Most movies have their own voices, and none of them was created to support a single aesthetic or theory.

THE CONQUEST OF THE POLE

The Giant of the Snows swallows one of the expeditioners in Georges Méliès' 1912 fantasy, one of the first shock moments offered by the movies.

THE CABINET OF DR. CALIGARI

Conrad Veidt, as Cesare the Somnambulist, abducts Jane, played by Dagover, in the Expressionistic sensation of 1920.

DEMONS, DEVIL:

Osgood Perkins as a New England Satan prepares to instill life into a scarecrow in *Puritan Passions* (1923).

A later version of a Yankee devil: Walter Huston as Mr. Scratch offers to buy James Craig's soul in *All That Money Can Buy* (1941).

The revolt of the angels in the prologue of *The Sorrows of Satan* (1925), directed by D. W. Griffith.

Werner Krauss as Scapinelli, the brigand from Hell, in *The Student of Prague* (1926).

A demon without a name as it appeared in *Night of the Demon* (1958).

The Witches' Sabbath staged for the classic *Witchcraft Through the Ages* (1920). The director Benjamin Christensen appears on the right as a fat, jolly devil.

THE RITES OF LUCIFER

Paul Wegener as the Master of the Revels delivers Alice Terry to the God Pan himself, played by Stowitts, in *The Magician* (1926).

Satan's Throne Room as depicted in *Seven Footprints to Satan* (1929).

Boris Karloff conducts a Black Mass in *The Black Cat* (1934).

Hazel Court offers herself to the Evil One in *Masque of the Red Death* (1964).

VISIONS OF THE PIT

These fanciful views of Hell were the high point of *Dante's Inferno* (1924).

Hades does not change. In the 1935 *Dante's Inferno,* the damned writhed in the same flames, albeit less clad.

DR. JEKYLL AN

Robert Louis Stevenson's novella remains the most oft-filmed horror story. In 1920, John Barrymore sacrificed his famous profile to play Mr. Hyde as a debauched roué.

Fredric March tormented Miriam Hopkins in the 1932 version.

In *The Testament of Dr. Cordelier* (1961), Hyde became Monsieur Opale, played with Chaplinesque impudence by Jean-Louis Barrault.

In 1941, Spencer Tracy managed the transition with hardly any makeup, relying instead on facial expressions.

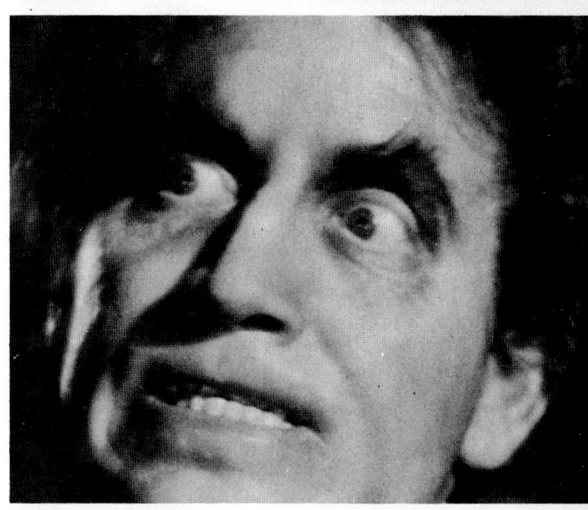

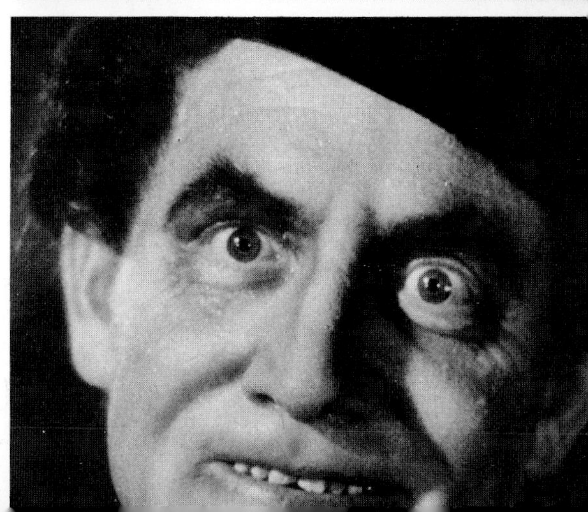

Lon Chaney as Eric the Phantom in the 1925 classic.

Chaney leads Mary Philbin, as Christine, into his underground lair.

Claude Rains remained discreetly masked throughout most of the 1943 remake.

The superfiend had degenerated into a seedy, potty composer, played by Herbert Lom, in the 1962 British version.

FRANKENSTEIN AN

The first version of Mary Shelley's *Frankenstein* was made in 1910 and featured Charles Ogle as the Monster.

Boris Karloff made the part forever his in the 1931 production, the most famous horror movie ever made.

HE GOLEM

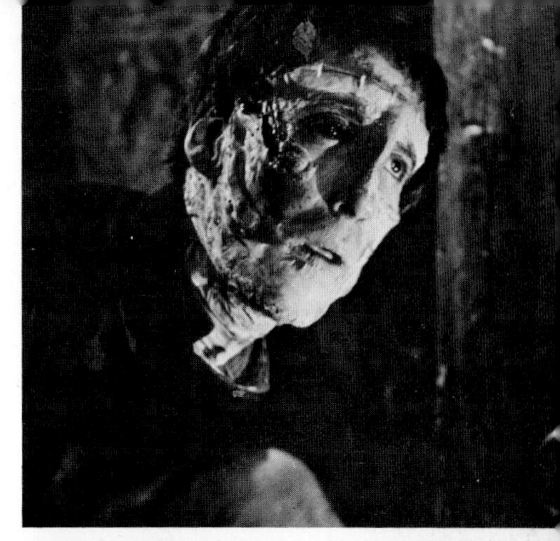

Christopher Lee in the British version of 1957, *The Curse of Frankenstein.*

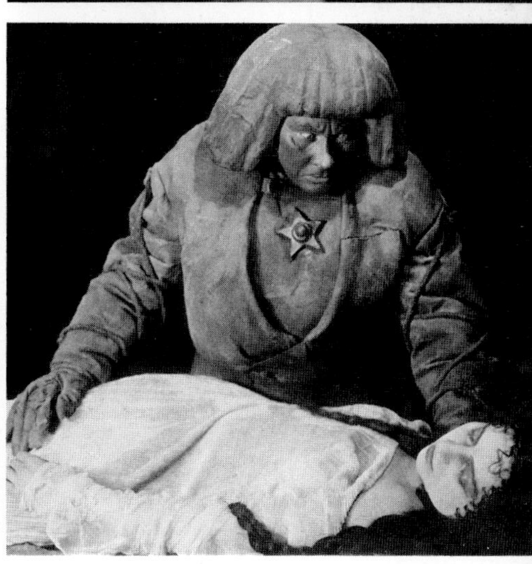

The mighty Golem of Jewish tradition was brought to life in several German films that featured Paul Wegener as the living clay statue. He appears here in the 1920 version.

CREATION OF A HUMANOID

The creation of the artificial Maria in Fritz Lang's *Metropolis* (1926). Rudolph Klein-Rogge as Rotwang the Mad Scientist, Alfred Abel as the Master of Metropolis, and Brigitte Helm as the two Marias.

CHAPTER 1

THE WIZARD OF MONTREUIL

Paris, 1895–1913

The muses were late for the birth of the movies. At first it seemed such a wonder when the figures really moved, when the trains actually roared silently past the camera eye (which we naturally made our own) that very little else was demanded of the invention in its first two years. Photographs that moved! The camera looked upon the everyday and returned it, fresh and silvery, to the screens of the world. City streets, city squares, workers, and cyclists. It was the real world of *la Belle Époque* and the Gay Nineties, captured forever, on celluloid in light.

But there was another world locked inside the Edison Kinetoscope and the Cinématographe Lumière, a veritable Pandora's box of marvels and horrors, waiting to be released. If there had been no good fairies attendant on the cradle of the cinema, there was at least a first-rate magician. He came from the ancient realm of the fantastic, the stage, which in the later years of the nineteenth century had become the last refuge of dragons, sorcerers, and magic. With the help of electricity, pantomime could go no further nor do any better: Mephisto would materialize in a puff of smoke, *daemon-ex-machina*. Cinderella's coach would change into a pumpkin in the wink of an eye, the time of a blackout. The last decade before the appearance of the motion picture saw the art of stage fantasy reach a perfection that was in itself a dead end. The stage was set to receive the film.

On the evening of December 27, 1895, the brothers Louis and Auguste Lumière invited a select group of Parisians to attend an advance showing of their invention, the *Cinématographe,* at the Indian Salon of the Grand Café at 14 Boulevard des Capucines. The program, scheduled to be shown the next day to a paying audience, lasted only a few minutes and the most impressive items in it were the arrival of a locomotive at a train station and a one-gag film about a mischievous little boy pinching a garden hose and relaxing his grip as the unsuspecting gardener inspects the nozzle, thereby releasing a spurt of water in the man's face. The first claims on the film were thus made by the documentary and the comedic.

Among the invited audience there was Georges Méliès, a stage magician of great reputation and the director of a popular theater named after the dean of French illusionists, Robert Houdin, the same Houdin who inspired Erich Weiss of Appleton, Wisconsin, to seek world fame under the stage name of Houdini. Méliès was the last of the line of French "white magicians," conjurers who rejected any claim of the supernatural in their work. Wanting to interpolate moving pictures between the various vaudeville and conjuring acts, Méliès approached the inventors' father after the show had ended to ask about the cost of such an enterprise. "The cinema is an invention without a future" was Lumière *père's* discouraging advice.

Undeterred, Méliès went ahead and bought an English camera and an abundant supply of film stock. The first films he made were done in imitation of the Lumières: card players, bicycle riders, strollers. These sun-drenched scenes, often recalling the paintings of Manet, were shown at the Robert-Houdin. But between 1896 and 1897, more than a dozen halls had opened in the center of Paris. Movies were in great demand and, despite Father Lumière's pessimism, they were fast becoming a highly profitable proposition.

The magician in Méliès soon rebelled against a medium that seemed to exclude poetry, fantasy, and unbridled imagination. Surely, he thought, the motion picture could be used for something more than the mere recording of reality. An accident revealed the way: one day, while filming a street scene in front of the

Paris Opera, the camera jammed and the flow of film was interrupted for a few seconds. When he viewed the developed film later on, Méliès was astounded to see a bus change into a hearse. Film had stopped while time had not. This wonderfully macabre metamorphosis was the genesis of all film trickery. The fantastic film had been born.

Then, on May 4, 1897, a terrible fire broke out during a film performance at the Charity Bazaar in Paris. Two hundred members of Parisian society died in it, and film attendance began to decline, not only in Europe but in the United States as well, where such accidents were to continue well into the twentieth century. If the infant invention survived this baptism of fire, it may have been due in great part to the showmanship of Méliès; the public had soon wearied of travelogues, historical reconstructions, and faked reportages, the staple of early Lumière and Edison programs. But Méliès was to bring to the crowds "dramas, comedies, vaudeville, operas and operettas, *visual tricks and fantastic voyages.*" Méliès refused to copy nature; instead he built in the Paris suburb of Montreuil the first movie studio in the world, with walls and ceiling made of glass and equipped with all kinds of stage facilities, such as trapdoors and scrim curtains, which had become fully developed for pantomime performances throughout the nineteenth century. After the accidental discovery of trick photography, his own sensibility steered him away from the dreary topicality of his competitors and he ventured deep into the realm of the imaginative. He started writing complex scenarios, planning their execution in advance and filming them in logical order. In so doing, he became the first movie *director,* a recognition that came to him late in life. For the beginning few years, however, he was to earn such titles as the King of Fantasmagoria, the Jules Verne of the Cinema, the Magician of the Screen.

To Méliès, the camera became a machine to register the world of dreams and the supernatural, the mirror to enter Wonderland. In 1896, he made a woman disappear into thin air without the help of a trapdoor; he simply stopped the camera long enough for the lady to step out of range. For *Battleship Maine,* he achieved an underwater effect by taking pictures through a large fish tank placed in front of a backdrop representing the sunken hull of the

Maine and in front of which actors in diving suits were made to emote. Double exposure was used in *The Haunted Cave* (1898) and multiple exposure in *The One Man Band* (1900), where Méliès himself appeared simultaneously in seven roles. Running the film backward, he achieved *An Impossible Deshabillé.* Fast, slow, and stop motion were brought to a high polish, as well as the gradual appearance or disappearance of the image (the fade) and the slow transition from one image to another (the dissolve). Most of these techniques were common practice among commercial photographers of the day and some of them had already been employed by the film-makers, yet Méliès seemed to make them very much his own, and for years afterward they were still referred to as "white magic" or "the Méliès effect."

Méliès alternated his *féeries*—as he called his fantasy films—with journalistic movies like his restaging of *The Dreyfus Case* or actual newsreels like *The Funeral of President Faure.* His flights of fancy were unequaled: *The Devil's Manor, Faust and Marguerite, Pygmalion and Galatea, The Man with Four Heads, The Devil in a Convent,* and the magic flame episode from Sir Rider Haggard's *She.* These films ran from less than a minute to under half an hour and were usually colored frame by frame. They were all surpassed by *Cinderella* (1899) whose "twenty artificially arranged scenes" sealed the doom of theatrical pantomime. How could the living stage hope to match the realism of the movie's fantastic effects? The entire bag of tricks of Méliès' repertory was dazzlingly deployed: a pumpkin was transformed by stop motion into a coach, the heroine's rags dissolved into a radiant ball gown, ballet dancers defied gravity through slow motion, and comedy was enhanced by reverse action or fast motion. But Méliès went even further with *A Trip to the Moon* (1902), now recognized as his masterpiece and one of the outstanding achievements of the first film decade. It was first shown to the public in a small film theater on the fairgrounds of the Place du Trône in Paris. Méliès himself had hastily executed the poster that showed a grimacing moon with a rocket sticking out of its eye. The film's success—doubted in advance by prospective buyers on the basis of its inordinate length and the novelty of the subject—was instantaneous and soon spread from Europe to America, where dozens of copies were illegally "duped" from the three prints Méliès had sold to his American agents. These unauthorized copies were issued through several film exchanges and, to curb this practice, Méliès was prompted to include a copyright notice for his firm, Star Film, in almost every frame. Since the copyright office required that a positive print on photographic paper be deposited for every entry, some of Méliès' best work was saved from destruction and preserved for posterity.

A Trip to the Moon derives in part from Jules Verne's *From Earth to the Moon* and H. G. Wells' *First Men in the Moon,* but the satirical wit and imaginative trappings were all Méliès' own. The film carries no titles whatsoever, relying on the visual to tell a more complex story than usual. In thirty minutes and sixteen scenes, it follows a scientific expedition from Earth to the moon and back. It is, then, the movies' first venture into science fiction and interplanetary travel; today it appears as a heady mixture of surrealism, humor, stage pantomime, and one amazing instant of pure cinema thinking. As the rocket is fired from the giant cannon atop the Paris roofs, the film cuts to the spaceship (in miniature) traveling against a painted backdrop of the sky, then cuts to the moon from viewpoint of the cosmonauts, getting larger and larger, and finally there is a cut or fast dissolve to the moon's face, wincing in pain as the bulletlike ship enters the eye. The audience is jolted out of the customary "orchestra center" viewpoint and drawn right along into the adventure.

From then on, invention never flags. When the Earthlings bed for the night on the surface of the moon, we see the Earth rise romantically in the sky. When they dream of heavens to conquer, the skies appear peopled with girls in Grecian garb to represent the various constellations, a chorus girl in tights sitting on a crescent while an old man peeks out from Saturn. An umbrella stuck in the soil of the moon takes root and grows like a giant mushroom. As the scientists descend into one of the moon's craters, they are met by the exuberant foliage of a Rousseau painting. The Selenites themselves, with their bird heads and lobster claws, could be sinister, yet, as played by a troupe of acrobats from the Folies Bergère, they are instead comical and knockabout, three new ones springing from every one that bites the dust. Indeed, Méliès announced that "there is not the least action in the film which would be obnoxious or shock the most sensitive audience." In general, Méliès seems to eschew the horrors of the Grand Guignol, then rampant on the Paris stage. Yet there is one chilling exception to this in his *The Conquest of the Pole* (1912), when the Abominable Giant of the Snows devours a member of the polar expedition. Although the Giant is a customary carnival figure, the total effect is gruesomely realistic.

The fantastic universe of Méliès could only exist within the glass walls of his studio and never again would his camera look upon a real landscape. Instead, it was Lilliput and Fairyland, Crusoe's island, the bottom of the ocean, and the North Pole—all designed by the master and executed under his supervision. Once the sets were painted, in all the shades of gray required by monochromatic film stock, they would be populated by ballet girls from the Châtelet Theater, music-hall performers, second-rank actors, and members of the family. The plum roles, such as conjurers, scientists, or the Devil would go to Méliès himself.

These were the vintage years. From the dream factory outside the gates of Paris issued *The Impossible Voyage* in 1904, a wild and wooly journey to the sun that contains a spectacular train wreck and seems closer in spirit to Edward Lear than to Verne. In 1907, it was *Tunneling the English Channel,* in which Edward VII of England and President Falguières of France dream (jointly) of an underwater tunnel between Dover and Calais. *The Merry Frolics of Satan* of the same year, is Méliès at his Surrealist best and contains, according to the catalogue of Star Films, "fifty new tricks, especially the extraordinary and phenomenal odyssey of the apocalyptic horse and the astral coach." *The Merry Frolics,* however, already points the way to Méliès' decline. Originally a long-running pantomime at the Châtelet, the entire production was recreated at Montreuil and simply embellished with trick photography. It remains stagebound in manner, betraying all of Méliès' shortcomings. The innovator of 1902 had become something of a curiosity by 1908. He seemed incapable of taking the next giant step, as others had, in particular the American Edwin S. Porter whose *The Life of an American Fireman* (1902) and *The*

Great Train Robbery (1903) pulsate with pure cinematic life. And films everywhere were acquiring a new sophistication. When, in 1909, both the Edison and Biograph companies released in New York their versions of *The Devil,* from the play popularized by George Arliss, audiences were confronted by an urbane gentleman in top hat and evening clothes, who went about his devilish business in a very elegant manner. A far cry from Méliès' Mephisto! In the same patronizing manner in which a modern reviewer might dismiss a cartoon, an American reviewer condescended at the time: "Méliès' films can always be counted to please a certain element of the audience and especially the children, who become spellbound by the magic and clever effects produced by this master of trick photography."

But for adult audiences with a taste for the macabre there was a welter of literary adaptations. In the spring of 1908, the Selig Polyscope Company of Chicago released *Dr. Jekyll and Mr. Hyde,* the first of many versions of the Robert Louis Stevenson novella, which had also served as the basis for the Richard Mansfield play of eleven years before. Another film thriller, *Sherlock Holmes and the Great Murder Mystery* was inspired by Poe's *Murders in the Rue Morgue,* and Edison adapted the same writer's *System of Dr. Tarr and Professor Fether,* removing all traces of horror and releasing it as a comedy under the title of *Lunatics in Power.*

Practically forced out of the American market by Edison, forced to release his films in France through Pathé, Méliès and Star Films went bankrupt in 1913 on the eve of the Great War which he had foreseen five years before in his *Civilization Through the Ages.* The Montreuil studio had to be sold and during the war, the army—which Méliès had criticized in *The Dreyfus Case*—requisitioned the company's warehouse. The negatives of many masterworks were either destroyed by a despondent Méliès or sold to a chemical manufacturer for their silver nitrate.

By the end of the twenties, Méliès had become a forgotten man. Discovered selling toys at the Gare Montparnasse, he was brought back to the limelight, his films revived, their value recognized and their creator acclaimed by the Surrealists as their spiritual father. A project was conceived to remake *Baron Munchausen,* one of Méliès' 1911 films, with the German Hans Richter as director and the grand old man as production designer and general supervisor. But the film was never made. Méliès retired with a small pension to a rest home near Orly and there he died at the age of 77 in 1938, after receiving the homage of fellow film artists such as D. W. Griffith, René Clair, Charles Chaplin, and Jean Cocteau.

Ghoulies, ghosties, all things that go bump on the screen, are forever in his debt.

CHAPTER 2

DOUBLES, DEMONS, AND THE DEVIL HIMSELF

Germany, 1913–1932

The nightmare world of the Gothic novel usually came to a logical end in the last chapter. With the light of dawn came the reasonable explanation for the supernatural events of the night. The shroud of mystery was pulled aside: cadavers turned out to be wax figures, the ghosts themselves were revealed as bandits, and the mysterious sounds were traced to an unhappy lover's mandolin. Our disbelief, suspended through the unraveling of the intrigue, was shatteringly restored in the closing pages.

And then Matthew Gregory Lewis intruded into the polite terror of Ann Radcliffe and Clara Reeve. His novel, *The Monk,* a tale of real horrors that was to win him the admiration of Coleridge, the friendship of Byron, and the praises of the Marquis de Sade, opened the door to the *Schauerromane,* the German "shudder novels" with their malignant catalogue of necromancy, diabolism, catalepsy, vampirism, and unbridled sensuality. These Teutonic folk tales and ghost stories seemed to issue from the darker recesses of the soul or, more accurately, from the lower depths of the subconscious which the Victorians had almost successfully repressed. Almost but not quite. For its influence was soon to be felt in the works of Wilkie Collins, R. L. Stevenson, and Sheridan Le Fanu, finding across the ocean a melancholy echo in Poe and Hawthorne. The nineteenth–century "penny dreadful" and the modern mystery novel are also descendants of the *Schauerromane.*

It is not surprising, then, that the first flowering of the horror film appears in Germany, land of dark forests and darker myths. The arts of each country feed on its own folk tales and legends. The German cinema of the early part of the century, after fumbling through a period of crude peasant humor and sentimental drama, found its way to the fantastic.

In 1913, early as that may seen, a German film company visited Prague to shoot some scenes on location for *The Student of Prague,* a variation on the theme of the *doppelgänger* or "double" that seems to preoccupy the Germans to a larger degree than it does any other nationality. Borrowing from E. T. A. Hoffmann's *The Sand Merchant* as well as from Poe's *William Wilson,* the writer Hanns Heinz Ewers had concocted the tale of Baldwin, an ambitious student in love with a highborn lady, who signs away his mirrored reflection to a mysterious mountebank, Scapinelli, in return for riches and power. Whereupon, Baldwin's reflection leaves him. The student achieves his heart's desire but is constantly haunted by his image, who follows him around in the night and even fights a duel for him, killing a rival for the lady's hand. Obsessed with fear, Baldwin lures "the other" to the old garret and there fires his pistol at him. A mirror is smashed and the student falls dead. Scapinelli appears and tears up the contract. In destroying the evil in his nature, Baldwin has also destroyed himself. And Scapinelli, Satan himself, has collected his soul.

Fortunately this remarkable picture has survived two European wars. It remains quite an achievement for a country as backward (in terms of cinema) as Germany was then. *The Student of Prague* was directed by a Dane, Stellan Rye, who succeeded in breaking away from studio interiors, filming many of its scenes in the tortuous alleys of the old quarter or on an ancient bridge dominated by the cathedral tower. The famous Jewish cemetery was reconstructed in a nearby forest when the Hebrew community of Prague refused to allow a movie to be made on their hallowed grounds. The final showdown between Baldwin and his alter ego, in a studio set representing the garret, is beautifully lit in "the Rembrandt manner." The use of double exposure, albeit crude, confers on these scenes a quality exclusive to the film: no amount of stage trickery can make an actor appear as two people at the same moment. The innocent tricks of Méliès are now seen in a sinister new light. Finally, the film gains immeasurably from the restraint of Paul Wegener, who played Baldwin and, of course, his reflection.

Born in Prussia in 1874, this massive actor with timeless Tartar features had played classical roles in Max Reinhardt's Deutsches Theater since 1906, among them Macbeth and Mercutio. He was that rarity, a stage performer with an instinctive flair for the film. Wegener was also quite knowledgeable about German myths and legends and later was to make a speciality of filming fairy tales (the *Märchenfilme*) like *The Pied Piper of Hamelin.* He married five times, and for thirty years his was one of the great names of the German stage. Like John Barrymore, he was to play *Svengali* in the movies and *Richard the Third* on stage. Also like Barrymore, his taste in roles ran to the bizarre, the twisted, the demonic.

While in Prague during the filming of *The Student of Prague,* Wegener came into direct contact with the legend of the Golem, that popular figure of Jewish tradition, "the body without a soul" fashioned from clay by Rabbi Judah Low Ben Bezalel, the great Talmudic scholar of the sixteenth century, in order to defend the Hebrew community of Prague against a pogrom, after false charges of ritual child murders had lost them the emperor's favor. In the old quarter of the city stood the twin statues of the Golem and its creator; rumor persisted that the original statue was hidden away in the attic of the Altneu synagogue. Gustav Meyrink, the Austrian writer who was to set down a modern version of the tale in 1916, was convinced that "something that cannot die haunts this quarter of the city and is somehow connected with the legend of the Golem." This chapter of Jewish folklore so fascinated Wegener, who was a Gentile, that he was to turn to it three times during his career.

Wegener and his screenwriter Henrik Galeen jointly directed the first version of *Der Golem* in 1915, Wegener himself playing the title role. The story was given a new twist: a group of workmen excavating the site of an old synagogue discovers the clay figure of the Golem. An antiquarian buys it from them and with the help of some cabalistic texts brings it to life again. The giant becomes the antiquarian's docile servant, but the old man does not know that the Golem should be brought to life only to accomplish certain noble tasks. Otherwise, his strength and power will become as uncontrollable as a force of nature. The Golem falls in love with the master's daughter but she, naturally, turns away in horror. The monster goes on a rampage and is finally destroyed when he falls from a tower. Wegener brought the Golem back to life for an encore, *Der Golem und die Tänzerin* (*The Golden and the Dancing Girl*) in 1917. All that seems to remain of both films are the still photographs, showing Wegener in his grotesque makeup and costume—the sculptured wig, heavy boots, and doublet with the engraved Star of David in its middle.

The Golem arrived in America under the title of *The Monster of Fate.* It opened in New York the same week the United States broke off diplomatic relations with Germany. The picture's career was a short one, yet it was still fondly remembered by critics years later when postwar German films were making a new bid for the American market. In 1917, Wegener devoted his attention to a subject safely devoid of racial overtones, directing a heavily Teutonic film version of *The Pied Piper of Hamelin,* which nevertheless had charming costumes and acceptable trick photography. But Wegener did not forget the Golem.

As is true of Mary Shelley's *Frankenstein* (which she subtitled *The Modern Prometheus*), the origins of the Golem legend can be traced back to the Greek myth of Prometheus, the titan who, according to certain versions, stole heavenly fire from the gods to infuse life into his own creation. Like the Golem, the man Prometheus created was a compound of the four elements: fire and water, earth and air. During the Middle Ages, these became the instruments of the alchemist, whose highest goals were the discovery of the philosophers' stone (which transmutes metals into gold) and the creation of the homunculus.

The most popular German film of the war years borrowed from all of these themes. Released in six parts, each lasting about one hour, *Homunculus* had for its hero an unnatural being, artificially created in a laboratory, who grows up to be a superman both in intellect and in moral nature but who, upon discovering his true origin, becomes a malevolent creature bringing disaster to those around him. In five of the parts, although his evil designs were thwarted, he still managed to escape retribution; at the end of the sixth, however, nature takes a hand in the affair and a bolt of lightning, no less, destroys the Homunculus. The films were directed by Otto Rippert who, surprisingly, cast a Danish matinee idol named Olaf Fønss in the title role. Somberly dressed but devoid of horrific makeup, and playing with untypical restraint, Fønss made the Homunculus as popular a figure in Germany as less ambiguous serial heroes were in France and the United States.

The end of the war plunged Germany into a period of social, political, and spiritual upheaval that was to be reflected in the spheres of philosophy, music, poetry, and the visual arts, all of which thrived after the war. For, although despoiled of provinces and colonies and headed for bankruptcy and inflation, Germany in 1918 was not the devastated nation of 1945. The short-lived Weimar Republic, which had succeeded the German Empire, was the first really democratic government the country had known.

It was a period of artistic unrest, especially among the younger generation coming out of the war, who rebelled against the stifling complacency of nineteenth-century ideas as embodied in art and literature by Impressionism and Naturalism. The malcontent rallied under the banner of Expressionism, a term that had echoed through European art circles since 1911 when it was coined by critics to describe the works of certain painters of the French school (such as Cézanne, Matisse, and Van Gogh) and a new group of German poets.

Unrestrained, violently emotional, and often pessimistic (the Expressionist poets had foreseen the war as early as 1911), the new movement sought to restore man to the center of things in direct opposition to the old tenets whereby matter and nature reigned supreme. Accordingly, everything—objects, light, the universe itself—had to be reshaped according to man's individual vision. This intensely subjective view of life was to flourish first in the field of lyric poetry and was soon to spread to all the arts including the theater whose language became poetically concentrated, so much so that actors had to evolve a corresponding style, one of "dynamic synthesis," a system of highly condensed attitudes from which all intermediate gestures had been removed.

As Expressionistic drama reached its peak, dialogue became succinct ideologues, similar to the printed subtitles of silent films. And consequently, acting came close to pantomime. The boundaries of the two dramatic media became hazy. The ultimate concentration of acting so desired by the Expressionists could clearly be found in the film. In return, the German film had found in Expressionism the style required to render in black and white the reawakened fantasies of the darkly romantic German soul.

In 1919, two young men named Hans Janowitz and Carl Mayer approached Erich Pommer, director of the Decla (Deutsches Eclair) Film Company of Berlin, with an original film script which Pommer immediately bought for less than $200. Like Franz Kafka and Rainer Maria Rilke, Janowitz came from Prague, a city that still haunted his vision. Mayer was a brilliant Austrian poet who thought in visual terms and who was destined never to write for a dramatic medium other than the film. The story they sold to Pommer sprang not only from their personal experience but also from the deeper collective feeling of despair the Great War had left behind. According to his *Three Chapters from Hamburg*, Janowitz had found the inspiration in a sex murder of 1913. Strolling one evening along the Reeperbahn in Hamburg, he saw a respectable-looking middle-class gentleman emerge from behind some bushes; next day the papers carried an item about a girl raped and murdered on the very same spot. Janowitz became convinced the bourgeois was the actual killer; he attended the victim's funeral and there he glimpsed his suspect again. The murderer was never discovered and Janowitz became obsessed by the thought of the many murderers freely roaming the city streets. Years later, he met Mayer, recently discharged from the army and still smarting after several unpleasant incidents with an army psychiatrist who attributed his rebellious attitude to mental imbalance. Inspired by Wegener's films, they wrote a script, bitter with the memories of four years of war and repression, dealing with a traveling hypnotist and his murderous tool, a somnambulist. The name of the principal character was taken from Stendhal's

Unknown Letters. They called the story *The Cabinet of Dr. Caligari.*

Pommer, the shrewdest film impresario in Berlin, decided to produce it and entrusted the direction to his top man, the Austrian Fritz Lang who was enthusiastic about the idea and suggested for the leading lady a lovely Java-born actress named Lil Dagover, who had played Madame Butterfly in one of his films. But soon it became apparent that Lang would not find the time to direct *Caligari,* occupied as he was with a lengthy serial, *The Spiders.* He recommended instead Robert Wiene, who had directed several movies without particular success, but who was conversant with Berlin's artistic circles. Pommer's decorators and costume designers, drawn from the avant-garde group known as *Der Sturm,* suggested distorted sets in the Cubistic manner, not only because it would make the film a timely conversation piece but also because electricity was an expensive commodity in postwar Berlin and a canvas set with painted shadows was a money-saving device. The painters Hermann Warm and Walter Röhrig were responsible for the celebrated decor and Walter Reimann designed the simple, matching costumes: black leotards for the somnambulist, white for the heroine, a slightly grotesque outfit for Caligari, that seemed to step out of a period illustration of Hoffmann's *Tales.*

As Caligari, Pommer chose Werner Krauss, who was under contract to Decla but had also worked for impresario Max Reinhardt at the justly famous Deutsches Theater. Conrad Veidt, another Reinhardt actor who had already appeared in many films, was selected to play Cesare the Somnambulist. The film was made for under $20,000 at a period of devaluated marks. Before it was completed, Wiene suggested a script change that the authors regarded as a betrayal of their basic intention, an indictment of Germany's ruling class who had sent the country's youth to the holocaust. But now, the core of the film would be framed by a prologue and an epilogue showing that the story issued from a madman's lips. Mayer's and Janowitz's message of anarchy was stifled and instead, the film preached acceptance of discipline and authority.

It opens with two men sitting in a slightly stylized garden. The older man mutters: "Spirits have driven me from home and hearth." A beautiful girl, Jane, walks like a wraith past the two. Francis, the younger one, identifies her as his betrothed, adding: "What I have experienced with her is stranger than anything you have encountered." Francis' tale unfolds on the screen:

The town of Holstenwall is celebrating its fair, and a traveling hypnotist, Doctor Caligari, applies for permission to exhibit his creature, a somnambulist named Cesare, on the fairgrounds. The town clerk grants it, but not before he rudely humiliates the evil-looking doctor. That night, the clerk is murdered in his room. Next day, Francis and his friend Alan take Jane to the fair. They are attracted to Caligari's tent where the sleeping Cesare, roused to a few moments of wakefulness, answers questions about the future. "How long shall I live?" asks Alan. "Until dawn" is the chilling answer. That night, Cesare breaks into Alan's room and kills him. Francis begins to suspect that the murders are the handiwork of the sleeping man and tries to prove it. In the meantime, Caligari sends out Cesare to murder Jane. The somnambulist steals into the girl's bedroom but finds himself incapable of destroying the lovely girl. He abducts her instead, fleeing over roof and field; and, pursued by the townspeople, he dies of exhaustion. Francis discovers that Caligari is the head of a nearby insane asylum. He finds a diary explaining how he became so obsessed with a medieval sorcerer who journeyed through Europe with a somnambulist completely under his control that he decided to emulate him. When Francis confronts the doctor with Cesare's dead body, Caligari becomes violent and has to be put in a straitjacket.

The original story began and ended with Francis' tale. Wiene added an epilogue in which the garden at the outset is now revealed as part of the asylum where Francis is an inmate. The young man is thrown into a fit of hysteria at the sight of the head psychiatrist, a benign-looking Caligari, who announces to his colleagues that since he now knows the nature of Francis' delusions, he will be able to cure him. Among the patients at the institution, we glimpse Cesare and Jane. The film ends with an ambiguous shot of Caligari's face.

Caligari opened in Berlin in the spring of 1920 and its Expressionistic sets and costumes impressed the critics. The film did not immediately enjoy the acclaim it was later to receive, but Pommer devised an intriguing publicity campaign, papering Berlin with posters, hypnotically inviting the public, "You must be a

Caligari!" Even the subtitles—scribbled by hand instead of printed—were widely discussed; and Cesare's reply ("Until Dawn") became as famous as "War's Peace," Griffith's wry comment on the aftermath of war in *Birth of a Nation*.

Because of *Caligari*, French theaters lifted their ban on German films and the Paris opening had the critics reaching for new adjectives, one of which, Caligarism, was coined and bandied about to describe anything distorted or bizarre. Film historians, however, quickly unearthed a precedent of sorts in *La Folie du Docteur Tube* (*The Madness of Doctor Tube*), a French film directed by Abel Gance in 1915, containing several scenes photographed through a special distorting lens to depict certain psychological states. In April, 1921, the film opened in New York, where it was received with a mixture of awe and confusion, the picture's style being labeled anything from "Impressionistic" to "Cubistic" and justified by the fact that it represented "A madman's vision of the world." (But then, why is the epilogue, after order and discipline have been restored, in the same Expressionistic manner?) A reviewer justified the unrealistic acting (by American standards) stating that "the ghostly performers were suspended by wires." The most informed among them, however, saw in *Caligari* "a revelation of what the motion picture is capable of as a form of artistic expression." The crowds that filled the Criterion Theater, attracted by the film's *succès de scandale*, often reacted with whistles and hoots, evidence of traditional American disgust for the avant-garde. The film's advocates claimed that motion pictures were mired in the tradition of Griffith and Ince and that *Caligari* was to redeem them. This rather bold prophecy never came true, but *Caligari* remained the most talked-about film of the twenties until the advent of *Battleship Potemkin* (1925).

What the film undoubtedly accomplished was a break in the naturalistic progress of the cinema. For a quarter of a century, the cinema's first concern—aside from such exceptions as Méliès—was the photographic reproduction of reality. What the theater could not reach, the film easily grasped: a field would be a real field, a street a credible reproduction of a street. *Caligari* leaned toward abstraction, looking for its inspiration in painting, sculpture, even music (the film was twice as effective when accompanied by selections from Schoenberg, Debussy, Moussorgsky, and Richard Strauss). It was, and still is, a highly sophisticated work and although most of the initial shock has been removed by our familiarity with the work of painters like Kokoschka and Munch (which share some of its qualities), what remains is still a dramatic ballet of light and shadow, a *Coppelia* in a sinister key.

Caligari was a milestone, indeed. But is it a film? Detractors claim that it is static, that all its effects could be achieved on the stage, that the sets are uncinematic, the acting theatrical. Although the camera moves several times and there are some close-ups, all of these criticisms are valid. Yet the film succeeds in fusing all of its elements into a filmic whole, creating an atmosphere of anguish and terror that goes beyond the queer, crooked houses and the winding streets, working its spell in the dark solitude of the movie house.

But Caligarism itself proved to be a dead end. The same year Wiene again attempted to experiment with distorted sets and pictorial effects. The result was a fiasco. Called *Genuine,* the film dealt with one of those totally destructive women that so often recur in German literature, a pagan priestess of great beauty, sold in an Arab market to a rich old man, who keeps her imprisoned in a glass cage until she lures his young nephew into slashing the old man's throat. Sets (by the painter Cesar Klein) and costumes (again by Reimann) did not match each other and an American actress named Fern Andra, who played the blood-thirsty vamp, did not fit into the Expressionistic style. Wiene had better luck with his *Raskolnikov* (1923), an adaptation of Dostoyevsky's *Crime and Punishment* that benefited from the presence in Berlin of a troupe of actors from the Moscow Art Theater.

If not to Wiene, to whom should go the credit for *Caligari*'s success? After Wiene was conveniently dead, Friedrich Feher, who plays Alan in the movie, claimed that he had directed most of it! Since both Wiene and Feher were never to approach its success, and the name of the cameraman (Willie Hameister) is hardly remembered today, the paternity of *Caligari* falls on Janowitz and Mayer, who captured the spirit of a turbulent moment in European history, and to Warm, Röhrig, and Reimann who so adroitly translated that spirit into visual terms.

Caligari was too impressive a movie not to have offshoots. The Russian director Jacob Protozanov returned to Russia after seeing the film in Paris and, with the help of his designers, turned out some fantastic sets in the Constructivist style of Naum Gabo for a satirical science-fiction picture called *Aelita* (1924) which had a long dream sequence set on planet Mars. The film's humorous mood, however, is the antithesis of *Caligari*'s. In Hollywood, there were some sporadic outbursts of Caligarism. One of these was *Human Wreckage* in 1923, which employed distorted sets to represent the world of drug addiction. And after the arrival of sound, *Caligari* served as the model for one of the most accomplished horror thrillers of the thirties, *Murders in the Rue Morgue.*

In its country of origin, the evil doctor launched the vogue of the *Schauerfilme,* the films of fantasy and terror. No sooner was *Caligari* completed than Janowitz adapted *Dr. Jekyll and Mr. Hyde,* albeit rather freely so that author's rights would not be paid to Stevenson's heirs. Retitled *Der Januskopf* (*The Head of Janus*) it opened at the same theater that had housed *Caligari* four months before. It had Conrad Veidt in the dual role of Dr. Warren and Mr. O'Connor and was directed by Friedrich Wilhelm Murnau. Only the script and a few photographs remain, a grievous loss since Murnau was soon to develop into one of the great directors of the silent cinema. Janowitz's screenplay reveals the many liberties taken with the Stevenson story: the good Doctor Warren is obsessed by a bust of Janus, the two-faced Roman deity, one of whose faces is that of a leering, hideous satyr. Under its influence, he becomes a lustful, murdering fiend: he drags his own fiancée to a brothel in Whitechapel and murders a little girl in the street. The evil Mr. O'Connor finally overtakes the doctor's entire personality but Warren, in one last moment of lucidity, swallows poison and dies, clutching the statue of Janus. Stevenson would have found it easier to recognize his brainchild in two other versions made the same year in the United States.

Like Méliès before them, German film-makers realized that the very nature of fantasy required the absolute control of every phase of film production, a control that only well-equipped studios could furnish. Within the walls of UFA Studios was assembled an extraordinary array of artists and technicians, whose collective talents lifted the motion picture to one of the summits of the Silent Era, the Golden Age of German cinema. This period, intimately bound to the *Schauerfilme,* saw fantastic constructions spring overnight on studio lots—cities of the mind, convulsive, hallucinating, bizarre. The first of these was an ancient quarter of Prague designed by the architect Hans Poelzig for Wegener's new version of *The Golem,* an anthill of gabled, weatherbeaten houses that seemed, like the clay giant itself, to have been molded by the hand of man. (Poelzig had just rebuilt an old Berlin circus into Reinhardt's fantastic showplace, the Grosses Schauspielhaus.) Equally effective were the interior sets: the Rabbi's cabinet, where the Golem is created, a vaulted womb of a room; a maiden's bedroom in delicate Pre-Raphaelite lines; a tapestrylike throne room for the Hapsburg emperor.

From his own *Märchenfilme,* which he largely filmed along the Rhine, Wegener had learned the importance of sunlight and air, and from Reinhardt he learned the techniques of dynamic grouping and chiaroscuro lighting. His movie alternates between dark, claustrophobic sets and sun-drenched street scenes, between nocturnal terror and airy fantasy. The best of *The Golem* scenes capture the mystery and remoteness of the Middle Ages: Rabbi Low (Albert Steinrück) standing in the flaming circle and invoking the name of Astaroth and the souls of the dead as he attempts to discover the life-giving word that will set his creation alive; frenzied masses of people swarming through the ghetto streets during a fire; the Golem's awesome entrance at the Emperor's court; and the lyrical last sequence where the rampaging monster comes face to face with a fearless child who offers him an apple and, a moment later, removes the Star of David from the Golem's chest and sends him crashing down to the ground, a lifeless statue once more. A contemporary critic wrote that Wegener's Golem was Wegener's face: broad, grim, yet almost beautiful when touched with humanity, as in his scenes with the Rabbi's beautiful daughter (played by one of Wegener's wives, Lyda Salmonova), or with the little girl who will be his innocent nemesis. Most of these situations were to reappear in later "monster" pictures of which *The Golem* is the most distinguished forerunner. All of the film's trick photography was done on the set through double exposure of the negative within the camera—the work of Carl Boese who shares director billing with Wegener.

The Golem was remade as a sumptuous French production in 1936, but director Julien Duvivier set it in a later period and departed from the original concept: it is the Rabbi's young wife who discovers the long-forgotten statue in the Emperor's own cellar and brings it back to life in time to save her husband from execution. *The Emperor and the Golem,* a Czechoslovakian film of 1951 directed by Mac Fric, brought a lumpish, inhuman Golem to life for comic purposes. The perennial giant has found its way into drama and opera and, undoubtedly, we have not seen the end of it. Like all true myths, this legend is subject to many interpretations; to Wegener, it seemed a poetic variation of the messianic theme, a medieval mystery play.

The vampire, the vilest, most detested, and, also, most popular of the creatures of the netherworld, was practically ignored by film-makers until 1921, when Henrik Galeen adapted Bram Stoker's 1897 novel, *Dracula.* To evade the copyright law, Galeen changed the characters' names and moved the location from London to Bremen. The resulting film, called *Nosferatu,* disregards most of the vampire lore contained in the Stoker novel. It is crude, unsubtle, and illogical, whereas the book is perfectly logical within the boundaries of fantasy. The film's ending, in particular, reeks of Nordic mysticism and betrays the genuine horror of the original. André Gide deplored the film as heavy-handed, absurd, and unimaginative, all of which it is. However, F. W. Murnau was incapable of directing a totally uninteresting film.

What attracted Murnau to the Stoker novel remains a mystery. He had already essayed a horror film in *Der Januskopf* and there was a chilling nightmare scene in *Schloss Vogelöd* (*Castle Vogelöd*) of the year before in which a large, almost Walpolean hand reaches out through a window to terrorize one of the characters. But the vampire legend, with its attendant hints of necrophilia, sadomasochism, and homosexuality, gets cursory treatment in the movie. Murnau robs the vampire of its aura: we see the shadow of Dracula/Orlock reach for the hero and we see the vampire's reflection in the heroine's mirror. As every reader of the novel—and there were already thousands—knew, the Undead cast no shadow and have no reflection.

Stoker laid his story in the contemporary setting of Victorian England, so that the sense of actuality, of things happening right before our eyes, is never lost. Murnau and Galeen place the action at the time of the Bremen plague of 1838, the safe, distant period of Goethe and Hoffmann. The story is basically unchanged: a young realtor, Hutter (Gustav von Wangenheim), is sent to the Carpathian Mountains to arrange the sale of a piece of property to a mysterious Count Orlock. Disregarding the peasants' warning, he reaches the castle and soon finds himself in the clutches of the Count, who is a vampire. Abandoning a terrified, half-mad Hutter, Orlock leaves his castle, taking several coffins with him, and boards a ship that will take him to Bremen. Back home, Hutter's wife, Ellen (Greta Schroeder), has all kinds of dark presentiments about her husband's safety while Hutter's employer (Alexander Granach), a student of the occult, goes insane and is put in an asylum. Hutter manages to escape from the castle and races on horseback toward Ellen. When Orlock's ship enters the port, there is not a living soul aboard and, soon thereafter, the plague breaks out in the city caused by an army of rats that follow in the vampire's wake. Hutter and Ellen are reunited. She listens to his story and soon realizes that the reason for the plague is Orlock's presence in the city. She resolves to destroy the fiend by enticing him to her bedside and keeping him there, at the cost of her own life, until the cock crows. Orlock is killed by the first rays of the rising sun: his body dissolves in the morning air. Hutter throws himself upon his wife's dead body. And the film closes with a twilight shot of a real castle in ruins.

Independently produced, which accounts for the picture's look of modest means, *Nosferatu* benefits from some good locations in Central Europe which bring the film geographically close to the sites mentioned in the novel. The indoor sets, however, are flat and uninteresting, which is surprising for a German film of this period. To increase the atmosphere of fantasy, Murnau makes effective use of the negative film during Hutter's ride in Orlock's hearselike coach through the land of the phantoms. He also employs fast motion (as the vampire piles up his coffins in a cart), but the effect backfires and the scene becomes ridiculous. Murnau has not attained here his later mastery in directing actors: the young principals are unattractive and, much too often, their terror gets in the way of ours. Alexander Granach, who plays Hutter's employer and the vampire's ally, is merely a grimacing mask. Max Schreck, as Orlock, makes us sigh for the comparative subtlety of Bela Lugosi. However, in his appearance, Schreck, with his emaciated body and rat's head, lends the film its few chilling moments. Doors open and close by themselves to reveal the vampire lying in wait, and, during the sea voyage, we glimpse him stalking the sailors on deck or slumping ominously on his coffin in the ship's hull. And there is one lovely shot, reminiscent of a Böcklin painting, showing Orlock on a barge, carrying his earth-box to a new abode.

In order to justify what was merely an excursion into fantasy and terror, German film critics were compelled to read all sorts of deeper meanings into the movie. Casting a cold eye on *Nosferatu* makes it appear, at best, a blurry Gothic romance. Looking already oldish when originally released in March of 1922, the film had the patina of antiquity by the time it was released in the United States in 1929 in order to profit from Murnau's Hollywood reputation. In the intervening years he had made his two masterpieces, *The Last Laugh* in Berlin and *Sunrise* in California. His last German movie was an adaptation of *Faust* (1926) based not on Goethe or Marlowe but on the older versions of the Faustian saga. And though he ignores the horror aspects of the myth (Goethe credits Faust with the creation of the homunculus) and his Mephistopheles is more comic than satanic, Murnau displays a command of the fantastic. Scenes such as that of the Four Horsemen of the Apocalypse riding the sky like a Dürer engraving come to life or that of Lucifer expelled from Heaven by a resplendent, winged archangel helped to make Murnau's *Faust* one of the most accomplished films of the Silent Era.

With inflation reaching its peak, German films seemed to retreat even more into the comparative safety of the past, as embodied in legend and myth. Some of the resulting films were based on anonymous folktales, such as *Der Steinerne Reiter* (*The Stone Rider,* 1923), adapted by Thea von Harbou and directed by Fritz Wendhausen with more than a passing nod in the direction of *The Golem.* Others were drawn from more recent novels, like Theodor Storm's *Chronik von Grieshuus* (*The Chronicle of the Gray House*), also adapted by von Harbou and directed by Arthur von Gerlach. A medieval castle and its surrounding moors were built at UFA from designs by Poelzig and Röhrig, and this massive decor all but overwhelms Storm's misty romance of two highborn brothers, rivals for the love of a bondswoman. Like Hanns Heinz Ewers, who scripted the first *Student of Prague,* Thea von Harbou was to develop into a major force in German cinema. A prolific writer of unbridled, sometimes visionary imagination and frequent lapses of taste, she found her best director in her husband, Fritz Lang. The apocalyptic climax of the trend was to be their two-part filming of the greatest Teutonic myth of all, *Der Nibelungen.*

With the reestablishment of social and economic order, the fantasy film declined and was gradually replaced by more intimate psychological dramas. The last gleams of the Romantic revival were Wiene's *Orlacs Haende* (*The Hands of Orlac,* 1925) and Galeen's remake of *The Student of Prague* (1926). In the first, which was based on a novel by Maurice Renard, Conrad Veidt played the part of a talented musician who, after losing both hands in a railroad crash, has those of a murderer grafted on to his wrists. A series of mysterious killings ensues until the artist becomes convinced that his hands have a life of their own and continue to perform their deadly task long after their master's death. The film has little of Wiene's *Caligari* in it but shares the director's obsession with the explaining of the supernatural. The whole thing turns out to be a plot directed against the pianist's sanity. Veidt, who since playing Cesare had made a specialty of bizarre roles like this, gave a powerful, hallucinated performance. He became the logical choice for the new version of *The Student of Prague* that Galeen was to direct: his tense, gaunt features and his controlled yet expressive acting made him an ideal choice for Baldwin. The film was done in high Romantic style and had excellent trick photography by Günther Krampf. Outstanding was a shot of Werner

Krauss as Scapinelli, an umbrella-carrying Satan in stovepipe hat, standing against the wind by the twisted stump of a tree. Or the sequence where his gigantic shadow spies on the lover's tryst in a moonlit garden. After the arrival of sound, *The Student of Prague* was remade in Vienna in the mid-thirties, with Adolph Wohlbruck (later Anton Walbrook) and Dorothea Wieck; there were some musical scenes which gave the film an operetta air that had little of the haunting quality of the two silent versions.

By the end of the twenties, some of Germany's best talent had left Berlin for Hollywood, where directors like Paul Leni and cameramen like Karl Freund were to discover that Old World fantasies could survive the sea change and revitalize the American mystery film, while waiting for the renaissance of horror that was to follow in the wake of the sound film.

The strands of mystery, terror, and fantasy are inextricably woven into the work of Fritz Lang—more obviously in his German films but also present, in subtler ways, in those of his later American period. It is rather easy to classify a film like *Nosferatu* as a horror movie or *The Golem* as fantasy; it is more difficult to do so with films like *The Spiders, Between Worlds, Der Nibelungen, Metropolis* or the Doctor Mabuse films, all created between 1920 and 1932 but often transcending the Expressionistic style of the period. The films of Lang, more than those of any director save Murnau, appear related only among themselves. The director's career is one of the longest in film history; unlike John Ford, Raoul Walsh, or Abel Gance, directors who share his artistic longevity, Lang has worked in countries as diverse as Germany (in the twenties and fifties), France (in the thirties) and the United States (in the thirties, forties, and fifties) and his films have changed accordingly, although they remain recognizable Lang films. There is more than superficial kinship between *M* and *Hangmen Also Die,* between *Doctor Mabuse* and *The Big Heat.*

Fritz Lang was born in Vienna (a city that never capitulated to Expressionism) in 1890. He attended several architectural schools there, deciding to follow in his father's footsteps. Before the war, he had already traveled around the world and made a name for himself as a painter in Paris. During the hostilities, he served in the Austrian army, was wounded three times and decorated. While convalescing, he began writing thrillers, some of which caught the attention of Erich Pommer, who hired him as screenwriter for established directors like Joe May and Otto Rippert. In 1918, he joined the rank of directors at Decla Studios, turning out four minor films in quick succession and a very popular serial, *The Spiders*. An avid reader of dime novels, Lang wrote four separate stories around a secret society of criminals, the Spiders, somewhat in the manner of the French serial classic of 1915, *Les Vampires*. The first two, *The Golden Lake* and *The Diamond Ship* were completed; *Secrets of the Sphinx* and *For the Crown of Asia* were to remain unfilmed. Combining the labyrinthine plots of Eugène Sue with the exotic locations of Karl May (actually filmed in North Africa), the two pictures are replete with Inca treasures, human sacrifices, and hairbreadth escapes. The most typical Lang qualities in them are reserved for the figure of Lio-Sha, an Oriental villainess played by Ressel Orla, a forerunner of later Lang super-criminals like Mabuse and Haghi.

At Decla, Lang came into contact with a talented couple, the actor Rudolf Klein-Rogge and his wife, the novelist Thea von Harbou. The former was to become Lang's favorite performer; the latter Lang's screenwriter and, after her divorce, his wife. Their first collaboration produced *Der Müde Tod* (*Weary Death*) in 1921, which made Lang's reputation abroad when it opened in Paris under the title *Les Trois Lumières* (*The Three Lights*). Shown in Great Britain as *Destiny*, it so impressed a young man named Alfred Hitchcock that he decided to become a film director. It reached America the following year under yet another two titles: *Between Worlds* and *The Light Within*.

Inspired by a line from the Song of Songs, "For Love is as strong as Death," the film was a macabre fantasy of two lovers separated by a mysterious stranger who turns out to be Death itself come to take the boy. The girl pleads for his life and weary Death makes a bargain: she will follow three lights into three moments of the past and in each of them she must try to save her lover's life. The three episodes were laid in Renaissance Venice, the Bagdad of the Arabian Nights, and legendary China. In all three, the girl loses her bet with Death. What appeared to be a dream ends as the girl awakens in an apothecary's shop, but, alas, Death still waits, offering one last chance: the boy's life will be exchanged for that of another person willing to take his place. Vainly the girl pleads with the old and infirm who, however, refuse to part with their wretched existences. As time's candle burns down, a fire breaks out and a baby is trapped in the flames. The girl hesitates but a moment—then she saves the child at the cost of her own life. The lovers are thus reunited in death.

Besides affording a chance to juggle time and space in the manner of Griffith's *Intolerance, Der Müde Tod* was a perfect vehicle for Lang's architectural flair. The many imaginative sets become the stuff fairy tales are made of the world over: the endless doorless wall that separates the girl from the domain of Death, or the cave behind it where every human life is represented by a candle, some tall and bright and others spent and flickering like that of the hero.

From the enchanting pantomime of the Chinese episode to the Expressionism of the contemporary sequence runs the leitmotiv of death as love's nemesis. Granting the climate of pessimism and despair prevalent among the youth of the day, and in spite of Lang's admission that his was the main responsibility for the screenplay, there is much of that sickly Romanticism that was to dominate Thea von Harbou's later work. In her *Stone Rider,* adapted from an old legend, the Lord of the Mountains and his shepherdess wife are turned to stone so that he will atone for the outrages he perpetrated while exercising his *droit du seigneur.* The lovers in *The Chronicle of the Gray House* are also reunited in the afterlife. Love can only be consummated in death seems to be what Von Harbou is saying. Lang's vision is more masculine, more matter-of-fact than all this wishful death-mooning.

A popular series of novels by Norbert Jacques was to furnish Thea and Fritz Lang with the character of *Dr. Mabuse.* Although the picture was laid in the postwar Berlin contemporary to them, it has an aura of timeless evil and total corruption that has lost none of its power today. Mabuse, the arch-criminal, rules the decadent, bankrupt city from behind multifarious disguises: we see him as a banker, psychiatrist, gambler, and drunken sailor. Although he plots to plunge the nation into chaos by putting counterfeit money into circulation, Mabuse's first aim in life seems to be the total control of the people who come into contact with him. Dreams of world conquest are reserved for later Lang villains.

Mabuse's only worthy adversary is District Attorney Wenk, a saturnine character unsympathetically played by Bernhard Goetzke, who played Death in *Der Müde Tod.* Wenk is not above resorting to some of Mabuse's unscrupulous methods to help bring about the doctor's downfall. But Mabuse, the genius of crime, can only be defeated by his own intellect: he eventually goes mad and is discovered in one of his subterranean hideouts surrounded by millions in counterfeit marks, haunted by the ghosts of his many victims. His associates are hunted down, one by one, and the film ends as one of them scribbles his defiance on the prison wall.

Released in two parts, *The Great Gambler* and *Inferno,* the Mabuse film comprised some five hours of running time and was an ambitious attempt at portraying depravity in high and low places. As such, the film scrutinizes the ultramodern apartments of the rich, the nude *tableaux vivants* of the fashionable casinos, and the spurious gaiety of the pleasure domes filled with monocled Lesbians and decorated with phallic symbols. Nevertheless, the film's social content takes second place to some magnificent melodrama. Less athletic than the American chapter-plays, less Surrealistic than the French serials, *Mabuse* succeeds better than they in depicting a claustrophobic closed world of evil, the fetid hothouse in which Mabuse alone can exist. Most of *Mabuse* was filmed in the studios, down to the street scenes. Only when it leaves the set, as when a hypnotized Wenk is ordered to wreck his own car, do we gain some sense of the real world outside. The movie does indeed have its quotient of secular snakes and time-bombs (there is also an ingenious automobile that, after hermetically sealing itself, fills with poison gas), but the touch is more sophisticated than ever before. Posing as a fashionable psychiatrist, Mabuse easily discovers his victim's weaknesses and exploits them accordingly. As a hypnotist, he can bend other people's wills to his own, although in at least one case he is not even required to exert his power: he orders his mistress to commit suicide when she is arrested and she willingly obliges! Mabuse, played moodily and effectively by Klein-

Rogge, appears as a cross between Conan Doyle's Moriarty and Count Zaroff (of *The Most Dangerous Game*), a civilized super-esthete, indulging in crime for thrills, and just as much at home in the aristocratic circle of Count Told as in the tawdry hovels of the underworld.

Mabuse put Lang in the front line of the German film industry. After Pommer's company merged with UFA, Lang followed his mentor into the new outfit and, when the vogue for traditional German themes swept the studios, he was entrusted with the most spectacular of them all, and made a two-part version of *Der Nibelungenlied,* scripted by his wife and enlisting the most distinguished talent available.

The film's two parts are very different: the first, *Siegfried,* seems set at the dawn of time, in a world not quite formed yet, where dwarfs, dragons, and the fantastic still hold sway. It follows the original Icelandic sagas and only incidentally the Wagner libretti. Siegfried, a brave warrior, obtains magical powers from the creatures of the mist called the Nibelungs, a race of dwarfs and custodians of a fabulous treasure. With his magical sword, Siegfried slays the dragon Fafner and wins the treasure. After tales of the exploit reach the kingdom of the Burgundians, King Gunther sends for him. Siegfried falls in love with Krimhild, Gunther's sister. To obtain the King's consent, he agrees to obtain the hand of Queen Brunhilde of Issland for Gunther. With the help of a magic cape which makes him invisible, he vanquishes the fierce virgin queen (a Walkyrie in earlier versions of the saga), who believes herself conquered by Gunther. When she learns the truth, Brunhilde reviles her royal husband and plots with Gunther's liegeman, Hagen, against Siegfried. From an unsuspecting Krimhild, Hagen extracts the secret of Siegfried's invulnerability: the hero bathed in the dragon's blood and no weapon can hurt his body, except for the spot on his back where a leaf fell and prevented Fafner's blood from touching his skin. During a hunting party, Hagen murders Siegfried and although Krimhild demands justice from her brother, Gunther realizes that the reason of state has been well-served by Siegfried's death and allows Hagen to go free.

This tale of demigods and mortals, dark deeds and heroic feats appears on the screen as a splendid, hieratic frieze, a triumph of sets, costumes, and mise-en-scéne, the only film to approach the *chanson de geste*. The rhythm is overwhelmingly slow as befits "this great and mighty poem, written in stone," which Heinrich Heine compared to the majestic dance of all the cathedrals in Europe. Lang reduces all movement to a stately walk, drains all humanity from legendary characters, making them serve passion only in an abstract way. In this, he borrows from Reinhardt's theater technique, but his own deployment of the human figure as another element of decor is unsurpassed: Brunhilde enters Worms over a bridge of shields held aloft by a hundred warriors, the love scenes between Siegfried and Krimhild take place in vaulted halls or espaliered gardens. Lang's sense of the wondrous brimmed over in the forest scenes (the set was built in the studio down to the last moss-covered rock and overgrown tuffet), while the flower-spattered glade where Siegfried meets his doom is as delicate and perfect as a Pre-Raphaelite painting.

"No tower is so high and no stone so hard as grim Hagen and vindictive Krimhild." The second part, *Krimhild's Revenge,* brings the myth down to earth in one of the most ferociously brilliant films in Lang's career. We are no longer in the misty no-man's-land where fact and fantasy are on speaking terms, but in Central Europe—in the iron-gray middle of the fifth century. Krimhild has remarried, taking for her second spouse Etzel, King of the Huns, known as Attila to the rest of Europe and to his enemies as the Scourge of God. The Queen invites her brothers and the Burgundian court to the Hun encampment and there she has them massacred. Thus, the last Burgundian, Hagen, is taken alive at the cost of half of the Hun army so that the bloodthirsty Queen can behead him with her own hands. Such an abject death for a great warrior enrages Etzel, who then has Krimhild killed. And so, what began as a heroic poem ends as a holocaust.

The first part revealed Lang the painter and architect; the second, Lang the film-maker. Both parts benefit from the almost unlimited resources put at his disposal, including some of the most accomplished camera wizardry in films. A special process whereby a real set is photographed through a miniature (painted on glass or built in reduced scale) was brought to perfection by Eugen

Shuftan and used to fool the eye into seeing unlimited grandeur. The sets themselves were from the beginning enormous and the trick photography impeccable. An experimental film-maker, Walter Ruttman, designed a dream sequence in which Krimhild sees in the battle of some falcons an omen of her husband's death. As wave upon wave of Hun closes in on the besieged Burgundians, Lang revealed himself to be a master of movement: there is a visual crescendo here worthy of Wagner's music.

Not surprisingly, the first part of *Der Nibelungen* became a huge success in its country of origin, where it was misinterpreted as an impassioned plea for "Germanism." Taking no notice that the saga is an endless succession of betrayals, murders, and perfidy, the Germans have usually regarded the *Lied* as an heroic example of courage (Siegfried's) and unflinching loyalty to the Fatherland (Hagen's). As early as 1815, the poem was issued to army conscripts. Ludwig of Bavaria sponsored Wagner while he wrote the four operas that were to make the saga famous around the world (and which do not include Krimhild's revenge). Later admirers included Kaiser Wilhelm and Hitler.

After the completion of *Der Nibelungen,* Lang and Pommer visited New York and Hollywood to study American film production methods. It was the first sight of Manhattan from the boat that inspired Lang with the idea for his next picture. Turning his back on the past, he ventured into the world of the future.

"A horror tale of the future," *Metropolis* was also the last gasp of Expressionism in Lang's work. Once more, Thea von Harbou scripted the story, which concerns a city of the future, year unspecified but close to the end of this century, a maze of skyscrapers built upon a subterranean "city of the workers," almost robotized in their hopeless existence of poverty and slavery. Among them flickers one last spark of humanity, a girl named Maria (Brigitte Helm), who preaches a gospel of love and understanding and tells them the story of the Tower of Babel, how it failed "because the toilers did not know of the dream of the planners." The news of Maria's disturbing influence reaches John Fredersen (Alfred Abel), master of Metropolis; her youth and sincerity captivate Fredersen's son (Gustav Froehlich) who, following Maria, stumbles into the universe of the machines and the city of subhuman wretches that run them. Determined to suppress the girl, Fredersen orders his evil adviser Rotwang (Rudolf Klein-Rogge), a builder of humanoids, to abduct her and make a robot in her image, a false Maria that will spread the seeds of revolt among the workers. (A typical example of von Harbou's faulty dramatic construction. If the workers are destroyed, who will work the machines?) Rotwang succeeds and Maria the Robot incites the workers to destroy the machines in an orgy of freedom. The underground city is flooded and only the intervention of the real Maria, who manages to escape Rotwang's clutches, saves the workers' children from drowning. The false Maria is then unmasked, Rotwang is killed, and Fredersen brought to reason by the love that has grown between his son and the good Maria. The last title in the movie carries von Harbou's placebo for the ills of capitalism: "The heart must mediate between the brain and the hands."

If the film now looks disconsolately dated in its naive pretensions and if time in forty years has given concrete shape to many of Lang's wild fancies, *Metropolis* does preserve some of its original grandeur. It does provide us with an accurate projection of the fears and hopes of the Germany of the 1920's, that time when the country finally achieved economic stability and German technology regained its peak, forecasting that television would soon replace the telephone and that the zeppelin would become the definitive means of travel and transportation. This first thoroughgoing excursion of the cinema into the future is marred by Thea von Harbou's narrow vision, embodied by a symbolic shot of the Machine as Moloch, feeding on rows of workers—a rather antiquated conception for 1926. Von Harbou dramatizes her tale of the future with the conventions of Victorian literature: Maria, the priestess of love, is a sweet innocent relic as laughable in her virginal simplicity as the hero, given to fainting spells and wearing knickers. The script calls for them to encounter one another in a cathedral when it should be obvious that the citizens of Metropolis have forsaken God for cybernetics. H. G. Wells dismissed *Metropolis* as "quite the silliest film" and, besides, claimed that Lang and von Harbou had borrowed from his tales of the future, such as *The Sleeper Wakes* and *A Story of Days to Come.* A decade later, Wells was to write the screenplay for *Shape of Things to Come,* a

British film that covers the same territory as *Metropolis*. This was a more logical, and sometimes just as impressive, look into the future. The important difference is that it lacks the hallucinatory power of Lang's film.

That science fiction ages fast and horror remains timeless is demonstrated by the most effective sequence in *Metropolis* in which Rotwang (Klein-Rogge in black leather gloves and made up to resemble a great bird of prey) chases Maria with a flashlight through the underground maze of tunnels until the terrified girl is ensnared like a moth by the beam of light. The famous scene of the creation of the false Maria, a riot of switches, dials, and electrical effects, was to reappear in the American Frankenstein films of the next decade. The entire sequence structured around the robot is outrageously absurd, yet the film's visual mastery and furious rhythm carry the viewer along: when introduced by Fredersen to the ruling caste of Metropolis, the false Maria executes a lascivious Oriental dance that inflames her audience. Later on, while the workers' city is being flooded, the robot presides over a frenzied revelry at the Dome of Pleasure, and when she is finally unmasked by the workers, Lang infuses the scenes of her burning at the stake with a delirious sadism that was to show up again in his first American film, *Fury,* as the lynch mob storms the jailhouse.

Combining miniature with photo enlargements, employing the Schuftan process and building the already vast sets in forced perspective, Lang and his designers created a breathtaking illusion of staggering size for this, UFA's most ambitious project. Masses of extras were mobilized in the Reinhardt manner, a faceless monstrous chorus, now slow-moving files of machine-fodder, now a rampaging mob. Accommodating this number of extras required the building of entire sectors of the underground city, the machine room, and the cathedral square. Shots of the fantastic city, with its heliports, neon signs, and Bauhaus-type bulk of architecture were pirated by countless science-fictions everywhere. This imaginary megapolis even inspired an American musical parody, *Just Imagine* (1930), which contained some impressive designs of its own.

The filming of *Metropolis* took the best part of two years and cost UFA more than a million marks. An exhausted Lang followed it with a refreshing return to the fanciful yet contemporary world of the serial, achieving in *Spione* (*Spies,* 1927) what Graham Greene called "Lang's simplest, purest thriller," an exciting duel between Haghi, a Mabuse-like super-spy and Number 326, a dashing secret agent. The pawns in this long and complicated game (the original version ran for more than three hours and was to be considerably cut for foreign release) are a beautiful lady spy, a treacherous vamp, a Japanese diplomat, as well as the bizarre assortment of characters usually found in spy fiction. *Spione* also contained a brilliantly constructed railroad crash and a music-hall climax that presages Hitchcock's *The Thirty-Nine Steps.* In fact, *Spione* can be seen not only as the forerunner of the Hitchcock thrillers of the thirties but, also, in its inspired gadgetry and wild schemes for world domination as the forerunner of the James Bond films of more recent vintage. In 1944, Lang joined talents with an admirer of *Spione* when he brought to the screen Greene's *Ministry of Fear,* another spy thriller. By that time, the genre had been dealt a deathblow by the Second World War; spying was no longer a romantic game of wits but a sordid reality.

With his last silent film, *Frau im Mond* (*Woman in the Moon*) Lang led science fiction out of the dusty medievalism so dear to the German Romantics and into the light of the latest advances in scientific research. Since *Metropolis* had raised violent criticism for its unscientific—albeit grandiose—vision of the future, the director enlisted as technical advisers Germany's two outstanding missile experts, the professors Hermann Oberth and Willy Ley. The first section of the film *Frau im Mond,* covering the design and construction of the rocketship, is reliably founded on astronautical theory as developed up to 1928; the second section, dealing with the voyage to the moon and the landing on its surface, is simply a visual elaboration of scientific conjecture. As such, the fantastic element is an extension of reality. The intervening third of a century has lent an even greater actuality to Lang's picture.

Convinced that it is possible for a man-made rocketship to reach the moon, Professor Manfeldt (Klaus Pohl) enlists the help of a young millionaire designer, Helius (Willy Fritsch). Another scientist, Windegger (Gustav von Wangenheim), joins the team to be near his fiancée, the Professor's beautiful secretary, Friede (Gerda Maurus). An international trust succeeds in placing one of its agents (Fritz Rasp) in the completed rocket. The five members of the expedition are joined at the last moment by a young stowaway (Gustl Stark-Gesettenbaur). The rocket is launched and eventually reaches the sandy wastes of the moon. The Professor discovers that the moon holds large deposits of gold; greed soon splits the travelers, who begin to fight for the vital oxygen supply. The Professor is accidentally killed, the secret agent unmasked. There remains enough oxygen for two people to make the return trip. Windegger and the child will travel back to Earth; Friede and Helius, who have fallen in love, will stay behind in the strange new world.

Once the astronauts reach the surface of the moon, the story deteriorates into routine melodrama which, however, does not blemish the building of the giant spaceship, fascinating in its almost documentary authenticity—so documentary, in fact, that eventually the Gestapo seized the beautifully designed models and recalled all prints from circulation. Professor Ley escaped to become a missile expert in America, but Oberth remained in Germany and contributed to the development of the V–1 rocket, employed with great destructive effect by the Germans during World War II.

As the shadow of Nazism grew larger and more ominous, Lang made his first talking picture, *M* (1931), the somber case history of a child murderer, inspired by the crimes, committed a few years before, of "the Vampire of Dusseldorf." The very theme of the picture excluded the introduction of fantasy and whatever horror there was derived from the pathology of its murderer, a role that catapulted Peter Lorre to international fame. The following year, Lang picked up where he left off a decade before in *Das Testament des Dr. Mabuse* (*The Last Will of Dr. Mabuse*) and this sequel showed Mabuse as a dying old man hypnotizing the head of the insane asylum where he has been confined into continuing his campaign to plunge the world into terror and chaos. In the words of Mabuse Lang was able to reflect Nazi ideology. Still, Hitler and Goebbels professed to admire the director's work, especially *Sieg-*

fried and *Metropolis,* and offered Lang, a Jew, the post of director of the Third Reich's film industry. The same night the offer was made, Lang crossed the border; later, Thea von Harbou divorced him and remained behind to write, and eventually direct, until well after the fall of the Third Reich.

Erich Pommer, who had resigned from UFA the day Hitler came to power as chancellor of Germany, joined Lang in Paris where they collaborated on a movie version of the popular Ferenc Molnar play *Liliom,* with Charles Boyer playing the part of the wife-beating hoodlum who dies, goes to purgatory, and is given a chance to return to Earth for one day and perform one good act. Lang infused this bittersweet fantasy with some characteristic touches—such as the sinister angels of death who transport Liliom to Heaven. Soon after this, Pommer and Lang left Paris for Hollywood.

In America, Lang's thrillers became less fanciful, the secret society being replaced by the crime syndicate, his vision becoming more sober and current. The universe of Lang's cinema is one of violence and, logically, his attention became vested in the most essentially violent aspects of American life: the Western, the gangster film, and the psychological thriller. The influence of his German films was felt in the horror and science fiction films that were to come out of Hollywood in great number during the thirties.

CHAPTER 3

A SILENT CONSPIRACY OF TERROR

America, 1900–1928

From the moment the film found a language of its own, a date that can be safely established around 1908, there was no work of literature, however involved or stylistically complex, that the cinema would not try to adapt. Lasting one or two reels and loaded with a profusion of subtitles that borrowed naively from the original source, the moving pictures could hardly do justice to the Bible, Dante, Shakespeare, Dickens, or Poe. In the flood of films released in the United States in the early period, horror titles are comparatively rare, crude approximations of Hawthorne, Conan Doyle, and Stevenson; but, unlike the Western and slapstick comedy, horror movies were not indigenous to the American screen. Horror is nourished by myth, tradition, and legend—all of which require centuries of rich elaboration. One would look in vain for the more macabre aspects of the fairy tale (as found in Perrault or the Brothers Grimm) in L. Frank Baum's serial fantasies of Oz, which were already being filmed by Americans in 1910. The far ghostlier tales of such native writers as Ambrose Bierce and George Washington Cable have remained almost untouched to the present day.

Not that American movies were devoid of horrific elements.

There were isolated moments of shock and terror in many of them, although usually of an exemplary nature: recurrent visions of the hell that awaited the philanderer, the adulteress, and the dope fiend. Such Dantesque scenes appear as late as 1915 in films such as *The Warning* and *The Devil's Darling,* tinted a sulfurous red and populated with grimacing demons or even—as in *The Devil's Assistant* (1917) a convincing depiction of the three-headed Cerberus. But horror for its own sake was frowned upon by the public, rejected by the exhibitor, and often attacked from the pulpit as well.

During the early twenties, the latent, submerged streak of horror began to surface as it was encouraged by the sudden interest in mystery novels and plays. One of the long-running successes of the decade was *The Bat,* a play by Avery Hopwood and Mary Roberts Rinehart. On the bookstands, Miss Rinehart joined the best-selling company of Sax Rohmer, Edgar Wallace, S. S. Van Dine, Earl Derr Biggers, and E. Phillips Oppenheim. There were sinister undercurrents throughout the Jazz Age: the Lon Chaney films, the steady content of macabre elements in the work of certain directors like Ingram, Tourneur, and Browning and, finally, the arrival of the German directors with their more sophisticated attitude toward the supernatural. Still, the flowering of the "chiller"—as it was termed by the trade publications—had to wait until the following decade, after two events that rocked both Hollywood and the nation: the admixture of sound to film and the 1929 crash of the stock market.

Among a profusion of innocuous titles, it comes as a surprise to see the name of *Frankenstein* in the Edison catalogue for 1910. A print of this film has not been rediscovered and all that seems to exist is the synopsis and a few photographs. The official press release mentions "the creation of the Monster in that cauldron of blazing chemicals" which sounds closer to the Mary Shelley original than to the electrical paraphernalia of later versions. It adds that "the scene in the laboratory is probably the most remarkable ever committed to a film." In a curious departure from the novel that anticipates the climax of *Nosferatu* a decade later, the Monster is defeated by the power of love and vanishes into thin air, leaving Frankenstein and his bride to live happily ever after.

The same publicity man—there was no film criticism in those days and most of the writing was done by studio hacks—assured the readers that "many repulsive situations have been eliminated," but one cannot help but wonder when confronted with the photograph of the Quasimodo-like Monster, played by an unidentified actor, probably Charles Ogle—a member of the Edison stock company.

The film may have evaded the most macabre aspects of the tale, but trade publications of the period comment on the reaction of certain exhibitors who found *Frankenstein* a bit too weird for their patrons. Still, there was another version of the tale released late in 1915 under the title *Life Without Soul,* produced by the Ocean Film Corporation of New York in five reels. The very human monster (played by Percy Darrell Standing) was made a more sympathetic figure, "awe-inspiring but never grotesque," but the picture's last scene proved that it had all been a dream of the hero. This was the customary ending for most movies dealing with fantasy. Even D. W. Griffith resorted to it in *The Avenging Conscience,* his grim adaptation of Poe's *The Tell-Tale Heart* which Mutual released in 1914.

Nor was Poe a single source of mystery and thrills. Wilkie Collins had four of his best-known works (*The Moonstone, The Dream Woman, The Dead Secret,* and *The Woman in White*) brought to the screen before 1915, presumably retaining only the crudest plot-lines and shorn of complexity and style. Sherlock Holmes came up as early as 1903 and was a popular figure in Danish, German, and French one- and two-reelers before William Gillette, the "official" Holmes of his generation, repeated his stage role in a 1916 Essanay film.

By far the most oft-filmed horror story was Stevenson's *Dr. Jekyll and Mr. Hyde*—with Merimée's *Carmen* and Hugo's *Les Misérables* the most adapted novels in film history. With its comfortable, well-defined separation of good and evil, Stevenson had enthralled an entire generation of readers, coating what was essentially a penny dreadful (but a superb one, at that), with enough moralizing to make it acceptable to the most timorous Victorian. Soon after, Freud and Jung were to split Stevenson's two halves into myriad strands, concurrent and inseparable.

In 1887, *Dr. Jekyll* was adapted by T. R. Sullivan into a play in which Richard Mansfield thrilled theatergoers with some quick-change artistry and hideous, greenish makeup. In 1908, the Selig Company hired the touring company in Chicago to reenact the play before the camera. The curtain rose and fell at the beginning and end of what was nothing more than a fifteen-minute photographed record of the play; yet it was regarded as a prestige production. The Great Northern Company (or Nordisk) of Copenhagen had another try at the story in 1910. In this, the last scene revealed that it had all been a delusion of the doctor's feverish mind. There were three more versions before 1915, one of which was made in England in a very early color process. After that, the good doctor and his evil alter ego were allowed a five-year respite before reappearing in 1920 in two different American versions as well as in the German *Der Januskopf*.

That year, John Barrymore undertook the double role in a Famous Players production made in New York, the first film to do justice to the original. At the height of his powers and more popular than ever before, Barrymore showed a preference for bizarre, richly theatrical roles. He preceded the film with his triumphant *Richard the Third* and followed it with a stage adaptation of Hugo's *The Man Who Laughs* in which he played the hideously deformed clown, Gwynplaine. Later in his movie career, he incarnated such physically or spiritually deformed characters as Captain Ahab (in two versions of Melville's *Moby Dick*) and Svengali. Barrymore's Jekyll is the handsome, posturing gentleman of a Whistler canvas, and as such, of little interest to him or the audience. But as Mr. Hyde, Barrymore enjoyed an actor's field day. With his misshapen skull, scraggly hair, and clawlike hands, Barrymore does not conform to Stevenson's bestial, apelike conception, but his Hyde is nevertheless a remarkable creation: a leering, demented-looking old man not too distant from the villainous roués of stage melodrama. Besides borrowing some of Oscar Wilde's epigrams for the subtitles, there are echoes of *The Picture of Dorian Gray* in the youthful doctor's quest for forbidden pleasures and, later, in Hyde's sinister forays into Soho. The Barrymore film's most radical departure from Stevenson—and one retained in subsequent versions—is to furnish Jekyll/Hyde with two leading ladies in the persons of Martha Mansfield, as the doctor's aristocratic sweetheart, and Nita Naldi, as Hyde's pathetic victim. The introduction of the latter, especially, serves to expand the character of Hyde from the child-beating murderer of the original into a more sexually complex personality.

Barrymore easily surpassed his movie predecessors, among them Alwin Neuss, King Baggot, and James Cruze, even matching Mansfield's onstage bravura by turning the crucial transformation scenes into a self-indulgent, but highly effective tour de force. The actor effected the change-over without the help of trick photography by dislocating his regular features and resetting them into the repulsive countenance of Mr. Hyde. Only then does the film resort to cinematic device, cutting away to allow Barrymore to complete his makeup. On the film's opening at the Rivoli Theatre in New York City, a reviewer commented, "One leaves the theater with the belief that motion pictures are on the verge of a new era." And so they were. Barrymore's prestige was to bring new luster to the horror film, and *Dr. Jekyll and Mr. Hyde* may well have been the beginning of a trend. A few weeks after its June opening, another version of the same story was released in an effort to profit from the Barrymore success. It featured Sheldon Lewis in the dual role, was set in New York, and it had been produced by Louis B. Mayer. It was distinctly second-rate and cheated even further by having the entire plot turn out to be another one of those infernal dreams. The German version (also of the same year) did not have such trickery.

That Barrymore's version is something less than a landmark may be credited to its director, the competent but less than masterful John S. Robertson, also remembered for his Mary Pickford and Greta Garbo vehicles. Had it been directed by Maurice Tourneur or Rex Ingram or Tod Browning—all of them craftsmen with a high content of the macabre in their films—the result would have been a film superior to this.

A conspicuous penchant for the fantastic turned up in the movies of Maurice Tourneur. Born in Paris in 1876, he had assisted the sculptor Rodin, the painter Puvis de Chavannes, and the stage director André Antoine before embarking on a film career. His first efforts were adaptations of the popular thrillers of

Gaston Leroux (*The Perfume of the Lady in Black, The Mystery of the Yellow Room*) and a gruesome Grand Guignol version of Poe's *Doctor Tarr and Professor Fether* which, when it reached America under the title *The Lunatics,* was judged by at least one reviewer as "too grim for Sunday showings."

During his American period (1914–26), Tourneur came to be regarded as one of the screen's great stylists. Always an "artistic" director, he adroitly employed all the visual resources of the stage (lighting, design, and composition) to the extent that his films, beautiful to watch, often appear to be a suite of exquisite tableaux lacking the essentially cinematic rhythm of his contemporaries, Feuillade, Griffith, and Ince. Acquainted as he was with Art Nouveau and the Pre-Raphaelites, he invested his adaptations of *Prunella, The Blue Bird* (both 1918), and *Treasure Island* (1920) with the charm of storybook illustrations. His 1915 version of Du Maurier's *Trilby* was one of the last American photoplays to open in Berlin before the United States entered the First World War. Its sinister hypnotizer, Svengali, echoes in both Caligari and Mabuse. In 1920, Tourneur completed *The Glory of Love* for Paramount, the tale of a waxworks proprietor bent on revenging himself against a young man by adding him to his exhibit. It took three years to obtain a release for the picture, as it was judged too weird for public consumption. Finally released by another company (Hodkinson) as *While Paris Sleeps,* it met with no particular protest or, for that matter, success. Tourneur's career in America was abruptly terminated when he was replaced by Metro-Goldwyn-Mayer on the filming of Verne's *The Mysterious Island,* whereupon he returned to France and continued directing well into the forties. His later credits include a stylish adaptation of Jonson's *Volpone* (1940) and a macabre *La Main du Diable* (*The Devil's Hand,* 1942), inspired by Balzac's *La Peau de Chagrin* and shown in America after the war as *Carnival of Sinners.*

As might be expected, the first masterpiece of screen horror is a Griffith film of 1914, *The Avenging Conscience,* an all-inclusive compendium of Poe stories, verse, and lore, that captures the spirit of the man while commenting on the works themselves. Juxtaposing the printed text, photographs, and his own imagery, Griffith accomplished what Seymour Stern has called "a Poe mosaic" and one of his best films prior to *The Birth of a Nation*.

The bulk of the seven reels of *The Avenging Conscience* is devoted to *The Tell-Tale Heart,* but there are interpolations, in the form of subtitles or dramatic incidents, from other prose works such as *William Wilson* or *The Black Cat* as well as poems such as *Annabel Lee, The Bells,* and *The Conquering Worm.* An orphaned young man (Henry B. Walthall) has fallen in love and his tyrannical uncle (Spottiswoode Aitken) opposes the love match. Observing a spider trap and devour a fly, after which some ants attack and kill the spider, the hero concludes that life "is a long system of murder." He kills his uncle and walls up the body in the fireplace. Later, as he is being questioned by a detective (Ralph Lewis), his conscience overcomes him. The ticking of the clock, the rhythmic tapping of the policeman's foot, and the reiterated screeching of a night bird—all these sounds become to him "the beating of the dead man's heart."

One expects from Griffith masterful editing and effective performances, and rarely has the silent screen so expertly evoked sound as in the confession scene. More surprising, however, is the introduction of a gruesome, sinister sequence—one of those symbolic asides that Griffith favored in his movies—in which the guilt-ridden hero envisions himself summoning the creatures of the night, the "ghoul visions" of *The Bells,* "neither men nor women, neither brutes nor human," and the film achieves what poet Vachel Lindsay called "a higher demoniacal plane." This crescendo of horror collapses when the hero wakes up from a nightmare, induced by his reading of Poe's poem. This evasion seems to have satisfied contemporary audiences; Lindsay, who was America's first movie critic, speaks of it as "a radiant climax" when in retrospect it seems about the only flaw in this exercise in terror.

After such an accomplishment, Griffith's next venture into the horror thriller, *One Exciting Night* (1922), is sadly disappointing. Publicized as "the first genuinely up-to-date mystery ever filmed, brimful of love, laughter, and thrills," it merely attempts to profit from the current vogue for mystery plays like *The Bat* and *The Cat and the Canary.* Most of the action is set in a Baltimore mansion during a stormy night; the characters are the usual stock figures of stage melodrama. The plot contains two murders, a hidden bootleg treasure, a variety of suspects, and a hooded figure stalking the heroine (Carol Dempster) from behind sliding panels and secret doors. Griffith failed where later (and lesser) directors were to succeed. His haunted house holds no real menace and the mood is constantly sacrificed to some unfunny interludes featuring a comedian in blackface. *One Exciting Night* does achieve some excitement in its storm-lashed climax, where Griffith intercuts some authentic footage of a real hurricane he had filmed on Long Island the previous summer.

In 1925, Griffith left United Artists and signed with Paramount to direct three films, the first of which was *The Sorrows of Satan,* adapted from a novel by Marie Corelli that had delighted Queen Victoria herself and already furnished Carl Dreyer with the inspiration for his grim *Leaves from Satan's Book* (1921). Originally planned for Cecil B. De Mille, the project was not of Griffith's choosing. It was a modern retelling of the Faust legend in which Satan, in the guise of the mundane Prince Riminez (Adolphe Menjou) tempts a struggling young author away from his faithful sweetheart (Carol Dempster) and into the arms of a temptress (Lya de Putti). Griffith managed to imprint his signature on some of the best scenes: the prologue, taken from the Apocalypse, with the rebellious angels being driven from Heaven, is an effective embellishment. As usual, poverty is depicted with warmth and affection but there is also an unexpected flair in the portrayal of the orgiastic, luxurious world of Riminez, and a sensuous elegance worthy of Josef von Sternberg in the scenes with the vamp. The long-awaited moment of shock comes when the Prince drops his gentlemanly pretense and reveals his true Satanic self to the hero. Griffith wisely realized that a graphic presentation of a medieval Satan, complete with bat wings and spiked tail, would elicit laughter rather than fright. He gives us, instead, the hero's terrified reaction as the winged shadow looms over him, thus establishing the first precept of psychological horror: never show too much on the screen.

Griffith's Satan was a Continental man of the world. The Devil had already appeared in typically American guise in *Puritan Passions* (1923), a commendable attempt to render fantasy in American terms. An adaptation of Percy MacKaye's stage play *The Scarecrow,* which in turn derived from Nathaniel Hawthorne's *Feathertop,* the film was a combination of the Faust and Frankenstein themes and was set in Salem, Massachusetts, at the time of the witch-hunts. A child, born out of wedlock to Gillead Wingate and Goody Rickby, dies when the father refuses to seek a doctor's aid for fear of scandal. Goody swears revenge on the hypocritical Wingate, whereupon a mysterious Dr. Nicholas (Osgood Perkins) appears to offer his help. He breathes life into a scarecrow, making him into a handsome gentleman (Glenn Hunter) and directs him to court Rachel (Mary Astor), Wingate's ward. The girl falls in love with the strawman and a marriage is arranged. Nicholas, Old Nick himself, knows that when the truth is found out, both Wingate and Rachel will hang for witchcraft. But the Scarecrow foils Nicholas by laying down his life for love of Rachel, thus earning a soul and dying a man.

Deprived of sound and dialogue, director Frank Tuttle retained a good part of the play's poetic quality by making the picture strikingly visual and borrowing the barest of influence (like a blacksmith shop set) from German films. There were scenes of a supernatural horror, as when the weird, misshapen creatures of the netherworld meet for the witches' Sabbath or the episode of the Mirror of Truth, borrowed from Goethe's *Faust,* where sinners see themselves as they really are. And in its engaging, cynical devil, *Puritan Passions* points the way to *The Devil and Daniel Webster,* Stephen Vincent Benét's story of a New England Faust who sells his soul to a Down East devil, made into an effective movie in 1941, *All that Money Can Buy.*

The chill provided by the 867 record-breaking performances of *The Bat* proved to be contagious when, in 1922, the Broadway season unveiled such exercises in terror and the supernatural as *The Cat and the Canary, The Charlatan, The Night Call, Drums of Jeopardy,* a revival of the perennial *Trilby* and *The Return of Peter Grimm*—to be followed later in the year by *The Last Warning* and *The Monster.* Film-makers in Hollywood and New

York took notice: all the above-mentioned thrillers found their way to the screen with varying degrees of success.

But the best horror film of the year did not derive from a play. It was Goldwyn's production of *A Blind Bargain,* which brought back to the movies the character of the mad scientist in a very contemporary guise. However melodramatic, the film was inspired by the then-current interest in the Voronoff theories of prolonging life and youth by the transplanting of animal glands (mostly from monkeys) into human beings. These experiments, well-covered by the press of both continents, had inspired a best-selling novel *Black Oxen* (later released in movie form early in 1924), as well as the dusting off of an old Marie Corelli novel, *Young Diana,* which served as a Marion Davies vehicle in 1922 and was beautifully designed by Joseph Urban. *A Blind Bargain* was more outrageously fantastic than either of these:

> Robert, a young man down-and-out (Raymond McKee) agrees to submit to an experiment to be performed on him by the eminent scientist Dr. Lamb (Lon Chaney) in return for which Lamb agrees to treat Robert's sick mother. The young man soon realizes that the experience may cost him his life after he discovers that the hunchbacked assistant (Lon Chaney) of the doctor is really an ape-man, the result of a previous experiment. The ape-man reveals to Robert the doctor's secret operating room and the hideous creatures kept in cages in varied stages of human completion. Dr. Lamb overpowers Robert and straps him to the operating table, after which the ape-man releases a gorilla-like monster who crushes the life out of the mad scientist.

Based on the novel *The Octave of Claudius* by Barry Pain, the film is basically a free adaptation of Wells' *The Island of Dr. Moreau* with its semihuman horrors, sympathetic man-beast, and grisly climax. It was to become the archetype of the mad scientist movies and it further enhanced the reputation of Lon Chaney, who played the dual role of Dr. Lamb and the Hunchback.

Already a well-known character actor, Chaney had entered the movies in 1913, appearing in some one hundred films before attracting attention as the villain in *Riddle Gawne,* a William S. Hart Western of 1918. Born in Colorado Springs in 1886 of deaf and dumb parents, he had learned to express himself in pantomime from an early age and to use his forceful, expressive face as well as his well-coordinated body. This ability served him well in his performance of the Frog, the false cripple "cured" by the power of faith in *The Miracle Man* (1919). As he advanced in his career, Chaney was often cast in roles that required him to change his appearance. He soon became a master of makeup and rightfully earned the title of "The Man of a Thousand Faces." Yet Chaney realized that no amount of putty and false hair can create a believable character. His monstrosities, however warped in body and spirit, were still resolutely human. As often as not, his best parts required no particular trickery, such as in *Tell It to the Marines* and *Thunder*. At the time *A Blind Bargain* was made, he was in great demand as a villain. Tourneur had used him as the pockmarked Ricardo of Joseph Conrad's *Victory,* as two pirates in *Treasure Island,* and as the insane waxworks curator in *While Paris Sleeps.* His nonracial interpretation of Fagin in the Jackie Coogan version of *Oliver Twist* won him the best reviews of anyone in the picture.

In 1923, Chaney rejoined Wallace Worsley, who had directed *A Blind Bargain,* at Universal for an ambitious, expensive adaptation of the Victor Hugo classic *Notre Dame de Paris,* in which he played Quasimodo as the hideous, lovesick gnome of a fairy tale. His makeup, however, was faithful to Hugo's description of the deformed bellringer: bristly hair, collapsed eye, uneven teeth, and "an indefinable mixture of malice, bewilderment, and sadness." He also wore a heavy rubber hump and a harnesslike contraption that prevented him from standing erect. During the three months it took to complete the movie, Chaney was in pain a good part of the time. For his pains, the film was selected as one of the ten best of the year, and his performance is regarded as a masterpiece. *The Hunchback of Notre Dame* is a historical spectacle rather than a horror film and hardly compares with the 1939 remake, a superior piece of Grand Guignol.

Quasimodo made Chaney a star and Universal gave him the leading role in a film version of Gaston Leroux's 1908 novel *The Phantom of the Opera.* A good deal of secrecy surrounded the making of this movie: the story leaked out that Chaney's makeup was so horrendous that no pictures could be released to the public, at least not until the film had opened. The truth of the matter was that Chaney had clashed with the director, Rupert Julian. Julian had replaced Erich von Stroheim in the direction of *Merry Go Round* (1923), and he adopted some of Stroheim's martinet manners without matching his talents. Another director, Edward Sedgwick, was called to complete *The Phantom,* but Chaney himself directed many of his own scenes. The film went through several versions before its official release in September of 1925. As expected, the show was patchwork. It went on, however, to become one of the Ten Best Films of the Year, a huge money-maker for Universal and one of the best-remembered movies of the Silent Era.

In spite of *The Phantom of the Opera*'s veristic setting, Leroux's mystery romance is actually a fairy tale that gradually spirals into nightmare fantasy as the hero is subjected to a progression of ordeals in order to liberate Beauty from the Beast. The film became more of a compressed serial than a true horror film.

Backstage at the Paris Opera, the body of a stagehand is found hanging in the flies. The entire company is thrown into a panic for they know that deep in the maze of cellars beneath the theater there lives a mysterious creature who has access to the thousand-odd departments of the building and for whom a private box is permanently reserved. Nobody dares descend to the lower levels, except an equally sinister person known as the Persian.

Christine, a beautiful young singer in the chorus has been advised and coached on the premises by a strange, unseen voice, who has promised to make her a diva. She calls her mentor the Spirit of Music. "Think only of your art and your master," whispers the voice. "Soon this spirit will take form and demand your love."

Christine gets her chance to substitute for the prima donna and is revealed as a singer of great talent and promise; in spite of this, the management replaces her with a better-known singer. As this replacement sings on stage against the Phantom's warning, a voice whispers to the terrified directors: "She sings to bring down the chandelier!" The massive lamp, freed from its moorings, comes crashing down on the audience. In the ensuing panic, Christine is lured by the voice of the Spirit of Music into entering his world. From behind her dressing-room mirror, a masked figure appears to conduct her through an underground labyrinth of ramps, stairways, and tunnels, leading to a subterranean lake. She soon realizes that the Spirit of Music and the Phantom of the Opera are one and the same. Upon reaching the Phantom's lair, deep under the Opera House, she discovers that a macabre bridal suite awaits her.

While the Phantom plays his composition "Don Juan Triumphant," an apprehensive but curious Christine steals to his side and tears off his mask. The face of the Phantom is that of a living skull and the girl recoils in horror. He reproaches her for her curiosity and discloses to her some of his past life; later, he allows her to return to the outside world on condition that she must not breathe a word of what she has seen and learned.

During the Masked Ball, held every year at the Opera, Christine leads her suitor, Raoul, away from the carousers and "the ever-listening walls" to the theater roof, and there she relates her adventure. The couple does not realize that they are being spied upon by the Phantom. Shortly after, Christine disappears, presumably forever. Raoul, with the help of the Persian, in reality an agent of the French police, follows her into the Phantom's lair.

Only Louis Feuillade, the creator of the great French serials, could have matched the delirious imagination of the closing chapters of the novel, as Raoul and the Persian fall into the Phantom's trap, escape death by fire and water to be ultimately saved through Christine's intervention. Julian *et al.* stumble upon as many rich effects as they miss entirely: the fall of the chandelier is unexciting, the love scenes, as usual, the weakest spots in this kind of story. Among effective moments, a shot of Raoul and the Persian, advancing in the dark with one arm outstretched to ward off the Phantom's deadly noose, brings to mind similar moments in such French serials as *Les Vampires* or *Judex.* The Phantom's entrance at the masked ball, costumed as the Red Death, is effective too, originally even more so since it was filmed in the early Technicolor process. Color was also used for the ballet and opera sequences and the Phantom's billowing cape was hand-colored crimson for the scene where he hovers over the lovers, perched on a statue of Apollo like the Angel of Doom.

Conscious or not, the influence of *The Phantom of the Opera* has been felt in most horror efforts since. A good deal of Cocteau's *Beauty and the Beast* (1946) obviously derives from the long, dreamlike descent into the Phantom's netherworld, Christine astride an incongruous white stallion, her long white veil trailing, or, gliding in a black gondola, the Phantom as Charon, along the vaulted canals. Cocteau, on the other hand, knows the value of his symbols (the mirror, the horse) and those at Universal did not know the value of theirs. *The Phantom*'s most immediate influence can be seen in Universal's horror series of the thirties. The character of *The Phantom,* combining the attributes of musical genius, master builder, and ruthless killer, is an early version of the sympathetic monster-villain, while the leading man (Norman Kerry) is merely incidental to the drama, requiring a secondary hero, the Persian (Arthur Edmund Carew), to match wits with the Phantom. And it is the Paris populace that storms the subterranean rooms and eventually kills the fiend, unlike the novel where the Phantom meets a quietly mysterious end. The splitting of the hero into different entities (lover, antagonist, executioner) was to be retained in most of the horror films of the thirties.

Whether reported faintings in the audience were real or dreamed up by the Universal publicity department, Chaney's characterization was everything the public had come to expect of him. In a daily, self-imposed ordeal, Chaney's features were distended, pulled apart, and disfigured into a livid, cadaverous face of Death itself. Since familiarity would diminish the effect, Chaney withholds the unmasking scene until the story is well under way. Also, he subtly increases the horror of his appearance as the movie progresses so that he is nowhere more impressive than in the closing scenes, as he frenziedly drives a coach past Notre Dame (a set left over from his previous success), or when he makes one last pitiful stand against the enraged Paris mob.

Phantom was the last movie Chaney made for any studio except Metro-Goldwyn-Mayer. That same year, he parodied his own mad scientist (of *A Blind Bargain*) in a comedy thriller, *The Monster.* Also working at the studio was Tod Browning, who had directed some of Chaney's earlier pictures. The combination of Browning and Chaney was to give the silent screen its best chilling moments and a wonderful gallery of grotesques. Among them, the crooked ventriloquist masquerading as an old lady in *The Unholy Three* (1925), the one-eyed reprobate of *The Road to Mandalay* (1926), and the crippled, sadistic magician of *West of Zanzibar* (1928).

A director with a leaning toward the macabre and the offbeat, Browning delighted in dreaming up impossible feats for Chaney to perform. In *The Unknown,* a circus story in which Chaney played Alonzo the Armless Wonder, the actor wore the tightest of straitjackets binding his arms to his sides and he learned how to hold cigarettes with his toes. However, Metro's claims that he also learned to throw knives and light matches with his feet seem nowadays an exaggeration, especially on seeing the film again, where the more difficult scenes are done either in extreme close-up or extreme long-shot, betraying the presence of a double. Chaney's suffering for his art reached a peak in Browning's *London after Midnight* (1927) in which he played a hideously grotesque vampire, prowling the moor in the company of his wraith-like daughter (Edna Tichenor). Surpassing his characterization as the Phantom, Chaney employed some painful devices, such as thin wires that made his eyes bulge and a bridge of animal-like teeth that made speech impossible and which he could endure wearing only for short periods of time. These macabre episodes of *London after Midnight* are finally exposed as a hoax intended to trap a murderer and staged by a Scotland Yard inspector, also played by Chaney, whose frequent double roles must have saved the producers a small fortune.

Like Chaplin and Garbo, Chaney held off against talking pictures until 1930 when he remade his silent hit, *The Unholy Three* as a "talkie," showing that his protean qualities were not reserved for the silent screen—Chaney employs four different voices as Echo the Ventriloquist, mimicking an old woman, a parrot, and a baby, while he gave his own voice the forceful ring of James Cagney's. He was considering a return to Universal in Browning's projected version of *Dracula* when a growth in his throat was found to be malignant. As his condition worsened, he lost the ability to speak, and Lon Chaney's on-screen voice was the last of him to be heard. Still one of the nation's top attractions, he died at the age of 44 in 1930, and for a while it seemed that with his death would disappear the tradition of screen horror, a genre to which he had helped bring acceptance and acclaim.

The line between science fiction and horror was still well-drawn in 1925 when *The Lost World* was released. An adaptation of Conan Doyle's "scientific romance," it concerned a British expedition to the Amazon jungle where the explorers discover a time-forgotten plateau, some giant lizards of the Mesozoic Era, and a hostile, hirsute creature who just might be the missing link. The movie was pure adventure and accepted by the public as such. After the arrival of sound, the same dinosaurs would become roaring creatures of horror, but in 1925 the silence that is their movie lot makes them less formidable.

In spite of practically nonexistent direction by Harry Hoyt, the picture was selected as one of the ten best of the year in a poll conducted by the *Motion Picture Daily*, a trade publication. It had a cast of sympathetic performers (Wallace Beery, Lewis Stone, Bessie Love, and Bull Montana as the Ape-Man), but the real stars of the movie were the prehistoric monsters themselves, animated by the special effects of Willis H. O'Brien which equaled, and were soon to surpass, the best from the German studios.

Born in Oakland, California, in 1886, O'Brien had started his career as a cartoonist and amateur sculptor. Soon after, he began experimenting in stop-motion photography with small clay figures of boxers. Transferring his interest to the Stone Age, he constructed crude models of a dinosaur and a caveman out of modeling clay around articulated wooden frames, and shot a jerky, imperfect film on the roof of the Bank of Italy (now the Bank of America) in San Francisco. One producer was sufficiently impressed to advance O'Brien $5,000 for a longer, more ambitious short, *The Dinosaur and the Missing Link*. It took two months to make the film, which ran some five minutes on the screen, but the Edison Company of New York bought it and released it in 1917. O'Brien followed his film to the East and made ten Stone-Age films for Edison under the label of Manikin Films, each running five minutes and costing $500. Most of them were humorous in nature, like *Rural Delivery, Million B.C.* and they helped establish

O'Brien's reputation. In 1919, his longer, more ambitious *The Ghost of Slumber Mountain,* which already anticipated *The Lost World,* brought in $100,000, although it cost only $3,000 to make.

For *The Lost World,* O'Brien perfected a process whereby miniature rubber models molded over wooden joints were photographed in gradual stages of movement against appropriately scaled sets. Real performers were then photographed, reduced in size on film, and matched with the trick footage. The best moments of the film made it all worthwhile—the monsters battling among themselves, a wild stampede of prehistoric fauna fleeing an erupting volcano, and the climax where a live brontosaurus runs loose through the streets of London. They made the movie an outstanding novelty and provided a fine blueprint for O'Brien's masterpiece, *King Kong,* in the following decade.

Probably the most elusive of lost films is *The Magician,* a 1926 film version of Somerset Maugham's early novel inspired by the legendary Aleister Crowley, novelist and famous practitioner of the black arts. In the mid-twenties, newspapers, here and abroad, were full of reports on Crowley's founding of a love cult in Sicily, a combination of sexual rites and old-fashioned demonology, that could not help but capture the fancy of Rex Ingram. After directing such Hollywood successes as *The Four Horsemen of the Apocalypse* (with Valentino) and *Scaramouche* (with Ramon Novarro), Ingram, with his wife, the actress Alice Terry, had settled in the south of France. A full-blown Irishman fascinated by the bizarre and the grotesque (he once employed a dwarf as his personal valet), Ingram was also a writer of some talent. At the beginning of his film career, a weird story of his, *Black Orchids,* served as the point of departure for one of his films; a second version of this particular opus, titled *Trifling Women* (also directed by him) with Barbara LaMarr as a necromancer-vamp, contained enough poisoning, satanism, and necrophilia to make it one of the commercial disasters of 1922. Frequently pedestrian and pretentious, Ingram's films nevertheless contain splendid flashes of macabre fantasy, such as the ride of the Four Horsemen in the Valentino epic, or the "ghoul visions" that bring about the death of the miser in *The Conquering Power.* His more or less mystical bent was apparent in *Mare Nostrum* and *The Garden of Allah* which he filmed in the Mediterranean and North Africa, respectively.

Made for Metro in France, away from all interference, *The Magician* was saluted upon release by a barrage of negative criticism, mostly on grounds of tastelessness, that sealed the picture's doom. The still photographs, all that are available to the present day, show Ingram at the height of his pictorial talent. To play Oliver Haddo, the obsessive seeker of the homunculus, Ingram secured the great Golem of German films, Paul Wegener. The high point of the film was a nightmarish sequence in which the hypnotized heroine (Alice Terry) sees herself in the midst of an orgiastic rite presided over by Pan himself, a prancing, naked satyr played by Stowitts, the American dancer at the Folies Bergère.

As Rex Ingram's films became more esoteric, his career declined. The coming of sound forced him to relinquish his studios in Nice. Rather than equip them for talking pictures, he chose instead to travel and pursue a writing career. His one sound film, *Love in Morocco* (1933), was also his last. Ingram died in 1950. Aside from his thinly veiled portrait in *The Magician,* Crowley's evil fascination has eluded the movies. More's the pity, for one of his own novels, *Moonchild,* seems to have marvelous cinematic potential.

The exodus of film talent from Germany, which began with Pola Negri and Ernst Lubitsch in the early twenties, had achieved considerable magnitude by 1927. Among the Berlin imports working in Hollywood were such directors as F. W. Murnau, Dimitri Buchowetzki, Lothar Mendes, Alexander Korda, Andre Edwald Dupont, Ludwig Berger, and Michael Curtiz. Among the performers were Emil Jannings, Conrad Veidt, Lya de Putti, and Camilla Horn. Some of these artists found a haven at Universal studios, run by German-born Carl Laemmle, where Dupont directed *Love Me and the World Is Mine,* a Viennese romance in the von Stroheim manner. Buchowetzki was assigned a Laura La Plante vehicle, *The Midnight Sun,* which contained a bizarre Ballet Russe sequence (to pop up unexpectedly in the *Flash Gordon* serials of the thirties). Neither of these men matched their European successes, but their compatriot, Paul Leni, did go beyond his well-known 1924 *Wachsfigurenkabinett* (called *Waxworks* in England and released in America as *Three Wax Men*) and made the grade in the United States with his first Universal opus, an adaptation of John Willard's Broadway play of 1922, *The Cat and the Canary.*

Having served as art designer for the work of other directors (for, as an example, Dupont's *Variété*), Leni knew the importance of sets and lighting as ingredients in the creation of mood. He brought a Germanic eye to an essentially American script. There had been previous haunted-house pictures—the year before *The Cat and the Canary, The Bat* had been filmed with uneven success. Leni filled his haunted house not only with the standard cobwebs and sliding doors but with a genuine sense of mystery.

> The relatives of the late Ambrose West assemble in Clifton Castle on the Hudson to attend the reading of his will at midnight on the twentieth anniversary of his death. West was an eccentric millionaire obsessed with hereditary insanity. His will names Annabelle West (Laura LaPlante) as sole heir, but if she should show any signs of mental unbalance, it is provided that a second envelope shall be opened and a second heir named. During the night, Annabelle is scared out of her wits by a hairy hand reaching for her throat from the curtains of her bed. The lawyer drops dead from behind a secret panel. To complicate matters further, an insane criminal, named The Cat, is said to have escaped from an asylum nearby. The other relatives try to pass Annabelle off as insane; only Paul Jones (Creighton Hale) realizes it is all a plot to deprive the girl of her inheritance. The night brings many terrors but with the coming of dawn, the mystery is solved: The Cat turns out to be the second heir, and Annabelle and Paul decide to renew their childhood romance.

Leni established the mood from the first frame: a hand wipes away the cobwebs to reveal the credits. Then, in a weirdly symbolic shot, we see Ambrose West encircled by enormous medicine bottles, while huge, malevolent cats—his greedy relatives waiting for his death—hiss and snarl beyond. One inspired double exposure shows the machinery of a stately clock about to sound midnight, as the lights dim and the apprehensive heirs gather around to hear the will being read. Leni's omniscient camera silently glides along empty corridors, where the wind agitates shroudlike, ghostly curtains. Or, with split-second timing, the camera becomes the murderer's eye, peering from behind a portrait, or the heroine's paralyzed with fear as a gruesomely masked figure advances from the dark.

Leni had updated *The Castle of Otranto* without disturbing the cobwebs. *The Cat and the Canary* became the cornerstone of Universal's school of horror. *Cat* not only influenced such films as *Old Dark House* but was itself remade twice, first in 1930 (as *The Cat Creeps*) and again, at the Paramount studios in 1939, as a vehicle for the comedic talents of Bob Hope. Both versions depended heavily on the Leni original which appears even now as the best of the three. The one thing that has aged ungracefully in it is its comedy. *The Cat and the Canary,* like *The Bat* and *The Gorilla,* is full of cowardly characters shivering under the covers or hiding under the bed. Creighton Hale, the comedian hero of the first version, lacked the acerbic wit of Hope and the rest of the players are undistinguished. But then, what American film could have matched the cast assembled for Leni's *Three Wax Men,* which included Conrad Veidt, Werner Krauss, William Dieterle, and Emil Jannings?

There were some eerie moments in *The Chinese Parrot,* Leni's next assignment at Universal, adapted from a story by Earl Derr Biggers, in which the Japanese actor Sojin played Inspector Charlie Chan of the Honolulu police. As a reward for Leni's fine mood work, Laemmle entrusted him with the direction of Universal's most ambitious production for 1928, an adaptation of Victor Hugo's *The Man Who Laughs,* which Leni smothered in decor and chiaroscuro and turned into an impressive recreation of the splendor and horror of seventeenth-century England. Conrad Veidt, in the role originally intended for Lon Chaney, played Gwynplaine, the kidnapped heir to an earldom, who was hideously deformed into a perpetually smiling clown. Mary Philbin was the blind Dea who loved him; Olga Baclanova, the voluptuous duchess who is both attracted to him and repelled by his deformity. There were the touches of horror expected from Leni, notably

Veidt's torture in the Iron Maiden, but the film was neither a critical nor a commercial success. In an effort to recapture the success of *The Cat and the Canary,* Universal gave Leni a very similar stage thriller, *The Last Warning,* which had some recorded dialogue and sound effects. The setting this time was an abandoned Broadway theater filled with trapdoors and red herrings—it was the same formula and, again, it worked, though in a more modest way. Leni had visual wit as well as a head for the macabre. In *The Cat and the Canary,* he pays tribute to *Caligari* by bringing in an obviously deranged psychiatrist made up to look like Werner Krauss. And in *The Last Warning,* a shot of a theater front changing into a montrous grimacing face is a humorous comment on *Metropolis.* Leni died of blood poisoning in 1929 right after he made *The Last Warning*—an abrupt end to the most promising film career in the annals of terror.

The demise of the silent film, following the spectacular success of *The Jazz Singer,* had all the major studios in Hollywood converting to sound in less than two years. Quite a few silents were lost in the change-over, among them *The Wizard* (1927) adapted from Gaston Leroux's *Balaoo,* which combined a mysterious manor with a mad scientist and his gorilla-man. The last horror film before silents disappeared was First National's production of Abraham Merritt's novel, *Seven Footprints to Satan,* released in 1929 when most of the nation's theaters were already showing "talkies" and silent films were beginning to be regarded as quaint curiosities. The film adaptation brought a light touch to the novel's serious mystery, revealing the devil-worshipping cult as a hoax perpetrated on the hero by his uncle. The picture mocked what thrills there were in the book—it was full to the scuppers with weird characters, fake orgies, trick stairways, and gorillas (no horror movie seemed then to be complete without one or two).

Benjamin Christensen, the director of *Seven Footprints to Satan,* was one of the most ignored talents of his generation. By 1920, his early powerful melodramas elicited praise from a fellow Dane, the distinguished Carl Dreyer. In 1921, Christensen directed *Häxan* (*Witchcraft Through the Ages*) in Sweden, a film which traced diabolism from the Middle Ages to the modern day and seemed an uneven mixture of illustrated lecture and imaginative movie-making. Its Black Masses, stomach-turning detail, and frequent nudity limited the showing of *Häxan* to very few countries. In Hollywood, where he arrived in 1925, Christensen directed a number of indifferent melodramas, among them *Mockery,* a Lon Chaney vehicle, and *The House of Horror,* a parody. At least, they appear indifferent to judge by the not always reliable contemporary reports. Although *The Devil's Circus,* a skillful if outrageous melodrama of 1926, and *Seven Footprints to Satan* have recently turned up in European archives, the rest of Christensen's work—including the films he made in Denmark after his return from Hollywood—remains an unknown quantity. To be fully chronicled, this history of the horror film must wait for their rediscovery and reappraisal.

CHAPTER 4

CHILDREN OF THE NIGHT

Hollywood, 1928–1947

The American silent film which for many years suffered from an inferiority complex in regard to the theater, felt that complex dissolve with the first tearful sobs of Al Jolson in *The Jazz Singer*. Everything that up until then had been denied to the motion picture suddenly seemed attainable. Consequently, in the first two years of the Sound Era, Hollywood films strove to forget everything they had learned in the past thirty—while struggling to master the syntax of sound. Drama was slowed down to endless conversation staged in front of tinny, not so artfully concealed microphones, followed by just as endless pauses for speechless reaction. Or, to break the monotony, the actors sang. In fact, the one genre that was new to the movies was the musical—sound in *The Jazz Singer* meant mostly songs. And Warner's first all-talkie, *The Lights of New York,* had its share of nightclub scenes. In 1929, Hollywood produced more than forty films that could be classified as musicals: operettas, musical comedies, revues, or melodramas sprinkled with songs.

Warner Brothers, then leading the field in sound films, released in 1928 their second all-talkie, an adaptation of Edgar Wallace's London success *The Terror* which dispensed not only with subtitles but with printed billing as well! The cultivated voice of Conrad Nagel read the production credits and also served to inform the public of the time and locale of each scene. *The Terror* was replete with "spine-chilling Vitaphone effects"—which meant the moaning of the wind, the screeching of doors, eerie organ music, piercing screams, and comedienne Louise Fazenda's irritating giggles, not to mention nonstop orchestral accompaniment. The picture may have been full of sound but it signified absolutely nothing. At one point, the leading lady lisped that she was "thick and tired of thuch thilly antics," and thus was lovely May McAvoy's doom sealed. All the male voices sounded alike. In substance, *The Terror* was just another haunted-house mystery. A fiendish criminal, known simply as the Terror, whose features were hidden until the last reel behind the customary black hood stalks the heroine through subterranean tunnels and secret passageways. Warners optimistically predicted that "there's gold in them thar' thrills," but the gold turned to dross in *The Terror,* the first all-talkie to receive lukewarm reviews.

This temporary setback left the field open for the detective film, but it fared no better. Paramount brought Philo Vance to the screen in the person of William Powell in *The Canary Murder Case* (1930). Metro delivered their own Philo Vance, Basil Rathbone, in *The Bishop Murder Case* (1929). *The Donovan Affair,* also in 1929, made some kind of history as the whodunit in which the butler *was* the murderer. All of these efforts, as well as Metro's *The Unholy Night* (1929), were slow-paced and cumbersome, relying entirely on dialogue to unravel the plot. To everyone's surprise, even Tod Browning's *The Thirteenth Chair* (1929) seemed crippled by its stage origins. It was a play in which a medium (Margaret Wycherly in both stage and screen versions) is used to unmask a murderer. The film was notable on two accounts: it brought Browning and Bela Lugosi together for the first time and it opened just as the stock market crashed in October. That sound *could* be used to effect was proved by Jack Conway's remake of *The Unholy Three* (1930) whose plot hinges on a ventriloquist (Lon Chaney) who is capable of changing his voice at will. The melodramatic climax had Chaney, disguised as an old woman, betraying his identity on the witness stand by letting his voice assume its normal masculine pitch. This and other such scenes made audiences realize the contribution of sound to a good story whose silent version had, until now, seemed quite adequate.

The death of Chaney robbed Browning of his favorite interpreter. Nevertheless, the director proceeded with his plans to film *Dracula* at Universal. The Bram Stoker novel had been adapted to the stage by John L. Balderston and Hamilton Deane. An American stage production with Bela Lugosi in the title role opened on Broadway in 1927. In spite of critical disapproval—what the reviewers seemed mainly to object to was that a nurse was in attendance at every performance—it ran for almost a year in New York and two years on tour. Browning based his script on this play version rather than on the novel, much to the detriment of his picture. Sensing a change in attitude toward the blackly supernatural, he presented his vampires as accepted facts of existence. There was no trick ending like that of his *London after Midnight* of four years before. Instead, at *Dracula*'s close, Professor Van Helsing (Edward Van Sloan) warned the audience from the screen that vampires *really* exist.

Not without trepidation, Universal released the film on Valentine's Day, 1931. At first, there was no mention of the picture's unusual theme—"The Strangest Love Story of All" the advertising posters hinted in a cautious tone. Over the novelty of the "Love Story" the critics were enthusiastic, and lines began to form at the Roxy Theatre in New York City. It eventually became Universal's biggest money-maker of the year. The film restored the true meaning to the word "vampire" which had come to stand for predatory females of the Theda Bara school.

Dracula begins well. A few snatches of Tchaikovsky's *Swan Lake* and we are on our way to Dracula's castle in the Carpathian Mountains. Then, as the sun sets, the camera wanders around the crypt, noiselessly watching the vampires leave their coffins. The sequence of Renfield at the castle has a pleasant Gothic flavor, but, as soon as the action moves to London, the picture betrays its origins "on the boards," becoming talky, pedestrian, and uncinematic. We are told, when we should be shown, about "the red mist" that heralds the arrival of the vampire and about the werewolf seen running across Dr. Seward's lawn. Marvelous opportunities are ignored—like the episode of Lucy (Frances Dade) turning into a vampire herself—and the ending is curiously halfhearted. A powerful villain like Dracula surely deserves a more impressive demise than an off-screen groan! Here is a case in which a little more blood and thunder could have been folded into the ingredients.

If *Dracula,* the film, has retained any power to impress after thirty-five years of repeated showings, it is due in the main to Lugosi himself. It is useless to debate whether he was a good actor or not; Lugosi *was* Dracula: the actor's identification with the part is complete. He may not conform to the Stoker description (as does John Carradine, for example), but he left an indelible mark on the role and, consequently, on the horror film as well. Where Chaney remained human and pathetic, Lugosi appeared totally evil. As Count Dracula, he neither asked for nor needed the audience's sympathy. Even Lugosi's nonvillain roles he imbued with malevolence, as in *The Black Cat* and *The Invisible Ray.* To his other roles—mad scientist, necromancer, monster, or mere red herring—he brought a kind of corn-ball, demented poetry and total conviction. At the height of his popularity, he received as many letters as any romantic screen idol, 97 per cent of which, he announced to the press in 1935, came from women. Quite effective too was Lugosi's melifluous, Hungarian-accented voice, which helped create a barrier of unfamiliarity (and something too ambiguous to be charm) that was as effective in its way as Chaney's doleful silence before the Sound Era. There is a world of difference between Christopher Lee's hoary, modern-English introduction of himself (in the British remake) and Lugosi's ominous, remote "I am—Dracula." Lee may indeed be the better actor but Lugosi pretty permanently claims the part. The movies do not often bring about such happy matches.

Even before *Dracula* was released, Universal contemplated a film version of Mary Shelley's *Frankenstein.* Robert Florey, a French director of considerable skill, had been assigned by Richard Schayer, then Universal's story editor, to develop a story-line from the novel. Florey even made some camera tests with Lugosi made up as the Monster and utilizing the standing sets of the work in progress, *Dracula.* The success of Browning's *Dracula* upon release dispelled the last doubt about the marketability of horror films. But the Frankenstein film was to emerge a quite different product from the one envisioned in these early attempts. First of all, Lugosi refused the part on the grounds that the heavy makeup would render him unrecognizable. At this juncture, the direction was entrusted to British director, James Whale, who had only two films to his credit, the successful war drama *Journey's End*—which he had also staged in London and New York—and the less distinguished *Waterloo Bridge.* As a consolation prize, Robert Florey was assigned to direct Lugosi in *Murders in the Rue Morgue.*

A highly sophisticated man with a streak of black humor and an unusual flair for casting, Whale had taken note of the work of a fellow Britisher acting at Universal in a gangster movie called *Graft.* His name was William Henry Pratt; his stage name, Boris Karloff. He had been in films for 12 of his 44 years, playing mostly character roles, among them a Caligaresque mesmerist in *The Bells,* a 1926 adaptation of the Henry Irving barnstormer. Whale had Karloff tested for the part of Dr. Frankenstein's Monster, and with the patience of the veteran, the actor submitted to a four-hour session with makeup man Jack Pierce. The result was more winning than had been gambled on. Whale then selected his friend Colin Clive—whom he had picked from a chorus line for the leading role in *Journeys' End*—to play Dr. Frankenstein because he looked suitably neurotic and high-strung.

Florey was responsible for the plot twist whereby the Monster is given a madman's brain, hence betraying the author's original intention. Mary Shelley's tale tells of a scientist who creates a monster, a hideously misshapen creature, harmless at first but soon driven to commit murder and perform other acts of terror through the fear and revulsion his appearance provokes in others. The movie Monster is a murderous fiend, devoid (at least in this first appearance) of reason and barely glimpsed as human during the episode of the child who befriends him and whom he gratuitously drowns in a lake. This scene with the little girl, incidentally, was the only one to be deleted after audience reaction proved too violently adverse.

A stark, gloomy film, unrelieved by comedy or music, *Frankenstein* is laid in a Central European locale, the outdoor scenes set in a rocky wasteland under a livid sky, while most of the interiors take place in the old mill that serves as Frankenstein's laboratory. From its opening sequence in a graveyard, the film carefully builds up to the first appearance of the Monster: never was Karloff more impressive than in this, his first entrance, with Whale cutting breathlessly from medium shot to close shot to extreme close-up, so that the heavily-lidded, cadaverous face comes to fill the screen. Pierce's conception and realization in makeup remain unsurpassed. Unlike many of Chaney's makeup jobs, so excessive they prevented speech, Karloff's sensitive features are practically naked under the built-up brow and the heavy eyelids, allowing him a wide range of expression. Destined to play the part three times, Karloff brought a different interpretation to each. His successors in the role—Lon Chaney, Jr., Bela Lugosi, and Glenn Strange—never seemed to realize that there was considerably more to the Monster than the flattened skull, the electrodes, and the lead-weighted boots.

Frankenstein went on to become the most famous horror movie of all time; to the mind served by mass media, the doctor and his creation became one and indivisible, at least in reference. The film also revolutionized movie advertising because Universal realized that the public could be frightened into buying tickets. The publicity carried "a friendly warning" advising the weakhearted not to see *Frankenstein.* Weakhearted or not, very few stayed away; yet there were no reports of heart failure, although a few mild cases of hysteria were fanned by Universal into an effective publicity campaign.

In the light of later films, there is little gruesomeness in *Frankenstein:* no dismembered hands or gouged eyes and absolutely no blood are to be seen. Its terror is cold, chilling the marrow but never arousing malaise. The camera (in the hands of Arthur Edeson) never lingers on the violent scenes, and this reticence makes them all the more effective, as in the sequence of the Monster's first killing, when a door is held open long enough to allow a glimpse of the pitiful body of the Dwarf (Dwight Frye), hanging on the wall like some terrible trophy. Whale's direction, perfectly assured in the more fantastic scenes, falters in the brief romantic interludes, which were obviously of little interest to him.

After *Frankenstein,* Whale was to become Universal's master of horror, an honor he accepted only halfheartedly. While pining for weightier subjects, he welcomed his position as the studio's "ace director" which gave him almost complete autonomy in the production of his films. As such, he improved the quality of his scripts by hiring such distinguished authors as R. C. Sherriff (of *Journey's End* fame), John L. Balderston (*Berkeley Square*), and

Philip Wylie. He backed his casts with a troupe of expert British players such as Charles Laughton, Raymond Massey, Ernest Thesiger, and Una O'Connor. His work had wit, elegance, and sharp characterizations. All these qualities were displayed in *Old Dark House,* adapted from a novel by J. B. Priestley (*Benighted*) which concerns a group of travelers forced to seek shelter from a storm in an isolated mansion in Wales. The Fenn family becomes the director's wicked parody of traditional English families: a bedridden patriarch of 102 (John Dudgeon); his sexagenarian son (Ernest Thesiger), obsessed, in his prissiness, with maintaining decorum at all costs; his fanatically religious sister (Eva Moore), an old hag who frequently invokes the wrath of God; and his younger brother (Brember Wells), a pyromaniac who is kept behind locked doors. Lumbering through the house is Morgan (Boris Karloff), a scarred brute of a man, half butler, half keeper, incapable of speech and not to be trusted around a bottle of liquor or an hourglass figure. During the night, the old dark house unveils its secrets. There is nothing supernatural in these terrors, arising as they do from madness, decrepitude and infirmity, natural human failings all. At Metro during the same year, Tod Browning made circus freaks appear human; in *Old Dark House,* Whale perversely inverts the formula and, reinforced by some good ensemble playing, achieves a dazzling display of grotesquerie for its own sake.

Karloff balked at appearing in Whale's next fantasy, an adaptation of H. G. Wells' *The Invisible Man,* which required a good speaking voice and a fair dose of modesty, as the actor would actually be seen only in the film's closing shot. A more self-effacing performer, Claude Rains, created quite an impression in the part, delivering the biting, literate dialogue (written by Sherriff and Wylie) as a sinister presence, his features encased in bandages, or as a disembodied voice.

> To the English village of Ipping comes a mysterious stranger in dark glasses, his face wrapped in bandages, his hands encased in gloves. He rents a room at the local inn and begins to work feverishly in quest of a mysterious chemical. The villagers, made uneasy by his presence, summon the town constable and intrude upon the enigmatic character. Whereupon, the man unwinds the bandages from around an invisible head, discards his clothing, and

totally vanishes under the very orbs of the terrified interlopers. The Invisible Man is Dr. Griffin, a scientist whose recent disappearance baffled his colleagues, Dr. Cranley (Henry Travers) and Dr. Kemp (William Harrigan), as well as Flora Kemp (Gloria Stuart) whom Griffin loves. Forced to seek shelter at Kemp's, Griffin explains to his uneasy host that while experimenting with an Indian drug called monocaine, he discovered that it had the power to render flesh and blood invisible when injected under the skin. However, he does not know that the drug eventually drives its user to madness. In the throes of megalomania, Griffin expounds his plans for world domination through terror. Kemp summons Dr. Cranley and Flora; he also informs the police. Griffin escapes once again, inaugurating his reign of terror by derailing a train, robbing a bank, and committing wanton murder. In spite of police protection, Kemp pays for his betrayal with his life. All plans to capture the Invisible Man are unsuccessful but a snowstorm forces him into a barn, where he falls asleep on a haystack. The sound of his breathing arouses the suspicions of a farmer, who notifies the authorities. The police surround the barn and, as footprints begin to appear on the snow, they open fire. Griffin is mortally wounded, and the effect of the drug dies with him.

The Invisible Man lent itself particularly well to film treatment; the special trick effects of John P. Fulton would have dazzled pioneer trickster Méliès. The scene where Griffin first flaunts his invisibility is the kind of cinema magic that paralyzes disbelief and sets the most skeptical audience wondering. It was primarily achieved by the combination of double exposure and masked negative, but there were other elaborate effects in the picture which required more complex techniques. Not only is the show a technical tour de force, *The Invisible Man* also contains some of the best dialogue ever written for a fantastic film. Dr. Griffin's credo of terror would stagger Dr. Mabuse: "We'll start with a few murders. Big men. Little men. Just to show we make no distinction." As his megalomania mounts, he exults to the terrified Flora: "Power! To make the world grovel at my feet, to walk into the gold vaults of nations, the chambers of kings, into the holy of holies. Even the moon is frightened of me, frightened to death. The whole world is frightened to death."

Side by side with such chilling polemic, there are flashes of the offbeat humor so dear to Whale, as when Griffin expounds on the less practical aspects of his condition, the do's and don'ts of invisibility: keep out of sight one hour after meals; avoid walking in the rain ("It would make me shine like a bubble."); keep rigorously clean to prevent appearing as a dark outline. The private lives of his monsters, the more prosaic side of his fiends plainly fascinate Whale. Long after many of the horrors are forgotten, one remembers the waspish effeminacy of Dr. Praetorius (Ernest Thesiger) in *The Bride of Frankenstein,* warning someone to take heed of a loose step or interrupting his ghoulish pursuits in a crypt by producing some wine and cigars, explaining apologetically to Karloff's Monster: "It's my only weakness, you know."

By 1935, Universal realized that they had been unnecessarily hasty in killing off the Frankenstein Monster and they decided to resurrect him for a sequel, *The Bride of Frankenstein,* again to be directed by James Whale. The original *Frankenstein* ended with the Monster perishing in the flames that consumed the old mill. There was even a happy epilogue, in which the old Baron Frankenstein (Frederick Kerr) toasted his son's recovery some time after the terrors of the night had vanished. Universal took a chance on the public's forgetfulness. The last scene was excised from circulating prints—the film's commercial career was nowhere nearly finished—and the happy ending remained almost forgotten in the Universal vaults until *Frankenstein* was released to television in 1957, whereupon it was restored.

But how was the Monster saved? The new screenplay (by William Hurlbut and John L. Balderston) had him fall to the mill's flooded cellar, escaping both the flames and the angry villagers. To make this unexpected twist more authentic, they included a prologue in which Mary Shelley (Elsa Lanchester) picks up the story where *Frankenstein* left off for the benefit of her husband (Douglas Walton) and Lord Byron (Gavin Gordon).

> The Monster rises from the smoldering ruins of the windmill to spread death and terror over the countryside. Pursued by the villagers, he finds refuge with a blind hermit, who teaches him to speak and enjoy human pleasure, such as music and tobacco. This peace-

ful interlude is interrupted by the arrival of some hunters from the village, who recognize the Monster as Frankenstein's creation, and force him to flee. Hiding among the dead in a cemetery, the Monster encounters Dr. Praetorius—necromancer, scientist, and grave-robber—who conceives the idea of giving the Monster a female companion. Dr. Frankenstein is forced to assist Praetorius in the creation of the She-Monster, when the Monster abducts his wife Elizabeth (Valerie Hobson). The scientists succeed in giving life to the artificial woman who, in a response they had not counted on, is repelled by her intended mate. The Monster allows Dr. Frankenstein to escape from the laboratory before blowing it to bits, destroying Praetorius, the Monstress, and himself.

If Universal expected Whale to deliver the formula as before, they got more than they bargained for. *The Bride of Frankenstein* is the high point of his career, a baroque exercise in the fantastic that periodically succeeds in parodying itself. For once, the sequel improves on the original. Where *Frankenstein* had hardly any music—a few snatches composed by David Broekman and heard under the opening credits—*The Bride* has a full score by Franz Waxman, which includes a leitmotiv for the Monster and his bride. The rather austere photography of the original is replaced here by the fluid, elaborate travelings of John D. Mescall. There are many embellishments to the plot, such as the tiny homunculi Dr. Praetorius keeps in labeled jars. Praetorius himself, as played by Whale's friend Ernest Thesiger, is a wonderful cartoon condensation of all mad scientists, past and present. The most fabulous element of all is the moment of the creation of the She-Monster, a riotous display of unusual camera angles, fast editing, and electrical effects that reaches its climax with the unveiling of the Bride, scored by Waxman with a cacophony of bells. Elsa Lanchester in her white shroud and Nefertiti hairdo is a truly fantastic apparition. With Karloff, she manages to communicate, in their brief courtship scene, a delicate suggestion of both the wedding bed and the grave.

The Bride was to be Whale's last venture into fantasy. During the filming, he met with some opposition from Universal, on grounds that he had made the Monster too human to be frightening. Even Karloff considered it a mistake to have the Monster talk, enjoy a smoke, and laugh. Whale's far-out humor shows itself in the episode with the hermit, making it a pastoral-grotesque interlude. It becomes more irreverent when the Monster, trussed up and raised aloft on a cross by villagers, becomes a queer Christlike figure. Later, the studio was to revive the Monster periodically, but as far as James Whale was concerned, this film brought the Frankenstein saga to an end.

Whale remained something of an enigma to the outside world. After directing successful screen versions of *Showboat* (from the play by Edna Ferber and Jerome Kern) and *The Man in the Iron Mask* (from *Le Vicomte de Bragelonne* by Dumas *père*), he retired in 1941 and after several abortive attempts at a comeback, he was discovered dead in his swimming pool in 1957 under mysterious circumstances. A multifaceted talent with a skill for painting, writing, and set-designing, Whale brought fastidiousness to his films, elaborating and refining the European tradition. His approach to the Frankenstein story—especially in the light of the recent stage adaptation by The Living Theatre in Europe—was a most modern one and *The Bride of Frankenstein* remains, along with *King Kong,* Hollywood's finest moment of unbridled imagination.

As a boy, Lon Chaney used to watch the clowns on the stage of a theater in Colorado Springs and years later, at the peak of his career, he gave them credit not only for teaching him the basic rules of makeup but also for the inspiration of his more sinister roles. Chaney contended that clowns are only funny when seen in context and that their painted faces and perennial smiles could project the same eerie quality of such characters as the Phantom of the Opera, for instance. There is nothing laughable about a clown in the moonlight, he used to say.

The world of the circus, the carnival, and the sideshow also attracted Tod Browning, who had made his start under the big top. It served as the background of such Browning movies as *The Unholy Three, West of Zanzibar, The Show,* and *The Mystic.* And, even more extraordinary than these, was his *The Unknown* (1927), in which Chaney had both his arms amputated for the love of a girl (Joan Crawford) who could not bear to be held in a man's embrace. Yet even this bizarre exercise in sadomasochism seems no more than a pale draft for *Freaks* (1932) which Browning directed on his return to Metro-Goldwyn-Mayer following the success of *Dracula.* The film, the strangest in his career and one of the most unique ever produced anywhere, was adapted from a story called "Spurs" written by Tod Robbins. The story was initially suggested to Browning by his friend, the famous German midget Harry Earles, who had created such a memorable portrait of diminutive malevolence in both versions of *The Unholy Three*

That *Freaks* was made at all is extraordinary. That it was made at Metro, the glamour factory that produced Garbo, Crawford, and Shearer, seems hard to believe. It appears that production manager Irving Thalberg backed Browning against massed opposition, for, this time, the freaks were to be played by real freaks assembled from all parts of the world. There were Johnny Eck, the boy with half a torso; Randian the Living Torso; Martha the Armless Wonder; the Siamese twins Daisy and Violet Hilton—and dwarfs, pinheads, bearded women, sword swallowers among others. Hollywood had never seen anything like it and, as it turned out, not many people were to get the chance to see it on the screen, either. The real thing proved too strong for some of the exhibitors, who flatly refused to run the film after a disastrous preview in San Diego, California, during which a woman ran screaming up the aisle. *Freaks* was cut in some states and banned in the United Kingdom for thirty years.

The story concerns the beautiful Cleopatra (Olga Baclanova), a trapeze performer in a circus who marries a midget (Harry Earles) in a scheme to get his inheritance. With the complicity of her lover, Hercules the Strong Man (Henry Victor), she poisons the midget within an inch of his life. Her plot is discovered by the freaks who wreak a terrible revenge on the guilty pair.

It is the kind of truculent story that might be heard over a beer from any sideshow barker, and the film appropriately opens and closes with such a character delivering his spiel. If the film were no more than a tour of a teratological universe, it would be as gratuitous and voyeuristic as the worst of *Mondo Cane.* But Browning also takes a compassionate look into the private lives of his creatures and finds them to be sensitive, vulnerable, and intensely human characters. His camera descends to their eye-level: one effective scene between two midgets, surrounded by their tiny props, communicates a sense of normality that is destroyed when a normal person intrudes on the scene. Freaks among themselves cease to be freaks. Unfortunately, although the grisly ending is intended as just retribution, it arouses a very different kind of horror. At the sight of the creeping, crawling creatures, we take our stand with the "normal" Cleopatra and Hercules. Our identification with the freaks has been purely intellectual.

This ambiguity apart, *Freaks* contains the most accomplished scenes of Browning's career. The wedding banquet brims over with Goyaesque vitality as the freaks sing, dance, and chant in rhythm their acceptance of Cleopatra as one of them, and a loving cup is passed from mouth to mouth to be finally presented to the nauseated bride by an exuberant dwarf. The climactic attack on the guilty couple takes on the aspect of a deadly ritual, scored to the reedy tune of an ocarina, as the freaks gather their forces in the rain and the mud, their knives revealed by the flash of lightning. Discarded was an alternate ending in which the Strong Man was emasculated rather than eliminated. As it is, the final shot of Baclanova transformed by the crude surgery of the freaks into a "human hen" is one of the shock moments of the decade.

In 1935, the peak year of Hollywood horror, Metro encouraged Browning to remake *London after Midnight* as *The Mark of the Vampire* dividing the old Chaney role into two separate parts for Lionel Barrymore (as the detective) and Bela Lugosi (as the vampire). The studio lavished its resources on this film, including some outstanding photography by James Wong Howe. Unluckily for the public, the recent failure of *Freaks* had made Browning forget the lesson of *Dracula*—he reverted to the old Silent Era theory that audiences would not stand for "the horrible impossible." And so, the ending of *The Mark of the Vampire* absurdly betrays some of the most hauntingly suggestive scenes found in the horror film during the thirties, such as the Vampire Girl (Carol Borland) being airborne on batwings like a Max Ernst postcard come to life. This and other scenes suffer from an ending which explains the Undead away as vaudeville performers, the pawns in an elaborate scheme to solve a murder.

In *Freaks,* Browning had made a film that brought him critical comparison with Erich von Stroheim. Paradoxically, the film in which both collaborated in 1936 resulted in a minor, if charming, excursion into the fantastic. *The Devil Doll* combined the bogus old lady of *The Unholy Three* with the pint-sized people seen in *The Bride of Frankenstein* in its story of a fugitive from Devil's Island (Lionel Barrymore) masquerading as the proprietress of a toy shop. The dolls that he sells to those responsible for his unjust incarceration are in reality tiny human beings, the end effects of some experiments in size-reduction. These lovely, lethal dolls (Grace Ford, Arthur Hohl) gave the film its delightful moments, as they move stealthily among the outsize furniture, steal pearls the size of boulders, and even drive a murderous pin into a man's heart. But much more was expected of Browning, von Stroheim, and Guy Endore, who diluted in whimsy the genuinely frightening mood of the original novel, A. A. Merritt's *Burn Witch Burn.*

Tod Browning finished his career with a minor mystery comedy, *Miracles for Sale* (1939), again peopled with stage magicians and fake illusionists. A quiet, reclusive man who had managed to save his considerable earnings, he retired to his luxurious Santa Monica home, where he lived until his death, at 80, on October 6, 1962, gently deprecating the films that had made him rich and celebrated.

Robert Florey brought a somewhat pedantic European taste to his *Murders in the Rue Morgue* (1932), a film closer to Caligari than to Edgar Allan Poe in its bizarre, Expressionistic sets and camera work. The story had a very Hoffmannesque Dr. Mirakle (Bela Lugosi) going about his way in the Paris of Daumier and Murger, trying to prove a theory of evolution that would have staggered Darwin and that involved the kidnapping of women for unholy experiments conducted with a gorilla that Mirakle exhibits in the Boulevard du Crime. At the time of its release, the film was criticized for its unrestrained ferocity. Compared to horror films of more recent vintage, Florey's handling of the theme—with its scabrous sexual implications—seems almost tastefully demure, although a sadistic scene in which a prostitute (Arlene Francis) is bled to death on a torture rack and her body later dumped into the Seine still carries some of the initial shock—

as does the most gruesome scene (the only one retained from the original tale) in which the hero (Leon Ames) discovers the body of the heroine's mother (Betty Ross Clarke), dead and stuffed feet-first up a chimney. There is always something a little too derivative in his work to support the theory that Florey's *Frankenstein* would have been an improvement on the James Whale version. From contemporary reports, it seems his conception of the Monster was very much akin to Wegener's Golem.

The success of *Dracula* and *Murders in the Rue Morgue* encouraged Carl Laemmle of Universal to offer Karl Freund, who had photographed both of these films, the chance to direct his first, *The Mummy* (1932), in which Boris Karloff played Im-ho-tep, a three-thousand-year-old mummy brought back to life when a British archeologist unwittingly reads an invocation from the sacred Book of Thoth. A priest in ancient Egypt, Im-ho-tep had been buried alive for a sacrilegious attempt to restore life to his beloved princess with the aid of the same papyrus. The Mummy appears next in the figure of Ardet Bey, an Egyptian archeologist stalking modern Cairo for the whereabouts of an English girl (Zita Johann) who is the reincarnation of the princess. Apart from its careful photography (by Charles Stumar), *The Mummy* is notable for its sobriety and refusal to shock, concentrating instead on mood. Although this was the picture that confirmed Karloff as Chaney's successor, the well-publicized make up of the Mummy is seen on the screen but briefly. Most of the time, Karloff is seen as the parchment-faced archeologist, enigmatic and stiff as a hieroglyph, one of his most restrained performances.

Unfortunately, Freund's career as a director was limited to one other film, made at Metro three years later, a remake of *The Hands of Orlac* entitled *Mad Love,* which marked Peter Lorre's American debut. Freund made this the antithesis of his first film, piling on absurdities and macabre touches, pulling it off by means of an overwrought Grand Guignol style. Following the Veidt-Wiene original but surpassing it, *Mad Love* had Lorre as Dr. Gogol, a surgical genius, in love with Stephen Orlac's wife (Frances Drake). When Orlac (Colin Clive), a talented pianist and composer loses both hands in a railroad crash, Gogol grafts to his wrists the hands of a knife-murderer (Edward Brophy), recently guillotined. When Orlac discovers the truth, he is haunted by the strange power of his hands and his worst fears are confirmed by a weird, steel-clad figure who claims to be the guillotined killer, brought back to life by Gogol's skill. A frenzied climax has Madame Orlac rescued from the now insane Gogol by her husband's inherited talents as a knife-thrower. Unlike its German predecessor, the film followed its fantastic theme to its gruesome conclusion. After the film was completed, Freund resumed his career as one of Hollywood's most sought-after cameramen, never to direct another film.

The inevitable matching of Universal's masters of horror, Karloff and Lugosi, finally took place in *The Black Cat* (1934) which, despite its title, had nothing to do with Poe's classic of murder and retribution. Sharing equal billing and screen time, Lugosi was dominated by Karloff's lisping, wolfish performance as Hjalmar Poelzig, an Austrian architect who has built his ultramodern home on the ruins of the same fort he betrayed to the enemy during the First World War. To this glass and marble mausoleum comes Lugosi as Dr. Vitus Verdegast, a sympathetic character in spite of his sinister bearing and ambiguous statements. The two adversaries exchange ominous pleasantries, stalk in and out of secret passages, and challenge each other to a game of chess that will decide the fate of the heroine. They finally come to grips when Karloff, about to officiate at a Black Mass with an American girl as unwilling offering, is robbed of his victim by Lugosi, gets tied to a rack and skinned alive just before the entire building—along with most of the cast and the outrageous plot itself—is blown to bits. A contrived catalogue of satanism, necrophilia, sadism, and murder, *The Black Cat* was nevertheless fashioned into a stylish resplendent silk purse by Edgar G. Ulmer, once an assistant to Murnau, who invested the proceedings with a sweeping visual quality, only here and there tagged by pretension. Mescall's mobile, subjective camera dashed up and down stairs, in and out of dungeons, now catching a silhouette and a shadow or looking modestly away when things seemed to be getting out of hand.

The commercial, if not critical, success of *The Black Cat*

prompted the studio to reunite the stars in *The Raven,* which somehow evened matters out by according Lugosi one of his meatiest roles, that of Dr. Vollin, a surgeon obsessed with Edgar Allan Poe, who has equipped his home with all manner of torture devices such as a bedchamber that descends into the cellar, a dungeon with walls that come crushingly together, and a slowly lowering, knife-sharp pendulum. Karloff gave support as the doctor's reluctant assistant, an escaped killer transformed into a hideous mutant by Vollin's surgery. *The Raven,* directed by Lew Landers (then Louis Friedlander), was at heart an old-fashioned serial, memorable mainly for Lugosi's unwitting self-burlesque. When the script has him exulting in such lines as "Poe, you are avenged!" without a shadow of tongue in cheek, the movie becomes its own deadly parody.

From then on, Lugosi's roles appear subservient to those of Karloff, as in *The Invisible Ray,* in which Karloff played a scientist who, having absorbed a deadly dose of radiation, becomes a man whose mere touch means instant death. Like the Invisible Man, Janus Rukh (Karloff) tampers with the secret of the universe and pays for it with his sanity and finally, with his life. More than any other horror film of the thirties, *The Invisible Ray* is concerned with the uses and misuses of science, uncannily anticipating the post-World War II science fiction thrillers. A foreword title explained that the scientific dream of today may well become the scientific fact of tomorrow, and the scenes between Karloff and Lugosi were stylized confrontations between "black" and "white" science. The picture ends as Janus, about to be consumed by his own radioactivity, fumbles with a life-saving antidote and his own mother (Violet Kemble Cooper) smashes the vital syringe as she reproaches him for breaking "the first rule of science." Unencumbered by its momentous subject, the picture was briskly directed by Lambert Hillyer, a specialist in Western movies. That same year (1936), Universal entrusted him with the direction of *Dracula's Daughter,* the long-awaited sequel to their first success. Hillyer rose to the occasion, delivering a serious, unpredictable horror film, that although lacking such distinguished names as Karloff and Lugosi, did not deserve to go unnoticed as it did, coming at the end of the first cycle of Universal horror. The picture stuck faithfully to the rules, even retaining Edward Van Sloan from the previous opus, as tireless a vampire-killer as before, uttering his by-now-familiar battle-cry, "We must find it and destroy it!," and always in perfect command of the situation. What is most remarkable about *Dracula's Daughter* is that a director as vigorous and straightforward as Hillyer could invest the scenes between the female vampire (Gloria Holden) and her victims (Nan Gray, Marguerite Churchill) with the subtly perverse overtones already present in Dreyer's *Vampyr* and later to be found in Roger Vadim's *Blood and Roses* (1959).

Throughout the thirties, Karloff and Lugosi shuttled back and forth between Universal and most of the other companies in Hollywood. Karloff exercised some care in the choice of parts; he knew when to play a role with just the right amount of humor (as in *The Mask of Fu Manchu,* which he did at Metro in 1932) or when to deliver a barnstorming performance (as in *The Black Room* for Columbia in 1935) or a quietly effective one (*The Walking Dead,* Warner, 1936). Building a reputation for versatility, he wisely interpolated some non-horror roles among the usual fare, such as *The Lost Patrol* and *The House of Rothschild.* Lugosi, on the other hand, wasted his newly won popularity in shoddy trifles like *The Death Kiss,* where he was required to do nothing but glare and look sinister. (The one marvelous exception was, of course, *White Zombie.*) Eventually, both performers crossed the Atlantic to appear in British films as well: Karloff in *The Ghoul* (1933) and *The Man Who Changed His Mind* (1936), Lugosi in *The Mystery of the Marie Celeste* (1936) and *Dark Eyes of London* (1940).

Next to the vampire, the werewolf is the most recurrent fiend in cinema mythology. As ancient and widespread as that of the Undead, the myth of the lycanthrope springs from an actual pathological aberration in which the patient identifies with a wolf or similar four-legged beast in order to gratify a craving for raw flesh, often that of human beings. It is usually accompanied by the delusion on the part of the lycanthrope that a physical transformation occurs during these crises. Plato, Herodotus, and Pausanias cite cases of lycanthropy; there is a typical werewolf story in Petronius' *Satyricon.* The origin of these beliefs goes back to primeval man and his aversion to man's traditional enemy, the wolf. Certain authors regard the werewolf as a creature closer to the witch than to the vampire—yet the latter shares with the lycanthrope the complicity of night, the fear of certain natural preservatives (such as garlic and wolf bane), and a method of ritualized destruction of a definite mystic order: the stake through the heart or the purifying rays of the sun (for the vampire), a silver bullet (for the werewolf).

Lacking a substantial source of inspiration—there have been no literary works dealing with werewolves that can compare to *Dracula*—Universal had to assemble its own set of rules from the numerous folktales available. A Balkan legend related the werewolf to a mysterious flower and the screenwriters seized on it, disregarding the more elaborate variations (which usually appear associated with cannibalism, satanism, or sexual perversion). *The Werewolf of London* emerged as a variation on the Jekyll/Hyde theme. An English botanist, Wilfred Glendon (Henry Hull), is attacked and bitten by a mysterious creature while searching for the *Marifasa Lupina,* an exceptional flower that blooms by moonlight on the Tibetan plateau. Glendon returns to London with the flower, and the next full moon he changes into a werewolf, a howling man-beast that attacks and kills a woman in the dark streets. An enigmatic Oriental named Yogami (Warner Oland) informs Glendon that the victim of a werewolf, if it survives the attack, will also become a werewolf, and that the *Marifasa* is the only known antidote for werewolfery. In spite of all his self-imposed precautions, Glendon escapes the following night to kill once again. With London in the throes of an epidemic of brutal murders, it soon becomes apparent that not one, but two werewolves are loose in the city. Yogami reveals himself as the other lycanthrope, in fact the one that attacked Glendon in Tibet. Both wolfmen struggle for possession of the flower. Glendon kills Yogami and is shot down by the police as he is about to attack his own beloved wife (Valerie Hobson). In death, he reverts to his normal human form.

Clumsily directed by Stuart Walker, the film fails to evoke a convincing mood of terror. Still, there are some effective touches. One eccentric sequence, worthy of Whale, has two gin-swilling Cockney landladies (Ethel Griffies and Zeffie Tilbury) investigate the howling behind Glendon's door. Lycanthropy is curiously conveyed to a degree equating it here with some sort of epilepsy or even acute alcoholism. In his sober, daytime state, Glendon is tortured by the vague recollection of the horrors of the preceding night, and the scenes where he feels the symptoms of the oncoming seizures are gripping and realistic. Like succeeding adaptations, the werewolf is made a sympathetic character, a victim of his condition. This is stressed to a point, rare in horror films, of quasi-religiousness: Glendon prays that he will not change again into a werewolf and his dying words are: "In a few moments now, I shall know why all this had to be." However, Henry Hull was a defeating choice for the part, one he obtained after scoring a certain success as Magwitch the convict in *Great Expectations,* an adaptation of the Dickens novel released by Universal the year before. As Glendon, he was neurotic and supercilious; as the wolfman, he seemed incongruous in his tweeds and cap. Also, lacking the patience and dedication (to the genre) of Chaney or Karloff, he refused to submit to the long uncomfortable hours of being made-up, and Jack Pierce had to devise for him a rather light makeup that gives him a curious, batlike physiognomy. The only first-rate things about *The Werewolf of London* are the special effects of John P. Fulton, a series of precise double exposures depicting the gradual transformation of man into beast.

Werewolves, however, proved to be too full of self-pity, torment, and remorse for contemporary audiences; a monster-hero with a touch of the mad scientist in him aroused in the public curiously mixed feelings. More successful was Universal's next try, six years later, with Lon Chaney, Jr. as *The Wolf Man;* it was invested with a more elaborate makeup job (also by Pierce), and the werewolf theme was endowed with a new set of rules. Chaney Jr.'s werewolf, which at times looked like a hirsute Cossack, could only be killed by a silver bullet or a silver-encrusted cane. But even this more mystical demise proved quite inoperative, as the Wolf Man was revived by accident (in *Frankenstein Meets the Wolf Man,* 1943) or simply by Universal fiat (in *House of Frankenstein,* 1944 and *House of Dracula,* 1945).

The unprecedented success of *Dracula* and *Frankenstein* made Universal the foremost producers of horror films in Hollywood, a position maintained throughout the decade, in spite of competition from the other studios, which were quick to follow the trend. Of these, Warner Brothers loomed large as Universal's most serious rival, at least in the first years of the vogue. Warners did not have Lugosi or Karloff, but they still owned the services of the illustrious John Barrymore. Shortly after *Dracula,* they released the first talkie adaptation of George Du Maurier's *Trilby,* the title fittingly changed to *Svengali,* with Barrymore in the title role. The character of the sinister Austrian Jew—mountebank, hypnotist, and musical genius—had already tempted many actors of stage and silent screen. Maurice Tourneur's version had featured Wilton Lackaye, the official Svengali of his generation. In 1923, the part was inherited by Arthur Edmund Carewe and in the late twenties, Paul Wegener appeared in a German version. But these mute performances could hardly match Barrymore's rich delivery of Du Maurier's fruity theatrical dialogue or the humorous bravado he brought to the part. More surprisingly, Barrymore touched Svengali with a sort of pathos, notably in the scene where he attempts to bend the hypnotized Trilby (Marian Marsh) to his amorous advances, only to recoil in self-disgust, muttering resignedly "It's only Svengali talking to himself." The Victorian flavor of the original was spiced with a good dose of the macabre. And the tragic but undramatic ending of the novel was replaced by a *coup de théâtre* as Svengali, dying of a heart attack, succeeds with a final surge of sheer willpower in taking Trilby along with him to the grave. Audiences accepted this uncompromising finale as the only demise worthy of one of the greatest villains of dramatic literature; they seemed to realize that both picture and heroine belonged to her menacer. Warners had unwittingly struck a genuine romantic chord.

Svengali had a success of the kind that spawns a sequel, in this case *The Mad Genius,* also released in 1931, and starring a more restrained Barrymore as a clubfooted puppeteer with the soul of a ballet dancer. This lame Diaghilev finds his Nijinsky in an orphaned child whom he raises to manhood (Donald Cook) and elevates to fame, and whom he loses to a young ballerina (Marian Marsh). The film was pure fabrication, but Warners backed it with a lavish production and a strong supporting cast that included Boris Karloff (in one of his last roles prior to *Frankenstein*) and an unusually sober Luis Alberni as a drug addict who becomes Barrymore's nemesis. Michael Curtiz, who directed, managed to bring this contrived story to a powerful ending which showed Barrymore's lifeless body dangling from the jaws of a prop idol during the performance of his masterwork, a modern ballet. The studio heads probably regarded Curtiz as another Browning, or a new Whale, for they entrusted him with two ambitious horror projects.

Universal had experimented with color by releasing a few prints of *Frankenstein* tinted a bilious green, "the color of fear," which reportedly increased its eerie quality. Warners, which had employed Technicolor—at that time a simpler, less perfect process involving only two negatives—in a few musicals, had both *Dr. X* and *Mystery of the Wax Museum* shot in that early process. The first of these dealt with a series of "moon murders" committed in the neighborhood of a medical college by an obvious maniac who kills only during the full moon. Even if *Dr. X* is closer to a thriller than to a horror fantasy, its murderer is truly a fiendish invention, a one-armed scientist (Preston Foster) who has discovered a synthetic flesh substitute from which he periodically fashions a murdering hand. A superbly goose-bumpy sequence involves the reenactment of the murders in the laboratory of Dr. Xavier (Lionel Atwill), an eerie play-within-a-play, during which the heroine (Fay Wray) realizes that she is acting out her own death—that the cloaked figure meant to represent the killer *is* the actual maniac! Throughout the movie runs a salutary vein of wise-cracking humor that very deftly places the horror element in modern Manhattan of the thirties, even though a good deal of the action takes place in the usual Teutonic old house perched on top of a Long Island cliff. Unfortunately, Warners decided that the film was effective enough in black and white and so they limited the distribution of Technicolor prints, at least in America, to the first theater engagement.

Yet color processing definitely enhanced the thrills of *Mystery of the Wax museum* (1933), the tale of a demented sculptor of wax figures, concealing his hideously charred features behind a lifelike mask as he exhibits to an unsuspecting public the wax-coated bodies of his murdered victims. James Agate, who resisted the more athletic blandishments of *King Kong,* found the film deliciously terrifying in its "charnel-house" gruesomeness and issued to his readers the recommendation (or warning) that "whatever your test [for horror], the film will live up to it." Although the film now seems irretrievably lost, the power of its best scenes lingers in the memory after two decades: the fire that destroys the waxworks, the figures themselves twisting and contorting into a chilling semblance of decaying flesh; or the heroine (Fay Wray) striking at the mask of the sculptor (Lionel Atwill) and exposing the ghastly face beneath it. The muted greens and blues proved to be a definite asset in establishing a psychological mood of anguish and foreboding; yet the uses of color remained unexplored in Hollywood horror films for almost two decades. There were a few exceptions, such as *Dr. Cyclops* (1940) as well as the 1943 remake of *The Phantom of the Opera* from Universal, where the excellent Technicolor photography served to support the spectacular, rather than the horrific aspects of the story. Only in recent years has color become an established feature of the genre, red being the predominant hue, the verdant color of terror getting replaced by that of blood and raw flesh. Therein lies the difference between terror and horror, between the Gothic creations of the thirties and the contemporary comic-strip style variations of Roger Corman and Hammer Films.

Early in 1932, after a well-deserved rest of more than a decade, Paramount released a new, talking version of Stevenson's *Dr. Jekyll and Mr. Hyde* as one of their prestige productions of the season. It was perfectly timed to boost the newly born vogue for horror films. Fredric March, then regarded as Barrymore's heir-apparent, played the dual role and the direction was entrusted to Rouben Mamoulian, who had scored a critical success with his first film, *Applause* (1929), and a unanimous one with his second, *City Streets* (1931). Even within the restrictions of a factory-size studio like Paramount, Mamoulian was regarded as something of an experimentalist, a reputation he carefully maintained with *Dr. Jekyll.* Besides his customary shadow work, visual symbolism and bold sound montage, there is an effective use of the subjective camera to introduce both Jekyll and Hyde, plus the novel scoring of the transformation scene by means of amplified heartbeats (an effect still impressive in 1964 when it was used on Broadway at the climax of Albee's *Tiny Alice*) . Time and repetition have worn out the novelty of some of Mamoulian's devices, but even so, the picture is the best of the many adaptations of Stevenson's story. The transitions from Jekyll's handsome, prepossessing face to the bestial, apelike features of Hyde are the most accomplished ever put on film—and the secret process by which they were achieved has not been revealed to this day by either Mamoulian or the studio. Other than skillful double exposure it may have involved the use of specially colored makeup which appropriate camera filters would have brought out. Be that as it may, these technical tours de force obscure a rather pedestrian performance by March that alternates between the priggishness of Jekyll and the broad overacting of Hyde—but which stark alternations inevitably earned him an Academy Award. The over-all felicity of the picture seems due more to the period in which it was produced, the decade in which films mastered sound and which in Hollywood corresponds roughly to the nineteenth-century full-flowering of the novel. (Not by accident, the period produced the definitive adaptations of such works as *David Copperfield, Little Women,* and *The Prisoner of Zenda.*) Visually, Mamoulian's film has all the chiaroscuro elegance of Victorian engravings, faithfully realized by Karl Struss' camera work.

On the printed page, the tale unfolds in an exceptionally cinematic manner, the story spun by several narrators, a method that was also employed by Wilkie Collins and Bram Stoker among others. As noted by critic John Mason Brown: "Stevenson plays hare-and-hounds with horror," dropping clues, giving hints, so that our apprehension grows steadily as we gradually perceive the truth, finally revealed by Jekyll's own posthumous confession in the last twenty pages or so. Like other adaptations before and after, the picture prefers to relate events chronologically, dispensing with mystery and suspense, substituting shock and, most notably here, a large content of sadism. Whereas Stevenson scarcely hints at the sexual components of Hyde's personality (and neither, for that matter, did the stage version and first screen adaptations),

Mamoulian's interpretation is remarkable for its heady sexuality, fully drawing and completing what was merely sketched in John Barrymore's interpretation. Accordingly, the object of Hyde's libido becomes of the utmost importance, and the role of Ivy, the lovely barmaid whom he sets up as his mistress, becomes the key to the Jekyll/Hyde character. It is Ivy's attraction, felt and rejected by Jekyll on a chance meeting, that prompts him to seek a way to release the lusting, repressed side of his nature. After the transformation has taken place, Hyde runs to pleasure, freedom unbound, a concept masterfully realized in a shot of an exulting Hyde receiving rain on his face.

In this light, it is easy to see why the Surrealists, in their quest for the absolute in love and freedom, were attracted to Stevenson's novella. For Mamoulian had realized that, in the long run, it is Hyde, ribald and repulsive, who represents the life force and that Hyde's sadism compensates Jekyll's prudery. Consequently, while the scenes of the good doctor and his fiancée (Rose Hobart) are sexless and stilted, those of Hyde and his mistress (Miriam Hopkins) provide the film with its best moments, one of which, in its unusual eroticism, transcends the limits of the genre: a vicious cat-and-mouse game in which Hyde's every word hints of the unmentionable, a taunting, mocking ritual that drives Ivy to a pitch of sobbing, hysterical terror.

From then on, would-be adapters of Stevenson had to contend with Mamoulian's version, although most remakes have failed to enlarge this ambiguous potential. Metro-Goldwyn-Mayer, which remade the film in 1941 with Spencer Tracy in the leading role and Victor Fleming as director, cautiously based it on the 1932 version, merely embellishing it with a good score (by Franz Waxman), a more literate (also wordier) screenplay and a voguish, Freudian "montage" of visions to bridge the passage from good to evil. Tracy's Hyde, relying on facial expression rather than face makeup, resembled nothing more than a snickering, lusty libertine, a cross between Aleister Crowley and James Cagney. But Ingrid Bergman improved and perfected the role of Ivy, thereby turning the film into a personal triumph. Nothing in the Fleming version matches the boldness of conception that marks Mamoulian's: the film is heavy, ponderous, and smothered in decor. There are fitful gleams of effective cinema: Ivy's song freezing on her lips as Hyde fixes her with his reptilian stare from across the pub; or Jekyll, whistling Ivy's polka, collecting himself as he tries to whistle a waltz, only to return to the polka after a few bars, a decisive way of conveying Hyde's final overtaking of the doctor's personality.

An English remake, *The Two Faces of Dr. Jekyll,* made in 1960 (and released as *House of Fright* in the United States) has Mr. Hyde (Paul Massie) as a dashing young rake unleashed by a middle-aged, spent Jekyll (also Massie), who yearns for the pleasures of youth; but this intriguing premise was hardly developed at all in Wolf Mankowitz's clumsy treatment of the original. Jean Renoir has come closest to a contemporary envisioning of the subject in his free-wheeling *Le Testament du Dr. Cordelier* (1961) by making his Monsieur Opale (a perversely engaging performance by Jean-Louis Barrault) part killer/part clown, impulse unrestrained, no longer the beast, but the anarchist in every man. (Not surprisingly, Renoir was associated with the Surrealist movement during the early stages of his career.) To date, the last film appearance of Jekyll/Hyde has been in *The Nutty Professor* (1963), in which Jerry Lewis wittily upsets the delicate seriocomic balance of the story (a feat often achieved in the worst of the horror genre), accurately lampooning both the dull, clumsy Professor Kelp and the grossly irresistible Mr. Love. Caricature is often the most devastating criticism and unless a new interpretation is found, the Lewis parody may well mean the end of the line for Dr. Jekyll and Mr. Hyde.

There is a passage in *The Island of Dr. Moreau,* one of H. G. Wells' earlier novels, where the hero, stranded on a remote South Pacific island as the guest of an enigmatic host, suddenly comes face to face with a ghastly apparition, half-human/half-leopard, covered with fresh scars and bloody bandages, howling in pain as it flees the operating room. Nothing in the film version, entitled *The Island of Lost Souls* and released by Paramount in 1933, approaches this climatic terror. Instead, the movie substitutes a demure Panther Woman (Kathleen Burke), the crowning achievement of Dr. Moreau (Charles Laughton), a mad scientist who is obsessed with the cross-breeding of animal species and whose unethical experiments have caused his banishment from civilization. The results of these experiments range from the almost perfect quasi-human (the Panther Woman) to a series of formless monstrosities kept in cages in the doctor's laboratory. The intermediate cases include a group of apelike creatures, a dog-man who devotedly lays down his life for his master, and other assorted mutants, freely roaming the island. Moreau would like to carry his theories to their ultimate conclusion by mating the Panther Woman with the American hero (Richard Arlen)—the result of this union would presumably carry him back to London society in triumph. With all these bizarre ingredients director Erle C. Kenton achieved a minor, not ineffective, film. Although in no way the "surging rhapsody of terror" announced by Paramount, the movie did achieve a climate of terror, and a sense of lurking menace, abetted by the screenplay of Philip Wylie and the photography of Karl Struss (who had recently shot *Dr. Jekyll* for the same studio). At times, Kenton adroitly blended fantasy and terror, as in the scenes where Laughton, whip in hand, leads his creatures in a primitive ritual that chillingly paraphrases the song of the *bandarlog,* the monkey people of Rudyard Kipling's *The Jungle Book:* "What is the Law?" "Not to spill blood; that is the Law. Are we not men?" The climax, reminiscent of *Freaks,* has the creatures revolt against Moreau and drag him to the House of Pain, from whence they all came, obviously contemplating similar surgical designs.

Judged unbelievably tasteless at the time of its release, especially in its sexual overtones, *The Island of Lost Souls* was banned outright in England, the country where vivisection is most carefully controlled. Wells openly repudiated the picture as a vulgarization of his novel, but in retrospect, the book reads like a horror story (and a very good one) rather than like "a scientific romance"—and Wylie's adaptation of it seems not only cinematic but temperate by modern standards. Other Wells adaptations, supervised by the author (such as *Shape of Things to Come* and *The Man Who Could Work Miracles,* both 1936) resulted in ponderous dogmatic bores. And although it is true that *Island* seldom convinces, it never bores. The fact that Lugosi, fresh from his *Dracula* triumph, appears only in a minor role as one of the ape-men, seems to indicate that some caution was exercised by Paramount before the film was released to the public.

Paramount was also responsible for the gentler fantasies of *Death Takes a Holiday* and *Peter Ibbetson* (1934 and 1935, respectively). The first, adapted from the play by Alberto Casella, has Death assume the guise of a man of the world (Fredric March) to spend a few days on the Italian Riviera, where he falls in love with a beautiful maiden and indulges in most of the pleasures reserved for humans, such as waltzing over exquisite gleaming floors to the strains of Sibelius' "Valse Triste." The immediate result of this escapade is that, for the duration of Death's sabbatical, no living thing on earth can die. When Death finally realizes that his function is needed, that indeed a whole suffering world clamors for it—a fact tritely conveyed on the screen by a montage of headlines and commonplace stock footage—he returns to his cosmic task, taking along the girl (Evelyn Venable) who has learned to love Death without fear. Born of Casella's actual war experience and originally conceived as a comedy, the play underwent considerable revision before it opened and became one of the popular successes of the 1929–30 Broadway season. Certainly there was nothing new in the idea of Death assuming human form—it had appealed strongly in this century to Maurice Maeterlinck and Fritz Lang, among others. Their success was measured by the amount of poetry or mysticism that could be instilled into the theme, usually demanding some pretty special dramatic gimmick more in the nature of stage presentation than filming. (After all, Death has been a stock theatrical character since the medieval mystery plays.) Another American film dealing with the same subject, *On Borrowed Time* (1939), marooned Death at the top of a magical tree, from where he could not set foot on ground unless he were invited. This film took on the aura of folksy, homespun fantasy and in that context succeeded rather well. Jean Cocteau's *Orphée* (1950) was a closed universe in itself where only the elements out of modern times—the Bacchantes as a feminist society in St.-Germain-des-Prés; the coded messages sent from the netherworld coming over the radio—seemed incongruous. *Death Takes a Holiday* lacks a definite dramatic stance: it is superficial, fashionable, and theatrical (not in the sense of juicy, masterfully written scenes but in that of staginess—one can almost see the curtain drop after each *coup d'effet*) and Fredric March, then traversing his Barrymore period, is painfully inadequate as death incarnate. The all-too-few touches of horror the actor has to work with have Death reverting to his Grim Reaper plainness, and the film founders between the conventions of Romanticism and those of old-fashioned circuit theatrics.

More successful was *Peter Ibbetson,* adapted from the novel by George Du Maurier and the play fashioned from it, which, coming from one of Hollywood's overlarge studios at the peak of a style best described as utilitarian, strikes one as an extraordinary and imaginative achievement, a gossamer fantasy about love overcoming time and space.

As children, Mimsey teaches Peter how to "dream true." As grown-ups separated by his imprisonment and her seclusion, the lovers live out their romance in a dream world shared between them to the time of their almost simultaneous deaths. The film was rather irresolutely directed by Henry Hathaway, a specialist in "action" movies, but this was more than made up for by poignant, sensitive performances by Ann Harding and Gary Cooper. Paramount extended great care over this film which, nevertheless, proved unpopular in America. The popcorn public found *Peter Ibbetson* both too glum and too serene for their earthbound, wisecracking era, in which the taste for fantasy ran to more athletic, full-bodied variations.

In the wake of *Dracula* and *Frankenstein,* a spate of minor, derivative horror movies began to issue from the independent studios of Hollywood's "poverty row," shoddy little efforts usually built around an established performer, such as Lugosi or Atwill, borrowed from the major sound stages. Most of these—like *The Death Kiss, The Monster Walks* (both 1932), and *The Sphinx* (1933)—were dismal failures. Somewhat superior was *The Vampire Bat* (also 1933) which boasted a good cast (Lionel Atwill, Fay Wray, Melvyn Douglas, and Dwight Frye) enacting the story of a small town terrorized by a series of mysterious murders, blamed on a vampire bat, but in reality perpetrated by the village doctor, a mad scientist obsessed by his search for a "blood substitute." Most of these films were quickly produced and almost as soon forgotten. Not so, however, with *White Zombie* produced by the Halperin Brothers in 1932, starring Bela Lugosi, and an excellent example of the genre.

The zombie is a modern addition to the mythology of horror. Zombies are "the walking dead" of Haiti and other voodoo-dominated islands in the West Indies—corpses reanimated by witchcraft for the purpose of supplying cheap labor for the cane fields and sugar mills. Neither good nor evil, the zombie is a neutral character, a mere instrument in some sinister hierarchical design. The term gained currency after the publication of *The Magic Island* in 1929. Its author, William B. Seabrook, had spent one year among voodoo worshipers in Haiti, where his modern-day skepticism was put to a rude test—not only was he shown "the walking dead" working in the plantations (Seabrook at first saw them as totally feebleminded) but he was also shown the Haitian Penal Code whose Article #249 specifies that: "Also shall be qualified as attempted murder the employment of drugs, hypnosis, or any other occult practice which produces lethargic coma or lifeless sleep; and if the person has been buried it shall be considered murder no matter what result follows." The same paragraph was used in publicizing *White Zombie* but the producers, by interpolating the word *zombie* (in brackets) after *person*, changed the emphasis from the legal (the criminal sanctions against the use of drugs or other forbidden practices) to the supernatural (the possibility of recalling a corpse from the grave).

Such tricks were not necessary. Seabrook's Haitian chronicles lent a certain topicality to the picture, but *White Zombie* is only superficially concerned with voodooism. The concept at the heart of the movie belongs to the timeless tradition of sleeping princesses, evil necromancers, and benign wizards:

> Fresh from New York, Madeline (Madge Bellamy) arrives in Haiti to marry her fiancé, Neil (John Harron), a bank employee in Port-au-Prince. On board ship, she has met a wealthy plantation owner, Charles Beaumont (Robert Frazer), who insists the cere-

mony take place on his estate. That night, Madeline and Neil witness a strange ceremony far different from their nuptial one: a dead person is buried at a crossroads. When they inquire about the reason for this peculiar practice, they are informed that this location for a burial will prevent the body from being stolen out of its grave and turned into a zombie. The lovers also come face to face with a satanic-looking individual called Murder Legendre (Lugosi), who is the island's notorious zombie master. The reason behind the plantation owner's invitation is that he has fallen in love with Madeline. In order to prevent her marriage to Neil from taking place, he calls on Legendre for help. The sorcerer gives him a poisoned rose to be placed in the bridal bouquet. During the wedding banquet, Legendre stands in the shadowy garden of the Beaumont estate, fashioning a waxen image of Madeline, tying a shawl of hers around it, and finally melting the image with a flame. Bereft of her senses, the bride at this moment collapses, seemingly dead. Her body is placed in the Beaumont mausoleum; the following night it is abducted by Beaumont and Legendre, with the somnabulistic assistance of six hideous zombies who form the sorcerer's macabre bodyguard. Thus, Madeline becomes one of "the walking dead," a mindless, speechless wraith, drifting aimlessly along the endless corridors of Legendre's castle, a slave to the necromancer's will. Beaumont, who belatedly realizes the magnitude of his crime, also falls under Legendre's spell.

Neil discovers that his wife's body is missing from her grave and he seeks the help of Dr. Bruner (Joseph Cawthorn), an island missionary who has made voodooism his life study. With the aid of a native witch doctor, they locate Legendre's abode. In the ensuing contest of wills, the sorcerer is finally done away with when Beaumont, with one recovered spark of willpower, drags him over the castle ramparts to their joint death upon the rocks below. Madeline is released from the evil spell and reunited with her bridegroom.

Contemporary reviewers found *White Zombie* childish, old-fashioned, and melodramatic. They might have allowed that it was also a Gothic fairy tale filled with traditional symbols, dreamlike imagery, echoes of Romanticism, and (probably unintentional) psychosexual overtones. Inside this web, Madeline, Bruner, and Legendre appear, respectively, as the sexual object, and, on either side, the archetypes of good and evil, clichés in their pristine state, both economical and persuasive. The film's costumes and set are also properly stylized: the heroine in her shroud-long wedding gown, Lugosi in his somberest formal wear, while his mountaintop castle seems to come all intact out of a Gustave Doré engraving. In conception and execution, the movie is the superior of *Dracula,* although it was made on a much smaller budget. While Tod Browning's film about the bloodsucking Count was theatrical, garrulous, and devoid of mood music, *White Zombie* is fluidly cinematic, filled with lengthy, wordless sequences, and supported by an effective musical score. One scene makes haunting use of a chorus humming the spiritual called "Listen to the Lambs." Bela Lugosi throws himself into the part of Legendre with real relish, gleefully etching lines in venom.

The movie invariably fails when it tries hardest to horrify, as in the shots of the vulture which is the necromancer's "familiar"—or in the protracted close-ups of Lugosi's eyes exerting his evil spell. The zombie entourage seems to step out of an old-fashioned operetta: pirate chieftain, officer, judge, executioner—all of them played by Europeans. But these mistakes are outbalanced by truly poetic detail: the poisoned rose or Madeline's appearance on the balcony, giving us the timeless image of the captive damsel. One of these perfectly realized moments is the first encounter at the crossroads when the horses rear in terror at the sight of the zombies, yanking the coach away and separating Madeline from her scarf, now an ominous token left in Legendre's hand. Better than anything else, the film generates its own ambience, and this aspect has been enhanced by the passing of time. Whatever period feeling *White Zombie* possessed at the time of its release has been erased by the intervening third of a century, making the images more faded, the period more remote, and the picture itself more completely mysterious.

Victor Halperin, who directed it, turned up at Paramount the following year, where he made *Supernatural,* a story about the transmigration of souls between a murderess (Vivienne Osborne) and a normal young woman (Carole Lombard). But Halperin here directed a film that is glossy and ineffective. The Halperin brothers tried to repeat their initial success by producing *Revolt of the Zombies* in 1936, but this work did not follow a definite enough supernatural pattern. Its zombies were not "the walking dead" of Haitian lore, but a regiment of defunct Indochinese soldiers, killed and revived to perform some bloody feats for the greater glory of France during the First World War. A dim, trite, commercial effort altogether, *Revolt of the Zombies* was as highly unsuccessful as *White Zombie* had been highly original.

Not a nodding acquaintance with either zombies, vampires, or man-made monstrosities did the most accomplished thriller of the decade have. It was an utterly preposterous, utterly enthralling piece of showmanship, whereby the most colossal gorilla on earth plunges New York City into terror and destruction before it is shot down by an entire squadron of planes from the summit of the world's tallest building on 34th Street. The movie opened, appropriately, at the then largest theater in the world, the Music Hall, at Radio City in Rockefeller Center, and simultaneously at the then-nearby RKO Roxy, and it succeeded in mobbing both of these houses with delighted audiences, the start of a commercial success that has repeated itself the world over. *King Kong* became the best apology for Hollywood's technical proficiency, the perfect admixture of a multitude of talents—and the very antithesis of the director's picture.

Although no one person can claim sole credit for *King Kong,* it was originally the brainchild of Merian C. Cooper, one of America's foremost documentary film-makers, responsible (with Ernest B. Schoedsack) of such history-book classics as *Grass* and *Chang.* While Cooper and Schoedsack were on location in Africa shooting some animal footage for Paramount's version of *The Four Feathers* (1929), Cooper became interested in the habits of the gorilla. He conceived an idea about an outsized ape of superior intelligence running amok in the city streets of the civilized world. He embellished this concept with a few more specific scenes: the gorilla would fight one of the giant lizards of Komodo (then of widespread topicality because two of these reptiles had been brought alive to New York's Bronx Zoo where, with dispatch, they died) ; for a climax the gorilla would make one last stand on top of the recently finished Empire State Building. In Cooper's original conception, the picture would feature live gorillas and lizards, enlarged by trick photography.

In 1931, Cooper was brought to RKO Studios by his friend David O. Selznick, who had been appointed vice-president in charge of production. While reorganizing the new company, Cooper had to assess several projects that he inherited from the previous administration, among which was *Creation,* an animation epic that would trace the evolution of life on earth, and for which special effects technician Willis O'Brien had built some remarkable models and landscapes. Cooper was so impressed with O'Brien's work that he decided to film *King Kong* in the studio, thereby saving the expense of location shooting and the risk taken in filming dangerous wild animals. (*Creation* was never made but Walt Disney included a sequence very similar to it in his multipart 1941 cartoon *Fantasia,* moving pictures to illustrate Stravinsky's dance score, *Rites of Spring.*)

With Selznick's encouragement, O'Brien and Cooper prepared a one-reel test showing the battle between the gorilla and a prehistoric allosaurus, as well as scenes where Kong hurtles a bevy of sailors into a chasm by violently shaking a tree-trunk bridge. This test was an enormous success with RKO stockholders, and Cooper was entrusted with the production and the co-direction of the picture. Bringing his usual collaborator Schoedsack to the project, he began filming in May of 1932. Edgar Wallace, the well-known British author then under contract to the studio, was engaged to develop the scenario, but death from pneumonia cut short his collaboration. (The finished film, however, carried his name among the credits.) The final script was the work of James Creelman and Ruth Rose (Mrs. Schoedsack). It took exactly a year to complete *King Kong* at a cost of $650,000, an impressive sum for those days; most of the money went into the special effects—to this day unsurpassed.

The animation of Kong, the prehistoric monsters, and the doll-size replicas of human performers used in some especially complicated shots, was accomplished by stop-motion photography. Averaging sixteen inches in height, the models were built of rubber and sponge and, in Kong's case, covered with appropriately shaggy lambskin. An articulated metal frame allowed movements of the limbs, mouth, and eyes that ranged from a quarter of an inch to more than one inch depending on the action required. After each almost imperceptible movement, the model was photographed, the camera stopped, and the model reset. When run on the screen, these individual stages gave the illusion of life. Each of Kong's steps would require a dozen separate exposures, and twenty-five feet of film flashing on the screen for half a minute was the maximum result of a day's work. The live actors were then combined with the animated models by miniature rear projection, multiple printing, and traveling mattes; for close-ups, a full-scale bust and hand of Kong were built. Some of O'Brien's most spectacular effects were achieved in the utmost secrecy and some of his processes were not even committed to paper for fear of plagiarism, but they were basically the same ones employed by him for his first short, now brought to the final stages of refinement. All this technical wizardry did not, however, overwhelm the film and therein lies one of its major accomplishments. One questions, or marvels at, or wonders at the first sight of the monster, but thereafter one is caught in nothing but the sheer flow of events, each thrill surpassing the previous one in splendid outrageousness. The film's art is to make the technical tour de force seem effortless.

Kong's entrance is preceded by five reels of careful buildup. The plot takes the spectator—along with a film-making crew led by impressario Carl Denham (Robert Armstrong)—from Manhattan to Skull Island, an unexplored isle off the coast of Africa. It is here that the film's first great climax occurs as Ann Darrow (Fay Wray) awaits the appearance of the redoubtable deity to whom she is being sacrificed by the natives, a superbly mounted sequence in which Max Steiner's score seems to become the Gargantuan heartbeat of the approaching Kong. The horror of the scene is instantly dissipated by the first appearance of the giant gorilla—no apparition however hideous could match our vaunting expectation; nor (wisely) does the film aspire to be a horror tale. It is instead a most successful adventure romance.

The picture's unique quality, as well as the reason for its vast success, lies in the scope of its own absurdity coupled with a subconscious but nevertheless irrefutable eroticism. The literal-minded among critics, probably misled by a realistic prologue laid in the contemporary Manhattan of breadlines and the starving unemployed, failed to perceive that *King Kong*'s logic is that of a dream, that the picture is a visualization of the most recurrent dream fantasies: Driscoll (Bruce Cabot) and Ann dangling from a rope over a precipice and being slowly hauled by Kong, their subsequent fall into a chasm, a race through the jungle with something large and terrifying in pursuit, one cyclopean eye peering through the window of a midtown hotel, dawn-of-the-world landscapes, dizzying heights, and so forth.

Less obvious than these dreamlike effects is the picture's outré erotic content. There can be no doubt that its Beauty-and-the-Beast leitmotiv formed itself in the core of the original conception. The film opens with an "old Arabian proverb": "And the Beast looked upon the face of Beauty and lo! his hand was stayed from killing and from that day forward he was as one dead." It closes with a mournful Denham, standing to the side of the fallen giant, informing a callous cop that " 'Twas Beauty killed the Beast"—and this theme is reiterated and enhanced throughout the film by the secular liturgy of the myth: the golden-haired virgin offered to the barbarous demigod (variously a dragon, unicorn, minotaur or, here, an anthropoid) who is unable to spill this ritual-victim's blood, the sacrificial maiden then becoming the prize in a combat between beast and hero. Most of it is archetypical in the horror film, and both *Dracula* and *Frankenstein* contain scenes in which the fiends hover over white-clad reclining heroines. As it appears to be a time-honored sanction of Romantic tradition, this erotic content, being an intrinsic manifestation, usually eludes the consciousness of the film-maker as well as the vigilance of the censor. (Science fiction, on the other hand, rarely employs the tools of Romanticism and usually lacks these broodingly sexual overtones.) The makers of *King Kong* went so far they carried the Beauty-and-the-Beast premise to absurdity—the acute disparity of size between Ann and Kong puts any erotic rapport completely out of the question. And so, the film jumps to a substitute gratification in some spectacular sadism and whopping mayhem: Kong vents his frustration by razing the native village and, when really put out, he turns Manhattan into a shambles.

Through an extravagant and quite mad process of identification, the audiences of 1933 were plainly gratified by these scenes of urban destruction and *King Kong* triumphantly launched a fleet of catastrophe pictures such as *Deluge, The Last Days of Pompeii* (also by Cooper, Schoedsack, and O'Brien) and *San Francisco.* Reissued in subsequently less liberal times, *King Kong* was amputated of a few of its most sadistic moments (the giant gorilla trampling a native baby and tossing a hysterical woman several stories to the street below) as well as a charming scene where he rips Ann's dress off her body, then puzzledly sniffs the female scent that lingers on his finger.

The contribution of this sexual element to the success of *King Kong* was demonstrated by default in the all-but-forgotten sequel, *Son of Kong,* released later the same year and in which the purported offspring, a great white gorilla, is little more than an emasculated version of the great Kong—funny and endearing as a big teddy bear. Already the dazzling visual effects begin to look like pointless virtuosity. This also applies to an even later descendant, *Mighty Joe Young* (1949) which won O'Brien an Academy Award for his special effects and is most charitably described as *King Kong* for children. Like Kong, Joe Young is a gorilla, albeit only ten foot tall. But unlike Kong, Joe is the household pet of an orphan girl (Terry Moore) raised in an African ranch, and as docile and housebroken as a Great Dane. Both the girl and her ape are discovered by a showman (Robert Armstrong, of course) and his cowboy safari and brought to a temple-sized Hollywood nightclub where mighty Joe holds his mistress and a grand piano aloft on a platform while she plays "Beautiful Dreamer." The incongruous look of Texan cowpokes scouring the African veldt points to the source of some of *Mighty Joe Young*'s most spectacular trick effects. Back in 1942, after almost six months of work, RKO Radio abandoned the production of *Gwangi,* a story dealing with a band of cowboys who discover prehistoric life on a lost mesa, and some of *Gwangi*'s animation sequences, conceived and executed by O'Brien and his team, get exposure in *Mighty Joe Young* as well as in *The Black Scorpion* (1957). The latter's most impressive sequence, a gigantic scorpion wrecking a train, was obviously patterned after King Kong's similar attack on the elevated subway. O'Brien also revived his long-abandoned *Creation* project for

Warner's semidocumentary *The Animal World* (1956) and supervised the animation of the British-made *The Giant Behemoth* (1959) which elaborated on the last sequence of *The Lost World* by having an outsize dinosaur terrorizing Londoners. O'Brien authored the original story of *The Beast of Hollow Mountain* (1956) and his name also appears on the list of movie craftsmen responsible for the color, CinemaScope remake of the *The Lost World* (1960), which substituted live lizards and iguanas for his beloved animated models. The living breathing animals proved considerably less versatile, but by present filmmaking standards, the cost of such time-consuming craftsmanship has risen to the stars. As a result, the best animation done nowadays comes from the Japanese studios where costs are still held down somewhere within the realm of economic possibility.

Willis O'Brien's extraordinary career was marred by tragedy and disappointment. In 1933, shortly before the release of *Son of Kong,* his estranged wife shot and killed their two sons. Many of his most cherished projects were destined never to be realized—among these, *El Toro Estrella* which was to combine prehistoric reptiles with live-action bulls in a South American locale, and an adaptation of H. G. Wells' *The Food of the Gods,* in which a potion makes ordinary men and beasts big as a house. O'Brien was tooling on the intricate animation in Stanley Kramer's *It's A Mad, Mad, Mad, Mad World* when he died, at 72, on November 10, 1962. At the present moment, his successor would seem to be Ray Harryhausen, O'Brien's collaborator in *Mighty Joe Young* and the creator in his own right of some amazing fantasy broadjumps in such films as *The Seventh Voyage of Sinbad, The Three Worlds of Gulliver, The Mysterious Island,* and *Jason and the Argonauts.* (Harryhausen's animation for a Venusian monster in the minor *Twenty Million Miles from Earth,* 1957, was nothing short of superb.) His work, however perfect, so far lacks the exorbitant grandeur which made *King Kong* "the eighth wonder of the world."

Produced at the same time as *King Kong,* Merian C. Cooper's *The Most Dangerous Game* was directed by Schoedsack and Irving Pichel and released in 1932 well ahead of *Kong* whose special effects kept it in production until the following year. Adapted by James Creelman, the Great Gorilla's scenarist, from a short story by Richard Connell that had won an O. Henry Memorial Award in 1924, *The Most Dangerous Game* was an ingenious anecdote that concerned Count Zaroff, a Russian hunter who poured passion into the sport and then, weary of bagging lions and leopards, retired with a few loyal servants to an island in the Malay Archipelago. Here the aristocrat indulges in the ultimate refinement of big-game hunting: he periodically sees to it that yachting parties are wrecked on the surrounding shoals and thus is provided with something to satisfy his mania—human quarry. The survivors of the sinking boats, ordinarily the healthiest, strongest, and most apt to steer clear of the sharks and survive the long swim to dry land, are hospitably received by Zaroff and his staff. The next sunup, they are given one thing only—a sporting chance. Armed with a knife and a headstart of several hours, they must elude Zaroff's bloodhounds and his bow and arrows until the next daybreak. Those who see that light regain their freedom. But a game room heavily hung with macabre trophies testifies to Count Zaroff's unfailing mastery. The Count meets his match in Rainsford, another hunter who fights him with his own weapons: cunning and skill. Rainsford disposes of Zaroff's men one by one, ultimately cornering the big hunter in his lair where he impales him on one of his own arrows.

A tightly constructed, literate horror film, *The Most Dangerous Game* was well-played by Joel McCrea as Rainsford and Fay Wray, midway in her career between *Dr. X* and *King Kong,* as the female prize catch, a character written into the film in order to illuminate the complex cruelty in the character of Zaroff. To the pivotal part of the Count, the English actor Leslie Banks lent considerable style and deliberate restraint. Whether playing the piano for the pleasure of his guests, running his hand over the gash that scars his forehead, or expounding his philosophy ("First the hunt, then the revels"), Banks twisted Zaroff's hedonism to its most nerveless refinement, making it the equivalent on film of de Sade's lucid monsters and, as such, fathering a succession of similar fiends. The story itself was twice remade, as *A Game of Death* in 1945 and as *Run for the Sun* in 1956—in both cases, the role of

Zaroff was changed to that of a German Nazi, which was not so far off the mark since the character had its definite Nietzschean traits. Of the two remakes, the first was almost a carbon copy which employed liberal portions of the original footage (the chase through the swamps and several long-shots) and the second, filmed in color on location in the Mexican wilds, betrayed the sad fact that Zaroff and villains of his stripe irrevocably belong to the period between the two wars. The world was no longer divided into two kinds of people, the hunter and the hunted, as Zaroff liked to believe. The Space Age has done away with villainy as an individual pursuit founded on a perverted code of conduct. Nowadays, hero and villain are simply committed to rival factions, their methods similarly ruthless (the stakes are also considerably higher) and the fine line once drawn between them has all but vanished.

In 1939, after a two-year hiatus during which no horror pictures issued from the Hollywood studios, Universal launched a second horror cycle with *Son of Frankenstein,* bringing together not only Karloff and Lugosi but Basil Rathbone and Lionel Atwill as well. Three years before, the first surge seemed to have petered out with the tasteful, offbeat *Dracula's Daughter.* Inspiration had run dry and there appeared no new horror creations to match those of the first generation. So, in 1938, Universal jointly reissued *Frankenstein* and *Dracula* and they raked in higher grosses than they did in their original runs. A horror revival was in order.

Son of Frankenstein was an auspicious debut. It was a well-mounted production with eccentric, distorted sets that even then recalled those of the German silents. Longest of the Frankenstein series, it ran 93 minutes and was directed with competence by Rowland V. Lee in the post vacated by Whale. Contending defensively that each film of the series was to be judged as a separate entity, Universal had no qualms about reviving the Monster after its spectacular exit at the close of *The Bride of Frankenstein:* it just reappeared, in one piece, lying on a marble slab in the secret crypt of the Frankensteins. Lugosi had his last solid role—one he did again in another sequel, *The Ghost of Frankenstein*—as Ygor the Shepherd, a rogue who had already survived the hangman's noose to become the Monster's guardian. And Karloff played the character with hardly a shade of the humanity so winningly deployed in the previous episode, once again becoming a cold-blooded, deadly machine whose sole moments of tenderness were reserved for Ygor and for the baby son of Baron Frankenstein (Rathbone). The Monster howling with grief over the body of Ygor gave the film its one touch of pathos; and the climax, with all the principals converging on the laboratory—the Monster coming face to face with the Police Inspector (Atwill) and tearing his artificial arm off while holding the child under one of his boots—had the same choreographic excitement of Lee's best work (*Zoo in Budapest, I Am Suzanne*). Indeed, *Son of Frankenstein* succeeded so well that Universal followed it with *Tower of London,* again directed by Lee, which brought the mechanics of horror to historical spectacle and was, in essence, Shakespeare's *Richard the Third* minus the text but with every beheading, drowning, stabbing, and smothering lovingly intact. Rathbone made a fine sardonic Gloucester and Karloff appeared in support as a clubfooted, bald-pated executioner.

The same year (1939) saw revivals of such standards as *The Cat and the Canary, The Gorilla, The Hound of the Baskervilles* (most truly frightening of the Sherlock Holmes stories), and *The Hunchback of Notre Dame.* Warner Brothers, encouraged by the success of the Frankenstein saga, halfheartedly attempted a sequel of sorts, *The Return of Dr. X,* closer, however, to their *The Walking Dead* of three years before. At Columbia, Karloff appeared in a minor thriller, *The Man They Could Not Hang,* about a scientist convicted and executed for performing a criminally unethical experiment, who returned to life to avenge himself on those responsible for his death. Unpretentiously put together by Nick Grinde, the picture was judged successful enough for Columbia to follow it with a series of low-budget mad scientist thrillers which included *The Man with Nine Lives, Before I Hang* (both 1940), and *The Devil Commands* (1941), all starring Karloff whose career as a monster came to a close with *Son of Frankenstein.* (Although he was supposed to have played a hideous mutant in *Die, Monster, Die,* 1965, it is obvious that Karloff was replaced by an athletic double and the same goes for his dismal parodying in *Abbott and Costello Meet Dr. Jekyll and Mr. Hyde,* 1953.)

In 1940, Universal restored two more fiends to the screen with *The Invisible Man Returns* and *The Mummy's Hand,* pirating the best effects of their originals but not provided with controlling influences like those of their original directors, Whale and Freund, respectively. Still, Fulton's effects were as good as ever, and Tom Tyler, a cowboy actor, made an acceptable Mummy. A Paramount comedy with Bob Hope called *The Ghost Breakers* worked better than these sequels and it even had its share of thrills as a zombie (Noble Johnson) chased Paulette Goddard around and about a haunted castle. The film that had it all over these in 1940 for pure excitement was the charming, fabulous *The Thief of Bagdad* with its engaging hero (Sabu), its evil wizard (Conrad Veidt), and its storybook thrills, among those that can be counted: a flying horse, a magic carpet, a Djinn in a bottle, and a deadly, six-armed Dancing Doll.

As well they might have known, what Universal needed was a new Karloff or even better, a new Chaney. They found one in Creighton, Chaney's son, who had been acting in films since 1932, mostly in undistinguished small parts. The actor changed his name to Lon Chaney, Jr., in 1937, and, two years later, made an impression on the critics as Lennie, the half-witted, kind giant of John Steinbeck's *Of Mice and Men.* An inkling of Chaney's potential as a studio horror property came in *One Million B.C.* a spectacle of life in an imaginary prehistoric period when cavemen fought anachronistic dinosaurs for supremacy on Earth. D. W. Griffith directed this non-horror horror film which Hal Roach produced, although he later insisted his name be removed from the picture's credits. (Roach displeased Griffith by substituting gibberish on the sound track where the director had his cast of cavemen speak perfect English.) The film, however, still has the look of a Griffith picture, with the kind of naiveté and visually effective style one usually associates with him, and its trick photography of live lizards was well-matched and scaled to the human performers. Chaney played a crippled, scarred warrior looking much older than his 34 years. Universal producers took notice and put him under contract.

Contract player or not, Chaney's horror debut was somewhat tentative. Among unfilmed story properties of the Karloff-Lugosi era there was *The Electric Man,* a tale with more than a passing resemblance to *The Invisible Ray:* having survived a lethal charge of electric voltage after the bus he is traveling on crashes into a power tower, Chaney—the Electric Man in a sideshow—becomes the unwitting tool of an unscrupulous scientist (Lionel Atwill). Framed on a murder rap, Chaney is sent to die in the electric chair, which he walks away from, transformed into a lethal high-voltage monster. Released as *Man-Made Monster* early in 1941, the picture was only moderately successful at the box office, but Universal proceeded to cast Chaney as the werewolf of *The Wolf Man* which turned out to be the company's most successful film of the season. Chaney was overladen with publicity which stressed his daily five-hour ordeal at the hands of makeup man Jack Pierce. (Lon Chaney, Sr., had always created his own but union rules now prevented actors from creating or applying their makeup.) In quick succession, Chaney was to play all the parts made famous by Karloff and Lugosi in the preceding decade: Frankenstein's Monster in *The Ghost of Frankenstein* (1942), the Mummy in *The Mummy's Tomb* (1942), *The Mummy's Ghost,* and *The Mummy's Curse* (both 1944), and Dracula in *Son of Dracula* (directed to great effect by Robert Siodmak in 1943). Chaney even did a series of mystery thrillers that had supernatural overtones, inspired by radio's Inner Sanctum program, which included *Calling Doctor Death* (1943), *Dead Man's Eyes, Weird Woman* (both 1944), *Frozen Ghost, Strange Confession* (both 1945), and *Pillow of Death* (1946). In all of these, Chaney revealed himself as a monotonous actor of rather narrow range, possessing neither the voice and skill of Karloff nor the demonic persuasion of Lugosi, and his rash of films were themselves mechanical, uninventive, and hopelessly serialized in flavor.

The all too real horrors of Corregidor and Stalingrad did not kill off horror films but, in the hands of second-rate craftsmen, they were to carry on merely as the poorest kind of escapism, debasing and ultimately parodying the marvelous creations of ten years before. Universal and Columbia continued to produce their quota of chillers: they were quickly ground out, expected to bring in a small profit—with no alms for oblivion. The producers correctly figured out that there always would be an audience for this type of film, heedless of critical scorn. In this backwater, the horror movie stagnated. Here and there, another major studio would venture into the field, like 20th Century-Fox, who produced in 1942 a superior werewolf story, *The Undying Monster,* directed by John Brahm, and the less successful *Dr. Renault's Secret,* about one more mad scientist who succeeds in giving human appearance to an ape. Metro waited three years after *Dr. Jekyll and Mr. Hyde* before allowing Albert Lewin to make *The Picture of Dorian Gray,* a literate, elegant adaptation of the Oscar Wilde novel, with some chilling moments between periods of exquisite *langueur.*

A halfhearted try at infusing new blood into a tired genre resulted in Universal producing *Captive Wild Woman* in 1943 with a sultry starlet succinctly billed as Acquanetta playing a young woman fashioned by plastic surgery from a female gorilla but periodically reverting (especially when sexually aroused) to her simian ways and looks. This Monstress had her career extended into two sequels, both dismal, *Jungle Woman* (1944) and *Jungle Captive* (1945). The 1943 remake of *The Phantom of the Opera* divested the Leroux story of all fantasy and mystery, turning the redoubtable Phantom into a fatherly musician (Claude Rains) with an acid-scarred face. For genuine horror the movie substituted selections from Tchaikovsky, Chopin, and Flotow plus lush Technicolor which won itself an Academy Award. *Phantom* also had a follow-up in *The Climax* (1944) with Karloff as an opera physician who has kept in his home the embalmed body of the prima donna he murdered a generation before.

Rather than renew the by-now worn-out formula, the producers chose to increase the number of themes per feature, as if an excess of spice could save the brew. It was first done in *Frankenstein Meets the Wolf Man,* the most self-explanatory title of 1943, with Chaney as the Werewolf and Lugosi in the Monster role he had refused a dozen years earlier (although for the more violent scenes a double named Eddie Parker was used). Columbia watched the box-office returns and released the following year the somewhat better *The Return of the Vampire* which put Lugosi back on his coffin and gave him Matt Willis as a werewolf assistant. Universal held such yearly monster rallies as *House of Frankenstein* (1944) which had in its cast the Frankenstein Monster, Dracula, the Wolf Man, a mad scientist, and a hunchback—and *House of Dracula* (1945) which had every one of the above plus a dream sequence obviously inspired by the latest *Dr. Jekyll and Mr. Hyde.* Unconscious parody finally gave way to deliberate spoof when *Abbott and Costello Meet Frankenstein* was released in 1948. By then, Universal was flogging a dead horse.

In retrospect, the sole charm of these films resides in the very proficient contract players that populated them, portraying gypsies, mad scientists, lustful high priests, vampire-killers, or mere red herrings. Besides Lugosi (already relegated to supporting parts) and Atwill (happily ensconced in his mad scientist niche), this familiar group included Maria Ouspenskaya, once of the Moscow Art Theatre and now a wizened old gypsy warning the skeptics that "even though a man is pure in heart and says his prayers by night" he is still prone to becoming a werewolf; the very British George Zucco, whose suave manner and cultivated accent hardly concealed his lustful designs on the heroine, usually Evelyn Ankers who succeeded Fay Wray as the most persecuted heroine in films and always managed to appear unruffled in the clutches of the most current fiend; the real life acromegalic Rondo Hatton who proved that actual deformity could never take the place of Jack Pierce's makeup jobs; sinuous, talented Gale Sondergaard, the one woman in pictures who could outwit Sherlock Holmes and out-act Basil Rathbone; and John Carradine, Martin Kosleck, Turhan Bey, J. Carrol Naish, Ralph Morgan, Fay Helm, among others, all invariably bringing distinction to their routine roles and lifting their movies, however momentarily, from the level of the third-rate. They appear now as the real stars of these films, a most valiant troupe temporarily mired in the lower half of the double bill.

In 1947, the war over, Warner Brothers released the one horror movie produced in Hollywood that year. It was *The Beast with Five Fingers,* directed by Robert Florey; it had a gruesome story about the severed hand of a pianist crawling all over the floor and even performing Bach's Chaconne (for the left hand, of course) on the keyboard. It turned out to be a belated funeral march for the genre. Horror is a perennial, but the Monsters were tired. Caught in the interregnum between the Gothic period and the age of science fiction, the horror movie could hardly match the newsreel reality of the day, far more impressive than any special effect and far more terrifying than anything the art of the makeup man could devise.

CHAPTER 5

THE DEAD NEXT DOOR

Among the masterpieces (all too few, unfortunately) of the horror film, there is one that belongs to no industry or school or, for that matter, to no country at all. It was privately financed in France, had a Danish director, and was based on a story by an Irish writer dead for half a century. Yet in the thirty-odd years since its first showing in 1932, *Vampyr* or *The Strange Adventure of David Gray* has outgrown its subterranean reputation and become a pillar of the genre as well as a milestone in the career of its celebrated director, Carl Theodor Dreyer.

After completing *La Passion de Jeanne D'Arc* (*The Passion of Joan of Arc*) in 1928, Dreyer quarreled with his French producers, taking them to court. He won the case in 1931 and, although the success of *Joan of Arc* had made him world-famous, he resolved to work independently. With the financial assistance of a young film enthusiast, Baron Nicolas de Gunzburg, he started his own producing firm. It seemed odd at first that the first project of the new outfit—and the last, as it turned out to be—was an adaptation of one of the tales collected under the title *In a Glass Darkly* by the Victorian storyteller Sheridan Le Fanu.

It was the story "Carmilla," a tale of vampires and mysterious visitations, tinged with strong Lesbian overtones; both vampire and prey are beautiful young girls. Dreyer and his screenwriter, Christen Jul, jettisoned most of the original plot, retaining only the basic theme, that of the vampire who continues to live after death, feeding on the blood of the young.

The story of the film is dreamlike and vague:

> It opens with a prologue: "There exist certain beings whose very lives seem bound by invisible chains to the supernatural. They crave solitude. To be alone and dream . . . their imagination is so developed that their vision reaches beyond that of most men. David Gray's personality was thus mysterious."
>
> Gray arrives at the village of Courtenpierre where a bed has been mysteriously reserved for him at the inn. That night, he is awakened by a strange old man who enters his room, whispers to him, "She must not die, do you understand? She must not die," and leaves a small package in David's care to be opened in the event of his death. The old man leaves and David finds it impossible to return to bed. "Was he a ghost? A dream? Or just a troubled being asking for his help?"
>
> Leaving the inn, David sees the wandering shadow of a one-legged gamekeeper and follows it into a deserted building, where the shadow settles down next to its owner. The walls of the house are filled with shadows dancing to a lilting polka. David has stumbled upon the witches' Sabbath! The music stops and the shadows fade when an old woman enters and orders an end to it. The old woman is then met by the village doctor who, David discovers, lives next door to the haunted house. The one-legged gamekeeper is busy at work building a coffin. David sees the doctor hand the old woman a flask of poison.
>
> Again, he follows the shadow of the one-legged man to a nearby chateau. As the chatelain comes to the door, he is revealed as the mysterious old man who visited David earlier in the evening. A shot rings out and the old man drops to the ground wounded. He dies shortly after in the arms of his younger daughter, Gisele. Leone, the older daughter, is wasting away with a strange sickness. David opens the package left in his care. It is a book entitled *Strange Tales of the Vampires.*
>
> Later that night, Leone rises from her sickbed and is found prostrate on the castle grounds, the old woman briefly glimpsed by her side. The girl's condition is critical and the village doctor is called. He asks David for his blood for a transfusion. The young man agrees; later, weak from the loss of blood, he has a vision. The coffin awaits him. He feels himself locked in it and taken to burial.

The old woman peeks through the coffin's transom. She is the vampire and the doctor her accomplice.

David awakens in the cemetery. He has wandered in his delirium. With the help of an old servant from the chateau, he locates the grave of the old woman, as mentioned in the book of the vampires. Finding the body fresh and seemingly alive, they drive an iron pole through her heart. The body crumbles into dust. Back in the chateau, Leone is freed from her curse.

Left unprotected by their mistress' death, the doctor and the gamekeeper are pursued by the specters of their former victims. The gamekeeper is hurled down a flight of stairs and killed. The doctor is locked into the cage of a flour mill that fills rapidly with fine white dust. As he suffocates in it, with him die the terrors of the dark. David and Gisele walk into the morning sunlight.

Although *Joan of Arc* had been acclaimed as a peak of the Silent Art, Dreyer had been accused by certain critics of a preoccupation with surfaces, an excess of realism. In *Vampyr,* he resolved to go under the surface of realism and seek out the fantastic under the commonplace. The entire film is built on atmosphere and on an almost unbreatheable sense of evil. Unlike the Germans, Dreyer worked outside the studios, creating a fantastic film out of extremely common materials. The small company rented a semi-deserted chateau; other locations were discovered nearby.

To his crew, Dreyer described the film-to-be. "Imagine that we are sitting in an ordinary room. Suddenly we are told that there is a corpse behind the door. In an instant the room we are sitting in is completely altered; everything in it has taken on another look; the light, the atmosphere have changed, though they are physically the same. This is because *we* have changed and the objects *are* as we conceive them. That is the effect I want to get in my film."

The first results were disappointing. Rudolf Maté, who had photographed *Joan of Arc* under Dreyer's direction, came up with images that were too clear and precise. One shot, however, of the early scenes at the inn turned up fuzzy and blurred, unusable by usual standards. This was the effect Dreyer desired, so a piece of gauze was placed three feet in front of the lens and the entire film shot through it, so that the characters seem to be bathed in an eerie light as if they were at the bottom of the ocean or in perpetual dusk. To match this quality, Dreyer avoided brusque movements, pared the action to a few gestures and the dialogue to a few phrases, only half-heard. The camera followed the somnambulistic hero, David Gray, in and out of his "strange adventure" in long, tracking shots that somehow never pierce the white mist of the dream.

Every fantastic event in the story is treated matter-of-factly, defantasized as it were. The one truly supernatural incident in the film, the destruction of the vampire, is handled perfunctorily: The old servant takes the spike from David's hands, raises it, and brings it down off-screen / close shot of the head and shoulders of the old woman dissolving into a skeleton / shot of the night sky / Leone sits up in bed, a joyous expression on her face—"She's gone. . . . My soul is free." Originally, the film was to include a sequence in which the vampire summons the wolves of the forest, but once it was filmed, Dreyer thought it too jarring to the tone of the rest and it was dropped.

Physical shock has been eliminated: there remain two superb sequences of horror by suggestion. The first is the burial ceremony, as seen through the eyes of the corpse. The spectator, becoming the camera eye, takes David Gray's place in the coffin, watching in anguish as the lid is screwed on and wax drips over the glass pane as the old woman, holding a candle in her hand, peers through the transom. There follows the journey to the cemetery, the treetops and building corners glimpsed overhead. Then, awakening and relief.

The other climactic moment is the essence of the film captured in a few seconds. As Gisele watches over her sister, the lethargic Leone seems to awaken in the grip of demonic possession. Her lips part in a smile that bares her strong, white teeth, already thirsting for blood. She fixes her sister with a stare almost obscene in its craving. The nun in attendance spirits the terrified Gisele away and the smile in Leone's face disappears, giving way to a hard, threatening look. If Murnau equated the vampire with plague and pestilence, to Dreyer, vampirism is a sickness of the soul.

It was obvious to Dreyer that for the all-important role of Leone a professional actress was indispensable. Sybille Schmitz, a young disciple of Max Reinhardt, was summoned from Berlin and she acquitted herself beautifully. She embarked on a long career in German films and died a suicide in 1955. She and Maurice Schutz, who plays the chatelain, were the only actors in the film. David Gray was played by the Baron de Gunzburg under the pseudonym of Julian West; his passive face and slightly stooping stance perfectly suited the conception of the non-hero Dreyer had in mind. The rest of the cast was drawn from friends and acquaintances, selected for their "mental resemblance" to the characters.

Vampyr was Dreyer's belated debut in the talking film. Sound is used sparingly throughout: dialogue is elliptical, sometimes indistinct, increasing the sense of mystery of this tale of horror half-perceived. "I'm loosing blood," complains David Gray after the transfusion. "How can you?" retorts the evil doctor. "I have it all here." Or the ominous "Why must he always come at night?" that betrays the doctor's unholy alliance with the vampire. The night is full of sounds, mostly left unexplained. The score by Wolfgang Zeller, with the exception of a playfully sinister "Shadow Polka," is unobtrusive. *Vampyr* is not an easy film to grasp; it demands of its audience the same effort of co-creation Gothic novelists asked of their readers.

The film's career has been mainly subterranean. It opened in Berlin, disappointing most of the critics who thought a horror film, albeit a masterful one, beneath Dreyer's stature. It was released in the United States during the Frankenstein-Dracula period under the title *Castle of Doom* and found too offbeat by the Hollywood standards of action and gore. Some of its footage reappeared in a compilation film of the early forties, *Dr. Terror's House of Horrors,* which also included portions of *White Zombie,* Duvivier's *The Golem,* the Richard Oswald omnibus film *Unheimliche Geschichten* (*Extraordinary Tales*), and bits of Lugosi's serial *The Return of Chandu* (1934).

It was more than ten years before Dreyer was to direct again. *Vredens Dag* (*Day of Wrath*), made in Denmark in 1943 during German occupation, was also concerned with old age, death, and obsessive evil. In a Danish village of the seventeenth century, a doddering old hag (Anna Svierkier), suspected of being a witch, is tracked down, tortured, and finally burned at the stake. From the pyre, she hurls a curse at the stern middle-aged pastor (Thorkild

Roose) who tried and convicted her. The pastor has a young wife (Lisbeth Movin) who is resented by her mother-in-law and attracted to her own stepson. They become lovers and the wife brings about the death of the parson by revealing the liaison. "I wish you dead" she cold-bloodedly informs her husband, and the older man suffers a stroke and dies. Over his bier, the mother-in-law accuses the wife of witchcraft. It is as if the vampire had become the old witch. Both films are concerned with a death struggle between the young and the old; the curse of the old witch has tainted the wife and she, like Leone, is convinced of her own evil.

Day of Wrath illuminates both *Joan of Arc* and *Vampyr.* Its success revived interest in Dreyer's forgotten vampire film, which had survived mainly through the film museums of the world. It remained as darkly entrancing as ever, the work of a solitary creator faithful only to himself. But by the mid-forties, it seemed closer to the postwar sensibility. For one thing, we had had the admirable series of low-budget, imaginative movies from Hollywood's Val Lewton. *The Cat People* and *Isle of the Dead* were the spiritual children of *Vampyr.*

comprise eleven titles, nine of which are poised between the thriller and the horror movie, yet each resolutely turns its back on the fantastic. With the exception of the last three, which were more ambitiously literary, they were all compact little novellas set in a recognizable modern world, where man-made monsters, vampires, and werewolves had no place. In their stead, they substituted a very real fear of the unknown, the dark, of ancient superstition, and what Moncure D. Conway called "the reason of unreason"—for the night creatures themselves, these films substituted our dread of them.

From the first effort, *The Cat People,* the formula succeeded beyond Lewton's hopes for it. Directed by Jacques Tourneur (Maurice's son and worthy successor) from an original screenplay by DeWitt Bodeen, it had for its heroine a beautiful Serbian girl (Simone Simon), Irena, working as a fashion designer in New York. She is convinced that she descends from a race of Balkan women who, as a result of certain rites of bestial worship in the Middle Ages, are capable of changing into large, dangerous cats when their passions are aroused. Irena's obsession fascinates Oliver Reed (Kent Smith), a young naval designer who finally marries her; her fears, however, prevent the consummation of the marriage. An unhappy Oliver seeks the help of a psychiatrist (Tom Conway), eventually turning to another girl, Alice (Jane Randolph), for comfort. This arouses Irena's jealousy and, shortly after, an unseen animal makes several attempts on Alice's life. When the psychiatrist tries to dispel Irena's fears by making love to her, he is mortally clawed. Before dying, he succeeds in wounding the girl. Irena manages to reach the zoo to die among her favorite animals, the big cats. A variation on the werewolf theme, the case history of an obsession, a study in frigidity (or possibly repressed Lesbianism), *The Cat People* benefits from this ambiguity and keeps us guessing until the end. To an audience surfeited with puttied, gruesome creatures, Lewton was to bring in this and subsequent films a low-keyed and ominous mood, well-dosed moments of shock, and nearly subliminal hints of something almost too evil to be put into words and images. A large part of the action was set in Manhattan's Central Park and its surroundings: the brownstone apartment where Irena lives and works, the zoo where she compulsively sketches the felines, and the park transverse where Alice is pursued at night by something unseen and deadly (there is a magical moment of shock and relief as the doors of a bus hiss open to offer refuge). Later, Alice finds comparative safety in a basement swimming pool while the same malignant, growling presence claws her bathrobe to shreds at the water's edge. Even after Lewton's executive superiors insisted on the insertion of a shot of a black panther slithering under the drafting tables, as it stalks Oliver and Alice in a deserted office, the skillful editing of Mark Robson manages to preserve our uncertainty.

While *The Cat People* was being edited, Lewton and Tourneur embarked on their second picture, *I Walked with a Zombie,* a title borrowed from a series of newspaper articles dealing with witchcraft and voodoo in Haiti. The original script by Ardel Wray and Curt Siodmak derived from Charlotte Brontë's *Jane Eyre,* a novel much admired by Lewton. A young nurse (Frances Dee) is retained by a wealthy West Indies planter (Tom Conway) to care for his sick wife. Jessica (Christine Gordon) seems to be the victim of a mysterious malady which has left her a walking catatonic, speechless and mindless. To the superstitious islanders, she is a zombie—one of the living dead. The nurse decides to take Jessica to the island's voodoo priest, and their nocturnal walk through the cane fields, while the approaching drums drown out the rustling of the wind, constitutes the core of the film as well as one of the high-water marks of screen terror.

The Leopard Man, adapted from a thriller by Cornell Woolrich (*Black Alibi*), was an effective murder mystery about a series of killings in a small New Mexico town, blamed on a runaway leopard but actually committed by a psychopath. This time, the formula shows through in the mechanical repetition of the murders, however well-staged. Lewton's masterpiece may well be *The Seventh Victim,* which dealt with devil worship in Greenwich Village. Rarely has a film succeeded so well in capturing the nocturnal menace of a large city, the terror underneath the everyday, the suggestion of hidden evil. The anti-heroine (well-played by Jean Brooks in a cryptic sort of way) has defected from a secret society of Palladists. She endangers the safety and secrecy of the adepts by hysterically murdering an informer and is condemned by the society to death by execution or suicide. She takes the latter as the way out, hanging herself, alone and dejected in her dismal rented room while a consumptive neighbor (Elizabeth Russell) goes out into the night for one last, desperate fling. A hauntingly oppressive work, *The Seventh Victim* seemed to draw its inspiration from the John Donne sonnet that closed it: "I run to Death, and Death meets me as fast, and all my Pleasures are like Yesterdays."

Almost as unusual a film was *The Curse of the Cat People* (1944) which, far from being a sequel, was in many ways an improvement. To James Agee, it was "full of the poetry and danger of childhood." It was also psychologically sound and sensitively written and portrayed. It had nothing to do with cats or curses, the title having been imposed by the studio on Lewton. It did contain a terrifying retelling of the legend of the Headless Horseman by veteran actress Julia Dean in which the audience was subtly drawn into the world of seven-year-old Aimee (Ann Carter). Delicately perched on the very edge of terror—like *The Turn of the Screw,* it also concerns children and ghosts, imaginary or not—*Curse* never loses its poetic balance. The sole threatening forces in it are the lack of understanding of Aimee's elders, the pent-up resentment of wasted middle age, and the petty jealousies of an alien adult world.

The critical acclaim bestowed on Lewton's films (like the best producers in Hollywood, his stamp is stronger than that of his individual directors) brought him recognition, larger budgets, and first-rate stars. The later films became longer, heavier, and more literary. *The Body Snatcher* (made in 1943 but released in 1945 so as not to compete with other Lewton films) was an adaptation of a story by Robert Louis Stevenson, dealing with the notorious "resurrectionists" of nineteenth-century Edinburgh, Burke and Hare, who supplied doctors and students with cadavers for the study of human anatomy. (The same historical fact inspired the Dylan Thomas screenplay *The Doctor and the Devils.*)

Lewton's film was handsomely wrought and contained one of Karloff's best, unmade-up performances as a murderous coachman. But the one moment of real horror came at the very end and lasted but a few seconds; it was worth waiting for, but missing were the cinematic rhythm and engaging modesty of the earlier pictures.

The Lewton formula was to build a film around a horror sequence, balancing it with one or two minor shocks and allowing the tension to build in between. For this reason, the high points in terror always occur halfway through the film when the characters have been fleshed in and the audience is in command of the story. The best illustration of the method can be found in *Isle of the Dead,* ostensibly a tale of oddly assorted people marooned on a Greek island during a quarantine. Nothing much happens in the first half of the film, except that the audience is informed that the genteel wife (Katherine Emery) of a British consul (Alan Napier) suffers from cataleptic fits and lives in mortal fear of being buried alive. Later, when she dies or appears, to the other characters, to die, the cold eye of the camera comes close enough to her face for us to perceive the slightest tremor of the nostrils: she is alive and going to be buried as dead! Our knowledge and their ignorance turn the ensuing scene into a concert of terror, deadly silent except for the moaning of the wind, the creaking of wood, and the final, unleashed scream of the woman entombed alive.

With this suitable coda to his career, Lewton's brief reign as a master of terror comes to an end. His last effort at RKO was a straight, verbose exploration of *Bedlam,* the infamous eighteenth-century London asylum, in which the insane are treated as beasts and where a courageous, perfectly sane girl (Anne Lee) is confined by Bedlam's malevolent master (Karloff). Leaving RKO, Lewton made three non-horror movies for other companies before dying of a heart attack in 1951 at the age of 46. Although his kind of imaginative, literate horror seemed at first to die with him, Lewton's influence had already been felt in films like *The Uninvited.* More recently, it contributed to the success of *The Night of the Demon* (directed by Tourneur in England in 1958) and *The Night of the Eagle* (1962), both superior excursions into the field of demonology and witchcraft. Lewton's own films have lost little of their original haunting power and the titles that once seemed so incredibly lurid have gained through all these years an almost classical ring.

Among the seventeen horror films released in the United States during 1944, the best and most unusual was *The Uninvited,* which had Ray Milland and Ruth Hussey as a brother and sister who come across a charming vacant house on the Cornish coast and acquire it for a suspiciously low price. Moving into their new home, they come (in quick succession) to sense, smell, hear, see, and finally exorcise the evil ghost that haunts it. This is accomplished with the help of a beautiful young girl (Gail Russell) with mediumistic powers whose mysterious birth is the key to the enigma. An adult, polite ghost tale, lacking the disquieting undertow of *The Turn of the Screw,* the movie had a pleasantly chilling feminine touch (it derived from a best-selling novel by Dorothy Macardle) most evident in the deft dosage of its well-calculated shivers: a flower that wilts in seconds, a dog that refuses to climb the stairs, a scent of mimosa that impregnates a room, a moonlit romantic piano piece that develps into a somber concerto. The director (Lewis Allen) had learned the Lewton lesson well, although it is doubtful that Lewton himself would have retained the one shot of ectoplasmic apparition at the top of the stairs. Paramount, perplexed by a story in which ghosts turned out to be not only real but also evil (instead of the reassuring spirits of *The Return of Peter Grimm* or the funny ones of the *Topper* series), advertised their film as "the story of a love that is out of this world." The picture met with the success it merited but failed to earn ghosts a place in the cinema comparable to the one they enjoy in literature. Horror films, especially in Hollywood, prefer to steer clear of spiritual matters.

The British *Dead of Night* (1945) was a compendium of six tales dealing with the macabre and the fantastic, a film equivalent of the horror story omnibus. The trouble with films of its kind—especially when a different director takes over in each chapter—is that the merit of the episodes is quite variable. The one that succeeded the best was a short story (directed by Robert Hamer) about a mirror that at a certain time of night reflects a room from another place and another time, the setting of a murder committed long ago. Abetted by an ominous score by Georges Auric, the episode had all the evocative power of the best horror fiction. Another tale told about a girl (Sally Ann Howes) who enters a certain room she is not allowed into and there finds a sobbing, scared little boy who was murdered many years before. Still another concerned a young man (Antony Baird) haunted by a recurrent dream in which a jolly hearse driver (Miles Malleson) invites him for a ride with a spiritedly terrifying "Room for one more!" The remaining tales were a comic sketch about two golfers (Basil Radford and Naunton Wayne) whose rivalry transcends the grave, a heavily Expressionistic sequence about a ventriloquist (Michael Redgrave) dominated by his dummy, and a final farandole which redundantly mixed all the stories together. All in all, the film had a soft persuasive charm, like a tea party where some guests are excellent raconteurs and some are pretentious bores. One squirms at the latter and hopefully waits for the next.

CHAPTER 7

"KEEP WATCHING THE SKY!"

There is a world, if not a universe, of difference between the Martian romances of Edgar Rice Burroughs and the Martian chronicles of Ray Bradbury. Somewhere in between, man slipped from his position as center of the universe and human annihilation became a possibility when not a certainty. The cops-and-robbers fantasies tricked out against improbable galactic worlds all but disappeared, as science fiction moved from the pages of the comic books and "Thrilling Wonder Stories" into hardcover respectability and began to demand critical coverage in the pages of literary revues, *The New Statesman,* and *The New York Times.*

Hard to define abstractly, science fiction is instantly recognizable on the printed page. Its principal feature is extrapolation from the past and the present. It may take for a setting the human mind or the all-but-human cosmos. It can be subject to the stripes of many moods: satirical, sociological, humorous, philosophical. And although it has partly lost the admonitory gloom of a George Orwell or an Aldous Huxley, it still takes the tone of moral warning when it deals with the burning issues of control of the personality or of Earth's survival.

Science fiction, the one literary genre to have flourished since the war, is only one step ahead of the headlines. (Twenty years ago the preeminent scientists of the world questioned the possibility of accurate lunar landings.) To the classical soothsayers of old, a distinguished group that includes Verne, Conan Doyle,

Villiers de l'Isle-Adam, Rider Haggard, and Wells (not forgetting *their* forefathers: Swift and de Bergerac, and offbeat offspring like Karel Capek who introduced the robot to the world), we can now safely add the names of such first-rate authors as Poul Anderson, Isaac Asimov, Charles Beaumont, James Blish, John Christopher, Arthur C. Clarke, Jack Finney, Robert Heinlein, L. Ron Hubbard, Nigel Kneale, Richard Matheson, Judith Merrill, Lewis Padgett, Ian Stuart, and John Wyndham, among many too numerous to mention.

Lagging behind, motion pictures attempted to keep pace with science fiction during the fifties, matching in quantity—if not in quality—this fantastic output. During the 1957–58 season, more than forty films combining science fiction and horror themes were released in New York City and only now is the vogue abating. Their large number forces one into rough classification rather than individual analysis, though in spite of the lack of perspective a few more years might bring, some of the science fiction titles have achieved the prominence of popular classics. Also, the sad but inescapable fact remains that, until the last few years, few directors of importance were to attempt science fiction films. Quality takes second place to quantity and their staggering flow, lack of press coverage or even of advertising in the daily newspapers (not to mention the dismayingly low level of craftsmanship in most of them) make it well nigh impossible to cover the genre thoroughly. Children of the age, science fiction films lose the timeless preoccupations of the horror film and rise and fall with the trends of anxiety: *The Man from Planet X* may be negligible, but the Flying Saucer scare was not. Still, one may have seen *Terror from the Year 5000* or even *The Underwater City,* but who can claim such devotion to film research as to have sat through *The Space Children, War of the Satellites* and *Attack of the Fifty Foot Woman?*

The time for reflection may finally have arrived, but in the beginning science fiction demanded of the film-maker little beyond an awareness of the headlines and a technical dazzle. For the intellectual speculations of the printed page, the screen substituted color, lots of sound, CinemaScope, special effects, and even the third dimension. Science fiction films materialized the wildest fancies. Soon, logbook excursions into outer space in which Nature is the sole adversary began to look as outmoded as *The Swiss Family Robinson,* and a new element added itself to science fiction: horror. Flying, walking, crawling, creeping things festered up the screen, bastard offspring of nuclear energy or uninvited visitors from outer space. From then on, science fiction progressed on a curve of hysteria, masochistic wishful thinking, ritualized reenactment of dream catastrophes—accommodating to fear and ignorance of the controlling facts of modern existence, and evolving the new myths for our age.

Still, in 1950, the tone was considerably factual and mild. George Pal, for many years the producer of shorts that employed stop-motion animation techniques on puppets (they were called Puppetoons), joined the new Space Age with his soberly realistic *Destination Moon,* several moments of which bring to mind the distantly removed exploits of Lang's *Frau im Mond.* Akin to that venerable flight of fancy, Pal's movie was supported by the most advanced research on missile techniques and enlisted Lang's reliable Hermann Oberst among its consultants. Although the movie tried to stay apolitical, the realities of the Cold War creep into its plot with some very definite statements about the responsibility of America to reach the moon first ("Whoever conquers the moon will control the Earth"); and a minor episode concerns a sabotage attempt by an unnamed foreign power. The film reaches a climax when Army scientists and civilian industrialists, like mass-produced Columbuses, land on the surface of the moon and rather portentously claim her for the United States "by the grace of God" and "for the benefit of mankind." The blissfully innocent days of an unengaged Flash Gordon or Buck Rogers, launched to the stars and wandering beyond, were over and done with—as they left, a good deal of poetic imagination and convulsive excitement was carted off with them.

Destination Moon has no real heroes or villains (the cast does not contain any star names, either—what screen luminary would accept a job playing second fiddle to a royal flush of special effects?)—the story has the machines themselves as its raison d'être: the rocketship with its up-to-the-minute gadgets, well-researched paraphernalia, and the shiny well-designed look of pressure gauges, astronautical gear, and launching site specifications styled by Hans Knoll and Raymond Loewy. All very eye-catching but quite undramatic. Mildly exciting were such moments as the launching of the spaceship, the rescue of an astronaut who drifts onto the macrocosm (an anticipation of the actual walk into space performed by Aleksei A. Leonov in 1965), and the final successful landing on the sandy, pocked, and cratered face of the moon.

As soon as Pal announced his plans to film *Destination Moon,* an independent producer named Kurt Neumann rushed into production with *Rocket Ship XM,* which he wrote, directed, and produced in black and white (with some tinted sequences) on a low budget, pushing it into release two months ahead of its competitor and model. It was a gimcrack story about a spaceship detoured by a female member of the crew from going to the moon and reaching Mars instead. Putting down on the red planet, they discover the remnants of a civilization superior to ours that nonetheless succumbed to atomic warfare, leaving behind a handful of survivors who have regressed to the Stone Age. This would-be pawky moral warning had all the earmarks of cheap, last-minute opportunism.

Whether impersonal or overinvolved, the route to the stars was open. *Flying Saucer* (1950) and *Flight to Mars* (1951) were small-budget, inconsequential trifles, and it was left up to George Pal to map out the most ambitious, apocalyptic space exodus for *When Worlds Collide* (1951) from the novel by Edwin Balmer and Philip Wylie. With Earth doomed by an impending collision with the planet Bellus, the salvation of the human race depends on the safe removal of a select few to a wandering planet called Zyra which is charted to approach the Earth's orbit penultimate to the cataclysm. As this Noah's Ark to Zyra departs with its cargo of forty perfect specimens, we are treated so some spectacular views of disaster, including the destruction of New York by a tidal wave, which won an Academy Award for the Paramount Special Effects department. In what appears to be the morning after doomsday, the spaceship lands on the planet of its destination, an exuberantly tropical Eden, to start the building of a brave new world.

In spite of their updated jargon and the latest-model newness of their equipment, all the preceding essays on interplanetary travel are basically films of a kind—the straight, non-horrific science fiction of the prophecy films of the thirties, such as *Transatlantic Tunnel, F.P.1,* and *Shape of Things to Come,* concerned in varying degrees with some scientific or technological quest like constructing an underwater tunnel between North America and Europe, a vast floating platform in mid-ocean, or the look of the world of tomorrow. This nonviolent form of science fiction has now become rare, at least in the films of the Western World, although an occasional effort like Pal's own *Conquest of Space* (1955) or *Robinson Crusoe on Mars* (1964) appear now and then.

Following the Flying Saucer scare of midsummer 1947, and after the required incubation period in the public mind, the thought that two-way traffic between Earth and the rest of the universe was a possibility, if not (as many then believed and many more do now as the reports of U.F.O. sightings have increased over the last twenty years) an accomplished fact, injects into the genre the first symptoms of an hysterical, obsessive new fear. Danger, from now on, comes from the skies. The world must be warned, and the science fiction film has been called on its first mission. At the same time, the horror movie gains a new lease on life.

Things from other worlds offer unlimited variety as creatures of horror, untied as they are to anthropocentric codes. They can be protoplasmic monstrosities (like *The Blob*), figures of human appearance and superior intellects (Klaatu in *The Day The Earth Stood Still,* the Messenger of *The Twenty-Seventh Day*), or a combination of both (*The Thing,* the Martians in *The War of the Worlds*). Most of them arrive as either messengers from another civilization or as a vanguard squadron bent on reconnaissance for eventual take-over. When they arrive in full force, as in *The Mysterians* or *The War of the Worlds,* the films become eye-drugging fantasies of destruction, bolting and bounding with color, special effects, and big budgets.

In *The Thing* (1951) the tone is still persuasively intimate. A spaceship of alien and unrecognizable origin crashes in the Arctic wastes and its sole occupant, an eight-foot, man-shaped vegetable, is brought to an isolated Army research station, imprisoned in a block of ice. As the Army men debate what to do with it, the Thing awakens from its lethargy and escapes into the polar ice-deserts, leaving a trail of death and loosing a hand to one of the fierce Eskimo huskies. The astonished scientists discover that the Thing lives on blood, that it can regenerate its missing limb like any plant, and that the seeds found under the fingernails of the dismembered hand develop into gruesome organisms throbbing with life when nourished with plasma and capable of growing at alarming speed. At this point, the scientists clash with the military: the former would keep the creature alive and attempt some kind of intellectual exchange; the latter realize that a fast-multiplying, seemingly indestructible invader can take over the entire planet. Meanwhile, the creature lays siege to the base, destroying the heating system in its determination to obtain its vital supply of blood. How to combat it? Bullets cannot incapacitate a vegetable, and the sub-zero weather does not seem to slow it down. An inspiration comes from the practical, wisecracking secretary (Margaret Sheridan): What do you do with a vegetable? You cook it. The Air Force officer (Kenneth Tobey) takes command, overruling the scientists and rigging up an electric booby trap. When the Thing appears again, it steps on exposed high-voltage wires and is given a roasting of several thousand volts, which finally destroys it. One newspaperman, who has witnessed the entire adventure, broadcasts to an expectant world how the human race, as in Biblical times, was once again saved by an (electric) Arc (sic)—and the picture fades out with a question mark. Have we seen the end of the Thing?

Produced by Howard Hawks, directed by Christian Nyby, *The Thing* works best when the Creature is kept off-screen. Compared to the story that inspired it (*Who Goes There?* by John W. Campbell, Jr.) in which the Thing is so monstrous it defies visualization, the movie Thing (played by James Arness) bears a striking resemblance to the Frankenstein Monster and in itself becomes the film's only blemish and banality. Also, we cannot bring ourselves to believe that something supposedly so intellectually advanced could be a survival of the fittest if it depended for that survival on the life fluid of a species inhabiting an alien world. This onus of vampirism, however, works wonders in another context: the real new horror of the situation is not the roaring, bloodthirsty creature itself but the fact that an intellect superior to that of man's would be even deadlier, that omniscience does not mean human feelings, generosity, or understanding. In this respect, the film is something of a parable: superior science unencumbered by moral scruples will bleed us to death. Falling into place with this idea, the film's stirring near-tragic moment comes when the hysterical scientist (Robert Cornthwaite) makes one last desperate attempt to establish emotional contact with the Thing ("You're wiser than anything on Earth. Look at me and see that I'm trying to help you.") only to be violently brushed aside with a murderous uncomprehending gesture.

The newspaperman at the close of *The Thing* warning us to watch the skies was more of a prophet than he (or Hawks or Nyby) realized. *The Thing* was but the first of many such visitors. On the next spaceship over came *The Man from Planet X* (1951), a small rather vulnerable figure with a large head of inscrutable features encased in a glass bubble; his mission was to hypnotize the inhabitants of a Scottish island into forming a sort of fifth column that would pave the way for large-scale invasion. The Martians who land in the Arizona desert in *It Came from Outer Space* (1953) are capable of assuming many (even human) guises, but in their natural form they resemble an encephalic mass with one large unblinking eye in the middle. The *Invaders from Mars* (1953) wore velvety green monkey-suits and were kind to women and children. The *Phantom from Space* (also 1953) resembled nothing so much as a nearly naked body-builder; the creatures in *Killers from Space* (1954) were bug-eyed relics of the Flash Gordon period; and there was nothing animal or vegetal about *The Monolith Monsters* (1957).

But these small expeditionary forces can hardly compare with the Martian war machines deployed in *The War of the Worlds,* which George Pal adapted from the H. G. Wells novel in 1953, and which even now remains hardly surpassed (even by *The Mysterians* and other more recent Japanese science fiction) in its fantasy of mass destruction. A rocket ship lands in the California mountains and from it emerges a group of graceful, birdlike spaceships endowed with electronic eyes and an ominous ticking sound and emitting an exterminating ray. When a three-man parley approaches these machines, they are carbonized on their tracks; a priest who invokes the name of God and attempts to reason with the invaders meets the same fate (one of the few episodes retained from the original 1897 text). There are no possible truce terms—the Martians are bent on ruthless global destruction. This is seen in microcosm as Los Angeles is razed to the ground. Finally, after every conceivable terrestrial weapon proves ineffectual (even the Atom Bomb fails, for the alien spacecraft have their own protective atmospheres), the Martian invaders are felled by the tiniest organisms of our planet. Science cannot be trusted to defend Earth against more developed invaders, but Nature can. *The Thing* was destroyed by heat, *The Blob* (1958) will freeze to death, and the all-powerful Martians of *The War of the Worlds* are wiped out by contact with common, everyday germs. This is reminiscent of Wells' *The First Men in the Moon* (filmed 1964), one of whom destroys himself and lunar civilization by bringing with him the common cold. There is one old-fashioned horror sequence in *The War of the Worlds* wherein the hero and heroine (Gene Barry and Ann Robinson) find shelter in an abandoned cottage which is being probed by one of the Martians' electronic eyes. Although the persistent ticking on the sound track effectively builds up the breathless, life-or-death tension of the scene, the climactic coming to face with an exposed Martian, a thing that resembles some kind of crustacean with long fingers armed with suction discs, is a letdown. The film is more successful in its convincing depiction of carnage and obliteration. Bodily harm, death, even the loss of the soul have been replaced by apocalyptic destruction. The world, sometimes the universe, is now at stake.

Not all creatures from outer space are war-mongering, bloodthirsty mutants. Klaatu, the cosmic ambassador of *The Day the Earth Stood Still* (1951) is a well-spoken intellectual endowed with human form (played by gaunt, dignified Michael Rennie) and almost divine powers. He comes to Washington in a flying saucer, accompanied by his robot Gort, with a message of peace that brings with it a solemn warning. Either the nations of the

Earth put an end to all atomic testing (and consequentially, atomic warfare), which has endangered the delicate balance of the spheres, or Earth will be demolished to save the rest of the universe. To prove that his words are no mere boasting, electric power everywhere on Earth is neutralized for a day. That is, everywhere except on airplanes in mid-flight or in hospitals no matter where. This message, of course, exposes an underlying allegory: Klaatu is God's messenger come to Earth as in Biblical times to scold the modern Sodom and Gomorrah for their evil ways. While the heads of state deliberate these demands and the necessity of meeting them, Klaatu moves freely (under the watchful eye of the F.B.I.) among the people and, with the assistance of his terrestrial friends, a widow (Patricia Neal) and her child (Billy Gray), reaches a new understanding of his mission. He learns that the average earth person has no love of war, that war is mainly a large concern in the hands of a few men. These men, reaching their own conclusions, have decided that Klaatu is an impostor or a menace or both. The space messenger is shot down as he returns to his spaceship, and the robot Gort, especially instructed to destroy the Earth on the event of Klaatu's failure, is stopped in the nick of time, by the widow who was instructed to do so by Klaatu (the words she uses to save the Earth are *klaatu nikto barada* which have the familiar ring of the *mene mene tekel upharsin* of antiquity). After digesting this stop-signal, Gort retrieves the body of Klaatu. As the authorities and the crowd assemble around the flying saucer, they watch in astonishment as a resurrected Klaatu appears to deliver one final message: "I came as a messenger of peace and you did not understand me. I will return to my people." Klaatu has vanquished death, at least as it is known on Earth. The spaceship takes flight and disappears into the sky.

It is obvious from the above synopsis that *The Day the Earth Stood Still* is an attempt, albeit a rather confused one, to present the science fiction genre with its *lettres de noblesse*. The tone is more measured (as befits a philosophical allegory), the execution expert and polished within the limits of newsreel realism (part of the movie was done on location in Washington, D.C.), and there is a steady refusal on the part of the director (Robert Wise) to indulge in the more juvenile dreads and effects of his predecessors.

But the film trips on its own long seriousness and the religious parallel becomes embarrassing after a while. If Klaatu is God's angel on Earth, his rather conservative display of power simply is not enough to convince humanity of the power at the source of his words. And if he is a man, better than our men, the product of a civilization developed beyond ours, why does he not bring with him the formula for peaceful living that has supposedly succeeded so well in the cultures of other planets instead of an awfully earth-sounding ultimatum? Ambitious, intriguing, the movie is dramatically unequipped to deal with issues that most science fiction films leave unmolested.

Whatever its shortcomings, there was a sensible, level-headed attitude about *The Day the Earth Stood Still* which is tragically missing from the hysterical, inept "B" picture called *Red Planet Mars* released in 1952 at the height of the McCarthy era. The preposterously propagandistic plot-line concerns an American scientist (Peter Graves) who succeeds in establishing contact with Mars. Through his broadcasts, he learns that the Martians have reached a high level of civilization, attaining a life span of 300 years and exploiting all the peaceful uses of the atom. They are ruled, politically and morally, by a supreme authority, whose teachings paraphrase the Sermon on the Mount. The scientist makes public these disclosures and the Earth is swept by a religious revival ("God Speaks from Mars") as the Communist regime of Russia is overthrown. The film then brings in an Anti-Christ (Herbert Berghof), an absurd amalgamation of Nazism and Communism, a drunken scientist who serves only Satan, whose mission is the shattering of world peace, and who claims to be the one responsible for all the messages. The good scientist, rather than see his work undone, blows himself up along with his wife (Andrea King) and the villain, as a last message from Mars confirms the validity of his reports. The President of the United States—the action is set in a future day so near that the President is made to sound like Eisenhower—delivers the eulogy for the dead hero as the world embarks on an era of peace and prosperity.

Red Planet Mars also marks the sad decline of two illustrious names once associated with the horror movie: the insultingly crude screenplay is the work of John L. Balderston, who collaborated on *Frankenstein* and *Dracula,* and the shoddy, low budget sets were designed by Charles D. Hall, who was responsible for the fine, atmospheric look of *The Black Cat* and *The Bride of Frankenstein.* The director of the film was Harry Horner, once a set designer himself. The more traditional horror movie seldom—if ever—concerned itself with issues, political or religious. But science fiction is bound by its very nature to contemporary anxieties and the interest of *Red Planet Mars* lies today in its own irresponsible, extravagant reflection of the times.

The flying saucer of *The Day the Earth Stood Still* and the Sputnik-like sphere that brought *The Man From Planet X* offered tantalizing glimpses of other worlds, ultra-developed civilizations light-years in advance of our own. Film excursions into the world of tomorrow have been few and usually seem limited, not only in scope (for budgetary reasons) but more crucially, by their lack of imagination. There have been, however, exceptions.

This Island Earth (1955) shuttles back and forth between Earth and Metaluna, a planet of super-intellectual beings in human form (except that they have extremely high foreheads and slightly enlarged craniums). Metaluna is in the throes of interplanetary atomic warfare with a neighboring world, Zahgon, and in desperate need of an uranium supply. A scientist-agent named Exeter (Jeff Morrow) is dispatched to Earth to screen the world's most advanced scientists before selecting two, one man and one woman (Rex Reason and Faith Domergue), to accompany him back to Metaluna, where they will pursue their experiments. But it is too late: Metaluna is doomed. The Supreme Authority of Metaluna decrees that Earth will be colonized by and for the Metalunians. The earth couple is to be brainwashed and escorted back to Earth by Exeter to prepare the forthcoming invasion. But Exeter, who has grown to understand these emotional Earthlings (and to enjoy the best of their culture—like the music of Mozart) returns them safely home before crashing his spaceship into the ocean.

This compendium of stock science-fiction situations (interplanetary travels, brainwashing, "metabolic" machines, atomic warfare) was to be found in the whimsical, comic-strip fantasy of the Flash Gordon serials, but *This Island Earth* takes itself quite seriously, even achieving a certain tragic grandeur in its depiction of the last moments of a doomed civilization. And Metaluna itself is a plausible surrealistic landscape of destruction, doomed to be overrun by gruesome mutants with large, exposed brains and pincerlike arms, the end product of some terrible biological evolution.

A rare flight of fancy from the ordinarily earthbound Metro-Goldwyn-Mayer, *Forbidden Planet* (1956) manages to resuscitate the classical elements of the horror movie in the ultramodern decor of intergalactic science fiction. The action takes place on the planet Altair-4 in the year 2200, but the film takes its theme from Shakespeare's *The Tempest,* adroitly transcribed into science fiction terms by screenwriter Cyril Hume. This is not so off-the-mark as it may seem. Like Prospero, Professor Morbius is a scientist/magician who has not mastered all of the forces he liberates. His Ariel is Robbie the Robot, a triumph of cybernetics only one step removed from total humanity. Caliban is a pure force of destruction, a projection of Morbius' id, the embodiment of all his subconscious hates and fears. Morbius has found out the secret of the Krells, the extinct inhabitants of Altair-4, who achieved such intellectual control of themselves that they were able to materialize their most secret desires out of the blue and were ultimately destroyed by the materialization of their collective unconscious. Morbius spares his daughter and a few Earthlings the same fate when he commits suicide.

Direction does not count for much that is essential in films of this genre, where themes can be put across successfully by the art director, the special effects department, even by the sensuousness of the color or the quality of the sound track. In these respects, *Forbidden Planet* is more than successful. Yet, in spite of its weird electronic tonalities and endearing, well-bred robot, it has to fall back, for its climax, on the most conventional monster fiction. Once materialized, the Monster of the Mind looks like a panther silhouetted in red (the work of cartoon designers from the Walt Disney studios), and this denouement is as incongruous as if Spencer Tracy's Mr. Hyde had strayed aboard Gemini X.

The less violent type of science fiction, the kind that does not depend on cataclysmic spectacle, seems more appropriate to the printed page, and usually succeeds better there. The subtler, most intriguing premises are usually botched somewhere in the production of cheap, undistinguished films. In *Journey to the Seventh Planet,* a mediocre Swedish-American co-production of 1961, a United Nations spacecraft lands on the unexplored planet Uranus, where the five-man crew is met with a peculiar power of this otherworld that renders substantial their fears and desires: e.g., a man mortally scared of rats will be attacked by a giant rodent. The morale of this expedition is further compromised by the materialization of their loved ones and even their familiar milieux: a Scandinavian cottage (with a windmill in back of it) appears to the Swedish member of the group, and so forth. These figments of their imagination are mirages controlled by the mysterious Brain which rules the seventh planet, Uranus. True to form, the Brain turned out when it showed up, or materialized, to be as disappointing (in an opposite way) as Morbius' id—it was the usual formless mess.

In Socialist countries, where science is held in the highest esteem and its validity never questioned, science fiction is rarely concerned with the horrific. There are few monsters in Socialist films, and none of an inexplicable nature, no debacles, and absolutely no mutants (mutants are walking warnings against the use of atomic energy). The interest of the films is that of the adventure story, where danger comes out of natural causes, such as meteorites or earthquakes, and wrong-headed human interference.

Ikaria XB1, a Czech film of 1963 shown in mutilated form over here as *Voyage to the End of the Universe,* is a day-by-day log of an odyssey to a distant star, a manual of intragalactic etiquette. Its spaceship equipment and accoutrements seem as prettily modern and smartly efficient as those of its American counterparts. Although speculative, *Ikaria* is never extravagant. Its most memorable sequence concerns the discovery, where it floats in mid-space, of a ghost spaceship, presumably once manned by a United Nations crew who fell to fighting among themselves with tragic results. This bit of archaeology into the twentieth century (the story is set in the distant future) is dismissed by the advancely civilized Ikarians as "a relic from the century of Auschwitz and Hiroshima"—a belated, almost casual riposte to *Red Planet Mars!*

In the Russian *Planeta Bura* (*Storm Planet*, 1962) an expedition lands on the planet Venus, where it is met with remnants of prehistoric life such as dinosaurs and a carnivorous plant. The cosmonauts search for remains of the high civilization that once flourished in Venus but they come across no survivors. Then, as the last spaceship takes flight on the return voyage to Earth, we glimpse the reflection of a Venusian on the waters of a lagoon. The film ends right there: where most American science fiction begins.

The monsters of the nuclear age are all creatures of the Bomb. Since *The Beast from 20,000 Fathoms* (1953) was accidentally reawakened from its lethargy of a million years by the underwater testing of atomic devices, the screen has been overrun by all manner of reanimated prehistoric colossi and raw biological mutants (the atom affects both past and future). The larger, supposedly extinct creatures whose millennia of hibernation are disrupted by nuclear explosions usually emerge from such remote parts of the globe as the polar regions or the bottom of oceans. They invariably thunder off first to smaller communities where they are seen by witnesses whose reports are dismissed as unreliable by the more enlightened, more skeptical authorities (who live somewhere else). Then these saurian enormities finally get somewhere when they storm the metropolis and wreak havoc (the staple of this type of film since *King Kong*) before being put to sleep in extremis by the last-minute most lethal atomic defense equipment (which could rarely harm a guest from outer space).

This reliable pattern was first established by Ray Bradbury, who wrote the original story for *The Beast* and by Ray Harryhausen who conceived and executed the special effects. The success of *The Beast* assured its lineage. No sooner had the dust settled on the ruins of Coney Island than it was time for *Them!* (1954). Atomic testing in the New Mexico desert produces fifteen-foot-long ants capable of killing humans with massive injections of formic acid. Part brisk documentary, part outrageous fiction, *Them!* is probably the most successful example of its class. It was followed by the enormous octopus of *It Came from Beneath the Sea* (1955), the stupendous spider of *Tarantula* (1955), the gargantuan mollusk of *The Monster that Challenged the World* (1957), *The Deadly Mantis* (1957), and *The Giant Behemoth* (1959).

These creatures, however imposing, were surpassed in bellicosity by *Godzilla, King of the Monsters,* a Japanese monster-movie of 1955, that featured a prehistoric (or mythical?) dragon capable of emitting an incendiary ray. Godzilla rises from the depths of the Pacific Ocean to raze Tokyo in an exorcistic reenactment of the catastrophe of Hiroshima. All weapons prove ineffectual to stop the beast; then, an idealistic young scientist who has perfected *the* final atomic device (short of the Cobalt Bomb) decides to immolate himself like the kamikaze of old and destroy Godzilla. It was a useless sacrifice, for Godzilla returned intact to the screen in several sequels (*Return of Godzilla, Godzilla versus the Thing, King Kong versus Godzilla*) when the film proved the greatest international success of Japan's movie history. And Japan, the only nation on earth to have actually suffered from atomic warfare, has become the world's foremost producer of filmic holocausts.

These cataclysms were devised and executed by Eiji Tsuburuya and his special effects department. At their best, as in *The Mysterians* (1957), a combination of *The War of the Worlds* and *This Island Earth,* the effects may even surpass the classical articulation of *King Kong.* Whatever their excellence, they are sheer displays of virtuosity: Tokyo, Osaka, Yokohama tumble like a deck of cards. It is all very pretty, but, obsessively thrust on the viewer without reason or buildup, they ultimately appear as gratuitous masochism.

A few science fiction movies reduce nuclear catastrophe to more intimate terms, individual dramas from which the spectacle is absent. *The Incredible Shrinking Man* (1957), imagined by Richard Matheson, is the most typical illustration. While sunbathing, a healthy young American (Grant Williams) is engulfed by a cloud of radioactive dust. He begins to diminish in size at the alarming rate of an inch a week. The immediate result of this is alienation: he becomes a freak in his own home, a doll-like stranger to his wife. Soon, it is merely a matter of survival: running from a cat, defending himself against a spider and killing it with a pin. Finally, he is a minute speck looking at the stars, the infinitely small looking at the infinitely large. This disquieting ending was marred by an inopportune, uplifting comment to the effect that as far as God is concerned there is no zero. The movie, directed with flat precision by Jack Arnold, had its quota of traditional adventure, as the hero becomes a tiny Robinson Crusoe in a world of threatening familiar things. The final effect, nevertheless, is hauntingly thoughtful. It certainly has become a sort of classic in a remarkably short time, and that in spite of lacking real excellence—perhaps because it introduced a very different type of fear into the dark solitude of movie houses, not instant annihilation but a gradual inexorable descent into nothingness.

In the British-made *The Quatermass Experiment* (made in 1955 and released in the United States as *The Creeping Unknown*), the sole survivor (Richard Wordsworth) of an experimental space flight returns to Earth a stunned wreck of a man who gradually begins to change into a slimy, walking, funguslike mass that feeds on the blood of his victims. The monster is finally brought to bay in Westminster Abbey and destroyed with electricity. As the picture ends, an undaunted scientist (Brian Donlevy), who has chased the man-turned-monster down, prepares to launch another spaceship. As Lionel Atwill used to say: "Who knows what tomorrow's madness may be?"

The astronaut (Bill Edwards) in *First Man into Space* (1959) crash-lands his craft and emerges from it a minerally encrusted fiend, gasping for oxygen and striking out at those who would help him. Finally brought into a high-pressure chamber, the meteorite-man blurts out the details of the flight and his subsequent ordeal, and before dying, pathetically gasps, "I was groping my way through fear and doubt." "I wonder if we've learned too much" mutters one of the attending scientists.

A variation on the theme of atomic threat relies on the almost abstract fear of nuclear weapons. The monster here is neither a mutant nor a prehistoric beast but the atom itself, a hungry growing element that threatens to consume all the energy of the world, as in *The Magnetic Monster* (1953) where newly liberated radioactive energy doubles its power every twelve hours. It is finally forced to destroy itself by generating an equal amount of antithetical electricity. Examples of this type are few and unpopular, relying as they do on endless expository dialogue; and nuclear reactors and atomic piles are rather undramatic in the long run. The best effects of *The Magnetic Monster* came too late in the film and from a very unlikely source: a German film of 1934 called *Gold,* which, with an old-fashioned preoccupation, devoted its elaborate resources to the transmutation of lead into gold.

The ultimate horror in science fiction is neither death nor destruction but dehumanization, a state in which emotional life is suspended, in which the individual is deprived of individual feelings, free will, and moral judgment. That the most successful SF films of the past decade seem to be concerned with dehumanization simply underlines the fact that this type of fiction hits the most exposed nerve of contemporary society: collective anxieties about the loss of individual identity, subliminal mind-bending, or downright scientific/political brainwashing. (Not by accident the trend began to manifest itself after the Korean War and the well-publicized reports coming out of it of brainwashing techniques.) We have come a long way from *Metropolis* and the encroachment of the machine. Nowadays man can become the machine himself. The automatoned slaves of modern times look perfectly efficient in their new painless state. From this aspect, they are like the zombies of old—only we never bothered to wonder if zombies were happy in their trance. Zombies, like vampires, seemed so incontrovertibly different; the human counterfeits of Don Siegel's near-classic *Invasion of the Body Snatchers* (1956) are those we love, our family and friends. The zombies are now among us, and we cannot tell them and the girl next door apart any longer.

To Dr. Miles Bennell (Kevin McCarthy), returning home after a holiday trip, the town of Santa Mira seems as quiet as usual. But little by little, something that he can only see as evil starts taking possession of the town. A child runs away from his mother in terror, a neighbor begins to wonder if Uncle Ira is Uncle Ira. To Miles, this new state of things seems at first an epidemic of mass hysteria. In the night, an urgent call summons him to the home of his friends Jack and Theodora (King Donovan and Carolyn Jones). And there, on the billiard table, is a *thing,* a pseudo-human body —"like the first impression on a coin, no details." While he debates its origin with Jack and Theodora, Miles notices that the thing has begun to look like Jack. The sheriff is called in, but not before the thing has been removed (by some person or by itself?). In the morning, Miles discovers in his own cellar huge seedpods that open and release the gruesomely imperfect alter egos of himself and his fiancée Becky (Dana Wynter). Terrified, Miles strikes at his effigy with a spade. The "things" seem to drain the likenesses and the minds from sleeping humans. Miles shows up in panic before the sheriff (Ralph Dumke) and realizes suddenly that the lawman has already been supplanted. The sheriff coolly advises Miles to abandon all resistance, to stop fighting the take-over. "There is no need for love or emotion. Love, ambition, desire, faith—without them, life is so simple." Soon, Miles and Becky are the last human beings left in Santa Mira. They manage to escape and hide in a cave. At dawn, Miles decides to try to get help from outside. Bending over to kiss Becky, he realizes that she has no emotion. "Stop acting like a fool, Miles," she says in a reassuring tone, "accept us." Miles runs hysterically onto the highway where, before too many cars have passed, he is arrested as drunk and taken to Los Angeles. He blurts out the whole incredible tale to a police inspector and is, of course, regarded as insane. Almost too late, a report arrives from nearby Santa Mira. There has been a highway smashup and one of the vehicles was heading for the city loaded with "strange, huge seedpods." The police inspector reaches for the phone. There might still be hope.

In *The Village of the Damned,* a British adaptation of John Wyndham's novel *The Midwich Cuckoos,* a mysterious force descends upon a small village causing every one of its denizens to lose consciousness for two or three hours. This incident is rendered more than inexplicable when, soon thereafter, all women capable of fecundity are found to be impregnated. The children these women bring into the world grow up to be totally emotionless super-intellects, sharing common traits such as blond hair and ebony eyes which acquire a phosphorescent glow during moments of extreme concentration. Except perhaps for a monolithic esprit de corps, which allows them to communicate among themselves telepathically, they seem unaffected by human feelings of any kind. When one of the mothers (Barbara Shelley) neglects her baby momentarily, the tot wills her to put her hand in scalding water. Grown older, the children can take over the minds of those they mistrust and order them to commit suicide. These handsome, murderous prodigies are capable of taking over the Earth. From knowledge of this, it follows that they must be destroyed—one of the nominal fathers (George Sanders) takes it upon himself to save the world and, with dynamite well-placed, blows them, and himself, to pieces.

The idea of the human body as the vessel of an alien force is as old as the stars. If nothing else, *Invasion of the Body Snatchers* and *The Village of the Damned* demonstrate the persistence of myths. There are many examples of such intimate visitations in Greek legend (the numerous human and animal forms assumed by Zeus), in Oriental religion (the avatars of Vishnu), in Christian theology (the Mystery of the Incarnation), and in Hebraic and medieval tradition (demonic possessions, dybbuks). The habitation of ordinary mortals by transcendent spirits was originally evolved as an explanation for recurrent examples of abnormal behavior, insanity, or perversion. They now reappear in their latest form, while yet retaining a distant echo of their former versions. One may not be surprised, then, when the tears of a female visitor from outer space in *The Unearthly Stranger* (1963) run down and burn her cheeks like acid. Witches, possessed by Beelzebub, were deemed incapable of tears. In many films of recent years, mysterious forces from outer space have replaced witches, gods, and demons, and they appear just as valid in the age of interstellar anxieties.

In some ways, the cheaper independently-made films can and usually do go further than their more serious, more cautious counterparts. *The Day Mars Invaded the Earth* (1963) is a ruthless version of *Invasion of the Body Snatchers.* A typical American family (Kent Taylor, Marie Windsor, and their two children) is caught in a frighteningly similar plight to that of Miles and Becky.

They are haunted and hounded by creatures who have assumed their forms and faces. The jolting surprise ending shows them to have been incinerated, their places in human society immediately to be taken by their doubles. (An additional, minor horror: their absence will not even be noticed.) The garrulous, unspectacular *Creation of the Humanoids* (1963) is the one science fiction film to carry the idea of dehumanization to its logical extreme. The hero (Don Megowan), believing himself to be the last man rebelling against robotization, is informed that he is already an android, an R96, definitely the highest order of cybernetical development, there being only twelve in the world, and, soon, even capable of procreating! We know not what we are, let alone what we may be.

CHAPTER 8

HORROR AROUND THE WORLD

The early-fifties revival of interest in stereoscopic films gave a new lease on life to the exhausted, non-science fiction horror film. There were 3-D remakes of such classics as *Mystery of the Wax Museum* (*House of Wax,* 1953) and *Murders in the Rue Morgue* (*Phantom of the Rue Morgue,* 1954) besides some original but mediocre material like *The Maze* (1953) and Universal's conservative addition to their family tree of monsters, *The Creature From the Black Lagoon* (1954), an improbable batrachian (played, or rather swum, by Ricou Browning) with the features of a frog, the stance of a man, and a vaguely lecherous design on the heroine (Julia Adams). Although the stereoscopic craze was quickly extinguished by the arrival of the more comfortable Cinemascope, stray examples continued to emerge as late as the early sixties. *Thirteen Ghosts* and *The Mask* (1960 and 1961, respectively) marked the end of the red-and-green filter fad.

Yet the very fact that three-dimensional films had concentrated on horror rather than on other less violent genres pointed the way to the next step: an increased audience participation was in order if the horror film was to survive. The producers organized a campaign of gimmicks that stopped short of nothing but actual frontal aggression on the public. The results, all rather ineffectual, were technical-sounding (although really only publicity) devices like Psychorama (for *My World Dies Screaming*), Hypnovista (for *Horrors of the Black Museum*), and Emergo (*The House on*

Haunted Hill). The latter consisted of nothing more technical than a luminous skeleton strung on wires and swung over the heads of the spectators in the theater, very much like the good old days of the Théâtre Robert-Houdin. One producer, the enterprising William Castle, actually dared to lay hands, figuratively speaking, on the audience.

Castle himself appeared at the outset of *The Tingler* (1959) to inform the public that, in cases of extreme terror, a scream might very well save a person's life by relieving tension and that he would advise the audience to scream for its life, or sanity. Then, a preposterous but ingenious story unfolded on the screen—a doctor (Vincent Price) discovers that fright actually creates a centipedelike organism at the base of the spine, a creature that pinches the nerves and eventually can cause death, but which, however, loses its grip if the frightened person screams. A perfect subject for a cruel experiment is found in the deaf-and-dumb wife (Judith Evelyn) of a theater owner (Philip Coolidge) who shows only silent films. Alone at night in her apartment, the poor woman is driven to panic by a series of ghastly apparitions. When she goes into the bathroom, blood flows from the faucets (the black-and-white film turns to color in this sequence) and a threatening hand emerges from a blood-filled bathtub. Opening the medicine cabinet, she is confronted with her own filled-out death certificate; incapable of screaming, she crumples on the floor dead. In one of those surprising twists which William Castle so obviously favors, her husband, and not the doctor, is revealed as the murderer-by-fear. And "the Tingler," liberated during the autopsy on the dead woman, invades a movie theater. At this point, as the story had proved somewhat unpersuasive, selected members of the audience were subjected to mild vibrations from electrically wired seats in the house—at least this is how it was done in the film's opening engagements, since the process of wiring an entire theater proved too costly and rather risky and this gimmick was soon abandoned. Castle, never daunted, seems ready to try anything despite the by now obvious fact that his most successful pictures are his more direct thrillers, such as *Straight-Jacket* (1964) and *I Saw What You Did* (1965).

Another unsubtle try at eliciting passive audience participation was attempted by a 29-year-old producer, Herman Cohen. Studying the results of a poll that earmarked the age group of a high percentage (70 per cent, to be exact) of the movie-going public as lying between 12 and 25 years, Cohen decided to adapt the well-known formulas of the horror movie to juvenile terms. In 1957, he released *I Was a Teenage Werewolf* and *I Was a Teenage Frankenstein;* the former, costing a paltry $150,000, grossed an astonishing $2,300,000 in a short time. The latter (just as successful) is worth a line or two: it marked the first time that anatomical detail was used as a horror element—although the picture's burlesque tone prevented this detail from becoming really disgusting. The monster of *Teenage Frankenstein* is assembled from selected anatomical parts of dead hot-rodders and various other teenage corpses by a mad doctor (Whit Bissell) who reputedly represents the American branch of the once illustrious Frankenstein family. The doctor's resultant creature (Gary Conway) has the physique of a fullback, the face of a Halloween mask, and a perfectly normal affinity for teenage girls and rock 'n' roll. The movie worked better than the more intentional parodies. It did not seriously scare its youthful public and it must have amused its more sophisticated admirers. The dialogue bears repeating: "He's crying, even the tear ducts work!" exulted the mad doctor at one juncture, adding a few moments later, "Answer me, you have a civil tongue in your head. I know, I sewed it in there." Cohen's sequels, *Blood of Dracula* (1957) and *How to Make a Monster* (1958) were not as inspiredly absurd but were nearly as successful. Shuttling between England and Hollywood, Cohen has been responsible for the screenplay and production of such undistinguished, but busy efforts as *Horrors of the Black Museum* (1959), *Konga* (1961), and *Black Zoo* (1963).

Because of several events, 1957 was to become an important year for the horror movie. The release of the old Universal classics to television in the package known as "Shock Theatre" was made in that year. The pictures were televised three nights a week, on Thursdays, Fridays, and Saturdays, presumably so that parents could screen them in advance of their offspring. An astonishingly high audience rating proved that horror was hardly a dead issue. Although abbreviated and interrupted by commercials, they still retained some of the genre's original power, if not to intimidate, at least to evoke the surrogate feeling of a nostalgic mood. They had been preceded by telecastings of the independent pictures like *White Zombie* as well as the Val Lewton thrillers, but these gems, however distinguished, lacked the dazzling mythical appeal of *Dracula, Frankenstein,* and their like.

At about the same time, in 1957, a new version of the Mary Shelley classic was made by the Hammer Studios in England. Titled *The Curse of Frankenstein,* it grossed more than one million pounds in the United States alone and initially helped establish Hammer as the successor to Universal as the world's greatest producer of horror movies.

Hammer Studios, a rather minor company with studios at Bray near Windsor, had been responsible for the first two science fiction films produced in Great Britain: *Four-Sided Triangle* (1952) and *Spaceways* (1953), neither put together out of more than the ordinary materials. *The Curse of Frankenstein* assiduously overlooked the tracks of its distinguished predecessor—the Shelley original may have been in the public domain, but the Karloff/Pierce creation was heavily protected by copyright. (Universal has, since the release of the James Whale *Frankenstein,* successfully brought suit against various commercial firms that had imitated the Monster's makeup on charges of copyright infringement.) As played by Christopher Lee in a makeup created by Phil Leakey, the Monster was a mass of collodiom scar tissue and greenish greasepaint and, what is worse, wholly negligible as a dramatic character. This movie version did restore the action to the original setting of the novel, Switzerland at the beginning of the nineteenth century, and its other assets were Technicolor, excellent sets (which have since, through Hammer usage, grown overfamiliar), and the crisp, mannered performance of Peter Cushing as Doctor Frankenstein. *The Curse of Frankenstein*'s extremely detailed laboratory scenes—eyeballs in alcohol jars, dismembered hands—were but an inkling of more explicit horrors to come.

Hammer did considerably better with their job on *Dracula,* made in 1958 and released in the United States as *Horror of Dracula,* which found even greater favor at the box office and consolidated Hammer's position and Hammer's style. Stoker's novel, scriptwriter Jimmy Sangster concluded, was old-fashioned, overlarded with symbols, and much too concerned with establishing the proper mood of terror and anguish. "It is a common fallacy that vampires can change into bats and wolves," announced a conceited Van Helsing (Peter Cushing) and to bury all the covert symbolism of the vampire the new *Dracula* substituted a blatant, almost athletic display of sadism and necrophilia—a young (physiognomically) uncadaverous vampire (Christopher Lee) slobbering blood over the naked throats of his victims ("The Terrifying Lover—who died yet loved," said the ads) ; the driving of a stake through the body of a beauteous vampire (Valerie Gaunt) ; all scenes swimming in a wealth of gory detail. As a result of this new approach, the movie failed where the others had at best made something of themselves, in the evocation of a timeless, intangible evil. It was most impressive in its physical aspects, in lushly colored sets and costumes and a distinct flair for period touches. It also had some eye-openers worthy of *Varney the Vampire, or the Feast of Blood,* such as Dracula's sudden appearance like a demon from hell, fangs bared and eyes bloodied, to the horrified stunning of his guest (John Van Eyssen). And sometimes even a whiff of Gothic survives Terence Fisher's pedestrian direction: Lucy (Carol Marsh) lying awake in her bed waiting the coming of the vampire while the wind rustles the autumn leaves on her balcony.

In comparison with this *Dracula,* the old classics began to look rather anemic. Hammer chose to infuse them with new blood, figuratively and visually. They have given us their remakes of *The Mummy, The Hound of the Baskervilles* (both 1959), *The Two Faces of Dr. Jekyll* (1960) and *The Phantom of the Opera* (1962), plus a few sequels to their own productions, such as *The Revenge of Frankenstein* (1958), *The Evil of Frankenstein* (1964), *The Curse of the Mummy's Tomb* (also 1964) and *Dracula Prince of Darkness* (1965). The effects of most of these were indistinguishable as well as undistinguished. Other Hammers, however, had some merit if not distinction. *Brides of Dracula* had a few nasty shocks but toned them down and was content to leave the thrust to the telling of a more unusual vampire tale. A girl (Yvonne Monlaur) spending the night at the castle of a sinister old Baroness (Martita Hunt) discovers that the noblewoman keeps her son, a sympathetic young man (David Peel), shackled to the wall of his bedroom by a silver chain. She steals the keys from her hostess, unlocks the son's shackles, and unwittingly liberates a blood-lusting vampire! *The Curse of the Werewolf,* from Guy Endore's novel *The Werewolf of Paris,* came closer to the mark than both of Universal's forays into the same theme, giving back to the lycanthrope many suggestive traits. A baby born on the Eve of Christmas, according to many folktales, will grow into a werewolf. One such child, the hero of the film in his earliest state, is about to be baptized when the holy water in the font begins to boil. Years later, a group of shepherds fire on a wolf that is attacking their flocks and six-year-old Leon limps home that morning full of buckshot. As a young man full-grown, Leon (Oliver Reed) manages to control the beast in him until he is denied the hand of the girl he loves. He is climactically killed by his own stepfather with a silver bullet forged from a crucifix.

These horror embroideries aside, a study of Hammer's adventure melodramas, such as *Stranglers of Bombay* (1959), *Terror of the Tongs* (1961), or even *Rasputin the Mad Monk* (1966), as well as their "straight" thrillers such as *Paranoia* or *Maniac* (both 1963), reveals that the common denominator of their product is not really horror but sadism. The more jaded the public's palate becomes, the ranker the banquet of effects. At one time, Hammer used to prepare three different versions of each film they produced: one for the United States, a milder one for Great Britain, and one considerably stronger for Japan. Such distinctions now seem a thing of the past. Mutilations, beheadings, gougings, burning flesh, and decaying corpses—all of these are arbitrarily spliced into the scenarios at the expense of characterization and plot. The story told in a Hammer film has become an utterly predictable and mechanical narration; Sangster has been replaced as top screenwriter at Bray near Windsor by the producer, Anthony Hinds himself, who signs his scripts either John Elder or Henry Younger. What can be said for director Terence Fisher except that his style (or lack of it) has neither softened, strengthened, nor sharpened from *The Curse of Frankenstein* to *The Gorgon?* The studio contends in the face of critical dismay that practically every one of their films has done extremely well at the box office—so Hammer does not intend to change the formula, or experiment with a new one, unless public taste changes first.

This may be sooner than expected; alongside the frayed jolts of *Plague of the Zombies* (1966) and *The Reptile* (1966) the company has already produced *The Nanny* (1965) and *Fanatic* (1965) (*Die Die My Darling* in the United States), both of them more immediate, more intimately gripping and sophisticated movies. The hybrid of wolfbane and festering black dahlia first exhibited by Robert Aldrich in his *What Ever Happened to Baby Jane?* seems to be the hothouse bloom influencing these marriages of Grand Guignol and the psychological thriller. Unfortunately, as Universal, finally realized, you can reanimate a monster but you cannot make it scare. The main interest in such films as *The Nanny* seems to be purely in the performances, as the horror precipitated is, in the long run, only of the kind to bother a pathologist.

Inevitably, Hammer's returns on each film's investment spurred other British companies to try a hand at the production of horror movies. Foremost among these are Amicus (producers of *The Skull* and a new, original *Dr. Terror's House of Horrors*) and Anglo-Amalgamated (*The Face of Fu Manchu*), both of whom unapologetically borrowed Hammer's formula along with Hammer's stars and directors. Still and all, the best examples of the genre ever made in Great Britain represent the diametrical opposite of the Hammer way of doing things.

Jacques Tourneur, for instance, knew that real horror is a fragile, glass-boned thing when he set out to direct *Night of the Demon* in 1957 for British Lion-Columbia. This was an elaboration on Montague R. James' short story "Casting the Runes," which is considered a classic of its kind. The plot hinges on an ancient parchment inscribed with runic symbols which have the power to summon primeval evils, demonic ghouls, from places outside of time and space. Tourneur conducts the spectator together with his hero (Dana Andrews) along the path from skepticism to uncertainty to terror. His experience with Val Lewton shows to a new advantage, and *Night of the Demon* abounds in prosaic situations turning implacably into nightmares. Every flourish is a touch not underlined but understated, ellipsed and just suggested. Unfortunately, the film's producers could not see that this was enough: against Tourneur's wishes, they inserted some atrocious shots of a demon at the very outset of the picture. It is a tribute to the director's skill that his movie survives such a monumental blunder. In America, *Night of the Demon* was retitled *Curse of the Demon* and released to the theater circuits in support of Hammer Films' *The Revenge of Frankenstein,* which in a wink it eclipsed.

Fritz Leiber's story *Conjure Wife,* which had already performed as the inspiration for one of Universal's Inner Sanctum mysteries (*Weird Woman*), was remade in England in 1961 as *Night of the Eagle* (retitled in America *Burn Witch Burn*). Since Sidney Hayers, who directed, has never nearly matched his work in this, the credit for its better than average success must go to the adapters which included such well-known names as Richard Matheson and Charles Beaumont. With skill in measure, the movie pastiched Dreyer's *Vampyr* (the cemetery seen through the eyes of the "dead" heroine) and Tourneur's aforementioned *Night of the Demon*—the hero chased by a huge stone eagle come to life parallels Andrews' panic-stricken race through a forest pursued by an omnipresently hovering, unseen demon—while it managed to dissipate the dread and presence of the supernatural with the logical and vice versa.

Although pathological case histories lie outside the province and proper spectrum of the pure horror film—as in the case of *M* or even the horrifying *Psycho*—Michael Powell's *Peeping Tom* (1960) almost bridges the gap, concerned as it is not so much with terror as with the face of terror. The hero, Mark (played by Carl Boehm) works as a technician in a London film studio and, as a sideline, takes pornographic pictures. A lonely, unfriendly, sexually repressed fellow, Mark is obsessed with the effects of fear and how they are registered on the face and behavior of the frightened. This obsession dates from the time when, as a child, he served as the subject of some cold-blooded experiments in the psychology of terror conducted by his own father. As a grown man, Mark becomes a compulsive murderer who kills women and records their contorted features and dying gasps on film. Alone at night in his rented room, he surrounds himself with the sights and sounds of terror: taped screams, black-and-white "home movies" of convulsed faces. *Peeping Tom* may well represent one of the few truly Sadian films, as opposed to merely sadistic. Bearing this out are various references to de Sade and his works, both overt and subterranean, throughout the picture. Associated in the past with such bizarre excursions as *The Red Shoes* and *Tales of Hoffmann* (not forgetting *The Thief of Bagdad* which he co-directed), Powell brought an elaborate technique to the realization of *Peeping Tom:* fanciful use of color filters, black-and-white films within the film, hand-held camera scenes from the vantage point of the first-person, etc. Although the film was conceived as a psychological thriller in the line of *The Lodger, The Sniper,* or *Without Warning,* Powell carried the implicit savagery of those earlier efforts to their logical conclusion, bringing to the type an unflinching absorption in place of the customary (and insincere) reticence. *Peeping Tom* was heavily censored in most countries; yet, in spite of its theme, the movie was far less gory than the most dignified of the Hammers. Critics and censors, united for once, seemed to find the display of terror more deplorable than actual blood-spilling.

Not often will a prestige picture attempt to lead the horror genre from the beaten path and raise it from the level of the penny dreadful to that of the distinguished literary work. In *The Innocents,* made in England in 1961, we are in the presence of a director (Jack Clayton) in evident awe of his material, and well he should be, the source being Henry James' fine 1897 novella *The Turn of the Screw*. The film speaks Distinction from the first frame to the last and is so carefully assembled, its shivers and shudders are so well-bred, that it ends up conveying no sense of evil at all. And evil is precisely what *The Turn of the Screw* is all about. And ghosts. But in *The Innocents,* Truman Capote had adapted James' narrative into post-Freudian terms. The ghosts are no longer demons from the pit as the author intended, "wooing their victims forth to see them dance under the moon," but the products of the sick imagination of a spinster and the horror (if horror there be, since a more accurate word would be tension) derives from the fact that a neurotic woman comes to be responsible for the traumatization or death of her infant and sensitive charges. The James story has suffered from overinterpretation and overanalysis, and every commentator has felt compelled to fill its gaps. The film, however, does not give its audience the sporting chance a reader of the tale is given—the viewer is never allowed to ensnare himself in his own interpretation. No sooner has the film begun than we are informed in terms far from inscrutable that the governess (played by Deborah Kerr) is a repressed hysterical type. Later on, when nine-year-old Miles (Martin Stephens) kisses her on the mouth she reacts with the breathless shock of a ravished heroine. The ghosts themselves are not visible until the lady in question conveniently finds their portraits, whereupon they materialize in short order and perfect faithfulness. (Needless to say, there is no such psychological alibi in the book.) The movie's cardinal sin is the overexplanation of all the things that James beautifully left in the dark. And failing literary art, Clayton falls back on the hoariest of dramatic devices such as thunder and lightning and overamplified sound effects: very poor substitutes for inexplicable terror. Carl Van Doren appositely termed *The Turn of the Screw* "the blackest of all nursery tales, the most terrifying of all ghost stories, the most pathetic of all chronicles of damnation." Clayton and Capote have reduced all its black sorcery to the conventions of the most banal narrative.

Hammer's main competitor for the horror film market is the American Roger Corman, the most prolific film-maker in contemporary commercial cinema, who between 1953 and 1963 directed more than thirty films (and produced just as many) ranging from hot-rod features to rock 'n' roll musicals to science fiction, before settling down as the foremost merchant of horror in the United States. Rapidity of output (and the skill that it develops) has contributed in part to the establishment of a Corman cult of admirers in France and Great Britain; yet some of his earlier work can stand up without apology on their own. Both his unabashedly lurid horror films and his juvenile thrillers were dynamically unpretentious and appropriately limned to the very contemporary world they were set in—a world that is usually ignored by Hollywood or blown up beyond recognition. *Bucket of Blood* (1959), in particular, was a valid transposition of *Mystery of the Wax Museum* to the typically Southern California milieu of jukeboxes, coffee shops, and Venice West beats. It was merely a quick sketch but it had style, a winning regard for locale, and even managed to satirize itself and the plethora of other teenage thrillers as it went along.

Then, in 1960, Corman picked up Edgar Allan Poe. Gathering to him a few reliable collaborators, such as the veteran photographer Floyd Crosby and the novelist Richard Matheson, he invested more time and money than ever before and turned out *The House of Usher* (1960), a ponderous drawn-out movie that seemed the antithesis of his earlier work. This was the first Corman movie to get extensive critical coverage and, although found wanting by most reviewers, its box-office appeal indicated to Corman that the way to the big-time was through Poe. Corman decelerated his output, dropped the swift bold touch of his juvenile melodramas, and embarked with a splash on his new career as Edgar Allan Poe's on-screen voice.

Through his next Poe adaptations, *The Pit and the Pendulum* (1961), *Premature Burial, Tales of Terror* (both 1962) and *The Haunted Palace* (1963), Corman began to develop a new manner if not a style. Constrained by larger but still limited budgets, the director has extracted the last ounce of effect from Daniel Haller's eye-deceivingly vast but far from spacious sets by his use of free camera movements. And with Crosby's assistance, he has exploited to their limit the possibilities of Pathecolor, obtaining sensuously sepulchral tones of blue, puce, green, and mauve. Corman's most ambitious film of his Poe period is *Masque of the Red Death* (1964) which he made in Great Britain with a generous budget, the luxury of Technicolor and superior technical facilities. The finished film demonstrated the extent of Corman's unmistakable talent and also his limitations. This time, the Poe text (combined with another story, *Hop-Frog,* for padding) afforded some visual sustenance. In his previous Poe adaptations, Corman had little more than a title to work with: *Premature Burial* had an original story by Charles Beaumont and Ray Russell, and *The Haunted Palace* was mainly an adaptation of H. P. Lovecraft's *Charles*

Dexter Ward. In the case of *The House of Usher,* Matheson had to elaborate an intrigue which emerged a total alien to the Poe spirit—a raving, maniacal heroine and a final conflagration simply work against the grain of Poe's damp, miasmic evocation from which all violence is absent. Contrarily, *Masque of the Red Death* is less this somber contemplation than an over-ornate macabre fable. The movie has all the flat undimensioned elegance of a well-drawn comic strip, brimming over with sparkling decorative effects in the chambers of Prince Prospero's castle (each done in one single resplendent color), and in this exploitation of decor Corman shows himself to be a true *metteur-en-scène.* Where he fails is in his more grandiose aspirations: Corman's grotesques are fairy-tale dwarfs out of figurine mold or theatrical wizards; his climactic *danse macabre* never becomes more than a listless third-rate ballet with the participant-guests twisting and turning to small effect. Obviously, Roger Corman is no Ingmar Bergman nor is he Luis Buñuel, both of whom he openly admires. In the long run, *Masque of the Red Death* is rescued from out-and-out imitation or heavy-handed pretentiousness by the brisk staging of many scenes and the current of irrepressible humor that swells up when least expected.

Corman must have been conscious of the more laughable aspects of his earlier Poe adaptations when in 1963 he directed *The Raven,* a burlesque at the expense of his usual crypt-and-coffin antics. The director—who cannot be said to control his players—brought the Poe ubiquity, Vincent Price, together with Boris Karloff and Peter Lorre to play magicians black, white, and gray, and gave them their heads. Relishing their absurd incantations, improvising their own bits of business, and lampooning their screen images, they emerge as monsters, but of a different kidney. To the sum of its credit, *The Raven* adds acceptable trick camera work and a childish sense of fun that covers a lack of any real wit—while the most unusual fact about the film is that it immediately begat another film. Finishing *The Raven* in sixteen days and three ahead of schedule, Corman had a few standing sets and Karloff on his hands. It seemed a pity to let the sets go to waste—not to mention the valuable services of the venerable Mr. Karloff—so Corman and two screenwriters hastily concocted a story-line and, with the assist of some fine seascapes taken in Monterey, California by Corman's assistant (Monte Hellman), they completed *The Terror,* a confusing but endurable horror thriller in color and CinemaScope, within the record time of three days! This would suggest that the medium for Corman, after all, is television.

Still that same year (1963) another Corman film flickered across the screen, a science fiction called *X, The Man with the X-Ray Eyes,* which left the intriguing possibilities of its story unrealized. A scientist (Ray Milland) perfects a serum that enables him to see through walls, clothing, skin, and bone, to diagnose diseases at first sight, to win huge fortunes at the gaming tables. But omniscience proves too much for this mere mortal and the hero, like Oedipus, plucks his eyes out in the end. It was as mechanically constructed and unimaginative as H. G. Wells' *The Man Who Could Work Miracles,* whose abject moralizing it echoed almost three decades afterward. That such a mediocre effort won Corman an award at the First International Festival of Science Fiction held in Trieste that year proves only that the crisis of this genre demands choices among an embarrassment of pittances.

Born in 1926, Corman is a shrewd movie-maker working in the pit between two generations: a younger one, which seems the more vocal nowadays and which forms the bulk of his audience, and an older world of critics for whose approval he spins his more ambitious and flamboyant pastiches. The reasons for this favor with the younger audience must be taken into consideration if the effect of Corman's films is to be justly assessed. His mise-en-scène (in the sense of a directorial design that utilizes all elements of film making to convey a definite idea) in film after film accentuates the putrid, the mouldy, the dusty—the crumbling of a hopelessly adult world. This overripe sphere of existence is almost invariably presided over by an epicene character played by Vincent Price (as in *The House of Usher* and *The Pit and the Pendulum*), enervated and haunted by dead or dying women. Such juveniles as there are to be seen in the shadows of these overdraped dramas are cardboard figures whose presence (or lack of it) silences any argument for audience identification. What appeals to the youngsters seems to be the pleasure of seeing the used-up, flabby gentlemen sink as the old order rots and crumbles around them.

Not a man to be bound to one type of film for long, Corman's interest in horror seems to be waning. His most recent passage through Poe, *The Tomb of Ligeia* (1964) was the handsomest of his color productions, but it polished off to a glaze the old Corman vigor. In any case, the mind boggles at the thought of having the Complete Edgar Allan Poe translated into Vincent Price star-vehicles. Corman may again have taken up with his first love, juvenile thrillers, but his influence on the Horror Film has already garnered *Die, Monster, Die* (1965), the directorial debut of his set designer, Daniel Haller. The film is an adaptation of "The Color Out of Space" by H. P. Lovecraft, and there are signs in it of an affinity that points the way to fresher, more adventurous collaboration.

The Fly (1958) stands out from the ordinary run of horror movies in nearly creating an authentic science-fiction monster and botching the job with an unscientific—and illogical—story-idea. Although a production slated for the minor budget of $350,000 by big studio standards, *The Fly* surprised everyone including 20th Century-Fox, its makers, by netting more than three million dollars during the first few years of its release—an unprecedented success that compensated for Fox's more expensive mistakes. In some ways the film's popularity is hard to account for. In itself it was rather a humdrum affair moving against its almost sole setting of a drab-looking laboratory, and it told an unbelievably absurd story in a genre that thrives on tall stories. A scientist (Al Hedison) has perfected a reintegration process for transposing atoms from one location to another. Having sent off and returned to shape unharmed numerous guinea pigs, he decides to take the big step himself. Unexpectedly, once inside the experimental chamber, the scientist unknowingly locks a fly in with him. The monstrous result of this mischance is that some of the fly's atoms are incorporated with the atoms of the man's body and vice versa, producing a man with a fly's head and a fly's foreleg together with a fly bearing the head and arm of a man. (The reintegration machine apparently blows up the atoms to size or alternatively reduces them to fly-size.) The whole scenario is geared to a climax that shifts the film inexplicably to another level. In the final scene, the fly with the scientist's head is trapped in a spider's web and cries, with the faintest squeak, for help. A police inspector (Herbert Marshall) and another scientist (Vincent Price) who stands for the less enterprising, more ethical side of science, deliver the hapless scientist from his terror by crushing both the spider and the fly under a rock. (Once again, "white science" joins forces with authority to destroy the transgressor of natural and divine laws.) This is presumably the end of both monsters, as the wife of the scientist (Patricia Owens), obeying her husband's orders, has crushed his hideous head, along with his human/animal life in a laboratory vice—bringing reassurance to all. *The Fly* was directed by Kurt Neumann, who failed to exploit the resources of CinemaScope and color, with one sole exception: the wife's terror as seen through the myriad eyes of the fly and stretching in multiple exposure from one confine of the wide screen to the other. And Neumann's pace lags so often that even the most willing spectator, anxious to suspend his disbelief, has time to wonder how the scientist who has lost his head to a fly manages to retain his mental powers. The film collapses under the weight of many such questions. The two sequels, *The Return of the Fly* (1959) and *The Curse of the Fly* (1965) were less ambitious (both were made in black and white) and less successful. The Kafkian climax of the first is the only thing in the series that remains lodged in the mind.

Robert Wise, who cut his first set of directorial teeth with Val Lewton on *The Curse of the Cat People* and *The Body Snatcher* and twice again ventured onto the domain of the fantastic with *A Game of Death* and *The Day the Earth Stood Still,* returned to the genre in 1963 with *The Haunting,* an adaptation of Shirley Jackson's novel *The Haunting of Hill House.* This return was prompted primarily by a renewed popular interest in extrasensory perception (referred to in the press, in a familiar mood, as ESP) and the psychic phenomena. But the picture plays a double game with this interest and loses at both. First, there is the house itself, a Victorian abortion architected into forced perspective and devoid of right angles. Its builder, an eccentric New Englander, is fated never to live in it; his new bride is killed in an accident when her carriage strikes a massive tree on the grounds. Since that time, and for a hundred years, the house has been the cause of many mysterious deaths, accidental or suicidal. Cognizant of its black reputation, a modern-day anthropologist, Dr. John Markway (Richard Johnson) arrives at Hill House with two mediums, hypersensitive young women, unusually receptive to supernatural or paranormal experience. Eleanor (Julie Harris) is a neurotic virgin haunted by a feeling of other-worldliness. On the other hand, Theodora (Claire Bloom) is telepathic, can conduct a séance, and happens to be a Lesbian.

The team settles down in Hill House to do a bit of psychic research and, just after the drop of a hat, all sorts and types of phenomena begin to manifest themselves. The first is a mere brush of a caress on Eleanor's cheek. Next, her name is written in the dust. Before you know it, night falls and the entire house shakes and roars with fury as a waving mass of invisible energy tries to penetrate the girl's bedroom.

So far so good. But Wise remounts in midstream; like an opportunist on horseback he grabs the chance to explain the whole affair. He unrolls an up-to-date rationale in the most current psychic jargon: these seemingly supernatural manifestations are supernatural in a sense, but have nothing to do with ghosts. They are merely the projection of Eleanor's subconscious desires and jealousies, something like the destructive "force of the id" in *Forbidden Planet*. This "projection" threatens to destroy Dr. Markway's wife (Lois Maxwell), a woman possessing a pretty skepticism, who arrives at Hill House determined not to be impressed by all this twaddle. In the end, naturally, the only way out for poor Eleanor is to go and crash her car over the very bole of the tree that wrenched Hill House's ill-fated mistress out of existence. This climactic sleight of hand obviates all the opening passages of the picture—the house is not the agent, it is merely the setting for Eleanor's (or Theodora's) psychic powers and/or secret obsessions. The house is not the living, breathing thing played up throughout the film. Or is it? In an effort to bend the theme to a preconceived idea of evil, Wise resorts to technical facilities in his use of anamorphic lenses and infrared film stock instead of allowing the horror to develop from the everyday, the horror of existence which helped to make the mysterious beauty and attraction of the Lewton films.

The obsession with blood and viscera exhibited by the Hammer films and rival exponents of the scalpel-and-formaldehyde type of sensation reaches a logical conclusion in the surgical thriller *Les Yeux sans Visage* (1960) and in garden-variety bloodbaths such as *Blood Feast* (1963). Both of these regale their audiences with views hitherto confined to medical training films or atrocity documentaries, but that is their only common trait. *Blood Feast* is a reactionary attempt to bring to films the obsolete trickery of theatrical Grand Guignol: on stage, a woman sawed in half is a source of amazement and wonder; on film, with all the resources of the editing room, the whole hocus-pocus falls flat. As a result, films like *Blood Feast* will continue to outrage middle-class proprieties, while titillating the more sophisticated members of the audience. *Les Yeux sans Visage,* a French film directed by Georges Franju, is a superior (if controversial) effort. Franju is famed for taking a camera into the charnelhouses of Paris for his documentary *Le Sang des Bêtes* (*Blood of the Beasts,* 1948) and coming up with an unflinching poetic commentary on conveyer belt death, a dark mirror held up to our eyes, a salutary shock for those kind souls and sensitive spirits who never wonder where steaks and beef hearts come from. He set out in *Les Yeux sans Visage* with a problem of another kind—how to make a horror movie that grabbed medical ethics by the horns. His hero, Doctor Genessier (Pierre Brasseur), was responsible for the disfiguration of his daughter (Edith Scob). To make amends, the doctor experiments with skin grafts to her face which fail to take. With the assistance of his nurse/mistress (Alida Valli) he kidnaps potential (if reluctant) donors, removes a layer of their facial tissue, and grafts it onto his daughter. Finally, the daughter rebels, accepts her fate (or loses her mind), stabs the nurse to death, and delivers her doctor father to the fury of some ferocious dogs who served him as subjects in other cruel experiments. From synopsis, the theme could be categorized as Guignol. It is that. Except in the French magazines circulated primarily among *cinéastes, Les Yeux sans Visage* was adversely criticized in just about every country it played. In America, it was dubbed, mangled, and released as *The Horror Chamber of Dr. Faustus* and dismissed, by those hardy reviewers who caught it at theaters specializing in nudist/sadist fare, as a nauseating piece of sensationalism. The basis for this complaint is a scene which covers the minutiae of a skin-grafting operation in detail and does it with operating-room clarity and without the customary tactics of shock. These moments, as unnervingly real as they seem, nonetheless were expertly faked and throw off an aseptic power which overcomes the revulsion. They are also indispensable to the film and not the least of Franju's talents is to convince us of their necessity. Elsewhere the movie is charged with suggestive poetry (one readily understands Franju's admiration for Cocteau and his eventual filming of Cocteau's *Thomas l'Imposteur*). A sinister little beetle of a Citroën stalks a young girl student through the Latin Quarter and its driver, the ambiguous nurse in her leather raincoat, takes on the bodeful presence of one of Cocteau's own messengers of death. A masked, ethereal figure goes among the cages, liberating their occupants in a flurry of doves that invests the scene with a fairy-tale grace. Tingling with Maurice Jarre's nervous score and superbly photographed in glacial black and white by the veteran Schuftan, Franju's movie treads horror territory with elegant assurance. It might not be the intended denunciation but something much more unusual: the elusive alliance of poetry and terror.

In the Mediterranean countries of Spain and Italy, horror is tied up in the public mind with the Gothic—that Gothic recognized as the undisputed domain of Anglo-Saxon writers and filmmakers. The film production of these nations has rarely turned out any works of this type, at least until the present. An exception, an honorable one, was *I Vampiri* which the Italian Riccardo Freda directed in 1957. The film was cut and dubbed beyond sense or recognition for export showings (as *The Devil's Commandment*) and was neglected by press and public alike in its country of origin. Freda concluded from this that his film's failure was due less to its own merits or lack of them (it lacked relatively few) than to the fact that *I Vampiri* was not the product of an English or American studio. In 1959, having completed *Caltiki Il Mostro Immortale* (*Caltiki, the Immortal Monster*), Freda insisted on appending to the film a set of credits with made-up English-sounding names. Thus, Riccardo Freda became Robert Hampton, his cameraman Mario Bava (soon to embark on a career as a director) was grossly translated into John Foam, and so forth. *Caltiki* was received, and reviewed, in Italy as an American movie (as it was, for that matter, in the United States itself) and proved a reasonably successful article. In retrospect, this modest effort seems a hybrid of *The Quatermass Experiment* and *The Blob*. However, its fame outlives it, since in its wake a wave of pseudonyms has swept over the Roman studios and, recently, has reached a high degree of confusion. Anthony Dawson turns out to be not the well-known character actor of that name but the director Antonio Margheriti, Thomas Miller hides the identity of Camillo Mastrocinque, and Jess Frank is none other than the Spaniard Jesús Franco!

In Freda's case, at least, the films themselves belie this imposture. They are strictly Continental affairs, and most successful where their Anglo-Saxon counterparts fail: in the evocation of mood through color and decor, and in a visual sophistication that reveals the director's earlier occupation as an art critic. On the other hand, Freda's direction of actors is without method and haphazard, while his pacing, at least by American standards, lags once too often. In spite of Freda's avowed preference for the genre, his horror movies are marked by a denial of the fantastic—they are in substance melodramas of jealousy and machinations, usually directed against the sanity, or the life, of the heroine. Freda's center is invariably the woman, either as victim or victimizer, and logically his work is subtle, unathletic, and velvet soft. The stories of both *Raptus* (*The Horrible Dr. Hichcock,* 1962) and *Lo Spettro* (*The Ghost,* 1963) are slices of Krafft-Ebing garnished with succulent Technicolor, the work of Raffaele Masciocchi *alias* Donald Green. For once, the film was accurately described by its publicity blurb: "His secret was a coffin named Desire!" read the posters for *Raptus,* adding, even more explicitly —"The candle of his lust burnt brightest in the shadow of the grave!"

Often the difference between the delicious shiver and the gasp of shock hinges on maintaining a certain dramatic distance, a perspective of both time and space. Would *Psycho, Peeping Tom,* or *Repulsion* be as effective had they not been set in the most contemporary of milieux, the world of motels, film studios, and modern flats? Freda is a master at making palatable the most lurid subject matter, be it necrophilia, sexual impotence, or sadism, by laying the action of his pictures within the safety of the Victorian era, in the claustrophobic manor houses and moldy crypts that are deeded Gothic country, decorating the sets with so much taste and opulent texture that they smother the most unsavory aspects of the plot. What Freda obviously needs, and what we should look forward to, is a solid literary source for his talents: Wilkie Collins or maybe even Charlotte Brontë. (There are echoes of both *Jane Eyre* and *The Woman in White* in *Raptus* and *Lo Spettro.*) In the meantime, given a tight shooting schedule, he can still give Corman a run for his money: *Raptus* and *Lo Spettro* were shot in twelve days and rather than ephemeral, both pictures achieve a permanence of lovingly wrought miniatures, the handiwork of a careless, but undoubtedly talented, minor master.

Mario Bava, Freda's erstwhile cameraman in *I Vampiri* and *Caltiki,* made his bow as a director with *La Maschera del Demonio* (*Black Sunday,* 1960), a fine set of neo-Romantic improvisations suggested by Nikolai Gogol's ghostly folktale, *The Vij,* which introduced the extraordinary Barbara Steele, eventually to become Freda's favorite interpreter. *Black Sunday* revolves around the one day in every century when, according to tradition, Satan is allowed to walk freely on Earth. It is the day when witches return to life to haunt their descendants and mete out revenge on their executioners. From the prologue where a young and desirable sorceress (Barbara Steele) is gruesomely punished by the Inquisition of a Middle-European province to the climax, two centuries later, when the same witch is finally burnt at the stake, the movie unreels like a relentless nightmare, a world of goblins and apparitions such as that of a black, ornate coach floating in slow motion through a misty forest like a hearse traversing a spectral landscape.

As might have been expected, the quality of the visual narrative was superb—the best black-and-white photography to enhance a horror movie in the past two decades. Bava also showed himself a director of a certain promise which, alas!, has not been fulfilled in subsequent works.

Black Sunday was very popular in America, as well as in Italy, and Bava can safely sign the best of his work with his actual name. *I Tre Volti della Paura* (*Black Sabbath,* 1963) rejected chiaroscuro in favor of lush Technicolor and developed the directorial flourishes of *Black Sunday* into mannered tricks such as gratuitous abrupt cuts and an unrestrained use of the zoom lens, an optical device that instantly bridges the distance between camera and subject. Recently, Bava has turned out a series of sadistic films, among them *Sei Donne per l'Assassino* (*Blood and Black Lace,* 1964) and *La Frusta e il Corpo* (also made in 1964 and released in England as *Night Is the Phantom* but as yet unknown in America), both deriving from the Hammer product. The former, especially, has minimal plot and consists of a string of brutal murders, each staged with relish and in the most redolent hues, attesting to the fact that Bava is simply trying to titillate a very specialized segment of his audience that requires neither rhyme nor reason. His *Terrore nello Spazio* (*Planet of the Vampires,* 1965) attempts to match science fiction and the vampire theme once more, and it brought good color to some elegant design, but there was a distinct feeling of a director uninvolved with his material. Bava probably assessed himself best when he claimed to be a mere photographer of fantastic scenes rather than a complete director. Of late, fantasy is woefully missing from the Bava films; his charnelhouse preciosity proves that if bad directors usually end up as photographers, the reverse of this axiom is just as valid and true.

Diametrically opposed to the luxurious decadence of the Italian horror films are the Mexican movies of Fernando Méndez, Alfonso Corona Blake, Chano Urueta, and José Cibrián (to mention but a few), destined for popular consumption all over Latin America and only occasionally seen in the United States in Spanish-speaking houses and (dubbed) on television. It is not surprising that these films were first noticed in European circles: they appeal to the polarities of the movie public, either to very plebeian audiences which relish their frenzied pace and top-heavy ramifications or to connoisseurs who delight in their disarming naïveté and their fairly frequent, and largely unconscious, felicities. In such quality they carry a great deal of conviction and are happily devoid of the self-contemptuous tone that often screeches in the work of more proficient competitors. In style, the horror movies of Mexico have assimilated the Hollywood tradition of the thirties and the forties, of which they appear a logical extension, and a touch of Freund and Stumar can be seen in many traces in the camerawork of Víctor Herrera and Raúl Lavista. Passengers of this style are a mixed company of vampires from Transylvania, Aztec mummies, werewolves of dubious origin, and even a bona fide Mexican spook like the Crying Woman, who first began her haunt of the Mexican cinema in the early thirties. Their most extraordinary feature, one peculiar to their country of origin, is the demented matching of all these venerable fiends with real-life champion wrestlers like Santo and Blue Demon, the Masked Marvels who have replaced bullfighters in Mexico as the popular figures of the day. This blending of the athletic and the macabre was most successful in Méndez's *Ladrón de Cadáveres* (*The Corpse Snatchers,* 1958) or Corona Blake's *Santo contra las Mujeres Vampiro* (*Santo versus the Vampire Women,* 1962). Méndez, the recognized master of this trend, has also directed more traditional stories such as *El Vampiro* (*The Vampire,* 1959) and *El Ataúd del Vampiro* (*The Vampire's Coffin,* 1961), unsophisticated but far from crude. Grafting to the arid locale the unlikely meteorological readings of a dewy English fen and to the landscape eternally gloomy mansions and haciendas, these films draw every ounce of effect from sets shrouded in artificial fog (which beside rendering them photogenic also conveniently hides their limitations) and borrow from Browning to Castle. Méndez especially (unlike Terence Fisher, *et al.*) is not afraid to have his Undead give the Vampire his due—the last shot of *The Vampire's Coffin* has Count Duval (played by Germán Robles) pinned to the wall by the proverbial stake, whereupon he turns into a pitiful bat flapping its wings. No matter how one qualifies their individual merits, these films form a Mexican horror tradition which throbs with vigor and self-conviction. The Italian Freda and his confrères may have exquisitely embalmed the horror movie in Europe, but there is one last outpost in Mexico of the old-fashioned, pre-psychological monster-rallying horror show in which science has not come to science fiction but is more the practice of black magicians and spirits of the night.

CHAPTER 9

NO END TITLE

Science fiction film-makers have, all too rashly, made and unmade worlds, so that at the end of the first big surge of science fiction films, a period from approximately 1950 through 1957, they must have realized that somehow they had burned their spaceships behind them. This span was the era of special effects. As was mentioned before, the films themselves do not abound in great stars and where the screenwriting was distinguished it has been duly noted. Plainly, the directors of these films played second fiddle to the technicians. Worlds smashed out of sight and collided, the Earth vanished in a welter of dazzling effects—never with a whimper and often with a loud climactic bang. Just as the cinema many years before had splurged its riches as the heir of theatrical tradition, it fell upon the freshly developed medium of television to take the hard-earned discoveries of the best science fiction movies and work them to death. On television the limitations and cinematic conventions of science fiction hardened into clichés: electronic twangs and booms, musique concrète, picturesque planetary locales, bizarre interior design, and a plethora of blinking, data-processing gadgetry. Nothing dissipates anxiety as well as a cliché can, and anxiety (on varying intellectual levels) is the root theme, and strength, of science fiction.

Predictably, the best of these TV programs survived on horror—a feeling not too different from anxiety. Some others depended on comedy, ordinarily by featuring some impeccably mannered robot or the proficient visitor from outer space with the homespun horse sense of a practical terrestrian. Romance usually came off badly, if at all, but this does seem endemic to the genre. The would-be lunar colonizers of H. G. Wells' *The First Men in the Moon* (published in 1901) are careful to include a mating couple of every domestic animal, yet neglect to bring along a woman. And science fiction ever since has fought a losing battle to find the woman's place in the Intergalactic Era.

It was inevitable that science fiction should finally become introspective. This happened rather early on the printed page, an equivalent maturity takes longer in coming to a graphic medium like the film. There will always be room in science fiction movies for the far-out imaginative, and enough of the child survives in most spectators to thrill to the engineered illusions of special effects. Yet, though a film like *Fantastic Voyage* (1966) may momentarily catch our fancy, it is soon obvious the more it changes, the more it remains the same. *Fantastic Voyage* has an enthralling central idea: in some future, but near, time, man has learned how to reduce himself and other objects to microbe size. (The utility of this discovery seems absurdly negligible in comparison with the complex, expensive, and impressive technology deployed.) The picture is a logbook of a voyage through the inside of man's body, from jugular vein to tear duct, a travelogue on an unexplored region that at one moment looks like a coral formation and at another like a majestically high-ceilinged cave. This innately fantastic concept collapses under the weight of the treatment's overliteralness and the film ends up seeming just another variation of *Twenty Thousand Leagues Under the Sea* and might have been written when that adventure was penned by Jules Verne back in 1869. Reinforcing this impression is the fact that *Fantastic Voyage* was directed by Richard Fleischer, whose direction was responsible for the film adaptation made of the Verne novel in 1954.

There now seems to be no place to go except inward, though not necessarily into the aorta. The present must constantly intrude into the future and Maeterlinck was not the first or last to realize that visions of the future are delimited by men, and by our concerns in the present. This realization has taken science fiction into the domain of more philosophical speculation and signals the arrival of the Director's Era—the period of *The Damned, The Birds, La Jetée, Alphaville,* and *Fahrenheit 451.*

One quality appears common to the above-mentioned films, and that is the scaling down of their themes to the limits of the immediately experienceable. Apocalypse, as it were, is now rendered in a minor key. The end of the world is decreed by the birds declaring war on the human race. The planet of tomorrow is no longer Altair-4 but Alphaville, and Alphaville is just another name for Paris, or New York—any capital city of our highly technological society. The future is just a breath away in *The Tenth Victim* or *Fahrenheit 451,* so close, in fact, that we find that we are wearing the same familiar fashions, that we are living in the same familiar apartment houses. All of these movies eschew the grandiose, the panoramic, the big statement. Of them all, only *The Birds* resorts to the more traditional trickery and, as it turns out, that is the film's weakest point.

In *The Damned* (1961) we have already caught up with tomorrow, the first mutants are among us, and what is more, they are man's own creation, a new generation conditioned to survive the catastrophe that, it is expected with premeditation in high places, will engulf their parents. Deep in a cave off the British coast there exists a government installation where a group of nine or ten children have been exposed from birth to gradually increasing doses of radioactivity. These well-bred creatures, superbly educated by a team of the most advanced pedagogues, are ice-cold to the touch and have never seen a human being other than themselves and those on the closed-circuit TV screen which, like omnipresent eyes, watch and gauge their every moment and activity. Into this top-secret establishment stumble a man and a woman (Macdonald Carey and Shirley Ann Field), fleeing from a more immediate danger. (The girl is the decoy of a band of thugs captained by her brother.) Not realizing that the slightest contact with the appealing youngsters means radioactive contamination, the pair try to help the children escape. The attempt fails, but not before the youngsters have glimpsed the outside world. Another outsider, a sculptress (Viveca Lindfors) who intuitively comes to suspect the truth about the installation, is ruthlessly executed by the civil servant in charge (Alexander Knox). The couple manage to escape out to sea, only to die there unaided as an ominous helicopter hovers over their boat like a vulture waiting for their last moments. All that is left of the blunder are the pathetic reiterating cries for help of the children, the self-containment of whose world is now shattered by the awareness of their condition.

Directed by Joseph Losey, an American who quit Hollywood during the McCarthy era and has since worked in England, *The Damned* was made for Hammer Studios, on whose shelves it rested undisturbed for a couple of years. Upon release, the picture had lost more than a reel and it took it another two years to open in the United States under the title *These Are the Damned.* An understanding of Hammer's puzzlement can readily be reached through a listing of all the things *The Damned* is not: a pure horror movie, a thesis-thriller about violence, an extravagant view of things to come. Instead of the hysterical type of political drama it might have been, the picture is one of the most lucid in Losey's career, and certainly one of his most accomplished. The director, once a disciple of Bertolt Brecht, achieves here a fine balance between the elucidations of the obvious and the enlightenments of the subtle. His technique is to bring a refinement to both by fluidly traversing various and parallel levels—the topography of the setting, the socially decaying resort town, the severe counter-society of the leather gang, the power-blunted rigidity and precision of the secret installation. Or, on the moral level—violence on the scale of the individual, irrational and done with a pained contempt; and violence, equally ruthless, done by the ruling bureaucracy fortified and supported by a dialectic. The film becomes ambiguous only at the center, or Losey wouldn't be its director. Bernard, the director of the secret project, is the totally committed man who will stop at nothing to safeguard the success of his cause. He is the killer without qualms, without enmity to serve, the superior intellect, as lacking in warmth as the children he breeds. Although he is never identified as a scientist, we somehow assume that he is one—so many facets, so many interpretations, and Knox's impersonal playing suits every one. Losey has wisely matched him with the picture's strongest character but one who, in a curious manner, remains, until the climax, untouched by the drama.

Viveca Lindfors' sculptress throughout answers for life against Bernard's nonchalant predictions of its logical end. The sculptress cannot, and will not, envision life beyond the immediate. Bernard's scheme for human survival strikes her as overprepared to the extent of guaranteeing the disaster it anticipates. Her affirmation of life does not restrict her vision of the age, for she sculpts birds of prey and twisted human structures. In this, she, too, has her paradox. However, she is sympathetic because she uses it to torture no one except herself. Hers is the most ringing speech in the picture when she berates Bernard, once her lover, ". . . you want to set your ice-cold children free in the ashes of the universe." There is a distinct resonance here of the final conflict in *Shape of Things to Come,* when Wells pits his eternal scientist /searcher against the cabal of the artists, headed by a sculptor. Wells' hero was the former. Losey, caught like his characters in "the age of senseless violence," has concern only for the losers.

The Damned, set in the present, looks grimly ahead into the future. *La Jetée* (1963) and *Fahrenheit 451* (1966) are set in the future looking back on the present and understandably the mood is of a different order. Both are primarily moved by nostalgia, full of a rueful longing for the beauties of the moment that was, our today. The hero of *La Jetée*—the film has retained its French title when shown abroad—is a man scarred by the memory of a certain Sunday afternoon when, as a child, he caught an unforgettable glimpse of a woman's face looking out from the jetty's end at Orly Airport near Paris. And almost simultaneously, he witnessed, without comprehending, the violent death of a man on the same spot. As an adult, he carries this haunting memory through life and cataclysm. He lives through World War III, which leaves every one of the world's great capitals a shambles. The victors (a handful of people) have taken refuge underground, although they realize that, even here, life on the planet is doomed. The scientists among them reach the conclusion that survival depends on flight, not into space, but into time. Memory, which keeps life in continuity, is the one remaining link with the past. Once they are able to find a subject with unusually strong mental images, they will propel him, according to plan, first into the past, then into the future. They discover the hero among the war prisoners and after he has been submitted to grueling experiments, he succeeds in reaching the past, his anchor in time being the girl he once glimpsed on the jetty. As a grown man, he takes up his life at that point, meeting the girl and falling in love with her. The experiment has succeeded; he is soon thereafter able to find his way into the future. Brought back to the underground laboratory, he is offered by his captors the chance to survive by advancing in time; he chooses instead to retreat into the doomed past. Once more, he finds himself on the jetty, at the starting point of his trajectory in time. Again, he glimpses the girl but also, this time, one of his warders—sent along to execute him. He runs toward the girl, looking for the child he was at the time, only to be shot down at her feet. The circle of time is joined where it links.

The French, with their penchant for bolstering film criticism with literary analogies, have correctly connected *La Jetée* with Bergson. Rarely has a film been so pursued by a theory of remembrance or so deeply inscribed on a philosophy of time. To convey this concept fully, an appropriate technique was employed—far from new yet never so well utilized: still photographs freezing movement the way that memory freezes images. The movie becomes an album of pictures that span present, past, future—even the future's future. Only once, and then briefly, an image unfreezes—a sensuous shot of the girl awakening in the early morning after a night of love. The effect of this is disarmingly moving, as if the picture's arrested stillness came to life in a burst of warmth. Chris Marker, the director, has attained in less than half an hour the film's unique quality of blending science fiction with a lament for love forever lost.

Fahrenheit 451, from the novel by Ray Bradbury, is a tale set in a society that has outlawed books, making a crime of their possession, and whose education and intellectual control is of the most totalitarian kind, education being restricted to television programs and captionless comic strips. Fire brigades are in charge of confiscating all printed matter and burning it on the spot. (Paper burns at 451 degrees Fahrenheit.) A fireman named Montag (Oskar Werner), on his way up in the ranks, has unquestioningly accepted this order of things, and his duties to maintain it, until the day he meets and is unsettled by a young schoolteacher (Julie Christie) who seems to him dangerously nonconformist.

During one of the book-burning raids, Montag for the first time spares a volume, Dickens' *David Copperfield,* and at home that night, he starts reading: "Chapter One: I Am Born." Montag is soon hooked on the reading habit, becomes a thinking fireman, and loses his unflinching devotion to the corps. Before long, he finds himself incapable of climbing up the fire pole and this arouses the suspicions of his colleagues. Next, he helps the subversive girl to escape. Betrayed by his own wife (also played by Julie Christie), he is finally forced to roast his captain (Cyril Cusack) during a raid on the Montag home. Montag escapes and joins a band of partisans known as "the book men" who hide in the woods and each of whom has committed one literary work to memory, perpetuating it for posterity. The film ends as Montag begins to memorize the *Tales of Edgar Allan Poe.*

Adapting the novel with loving care, François Truffaut directed this unrealistic plot in purely realistic style: his sole concessions to the picturesque are a few perfunctory scenes filmed on a futuristic monorail train and a squad of airborne, self-propelled pursuers. His neutrality also fits a tale so rich in parallels: *Fahrenheit's* obvious references (the book-burnings, the plucky little old lady who would sooner set herself on fire with her books than give them up) are played down and do not press themselves on the plot. Abetted by Nicholas Roeg's color photography, the picture has the unheroic look of the everyday, and Montag is a long jump to being an ideal hero for a film intentionally low-keyed and terminating with a sad impasse barely hopeful and none too reassuring.

Today's violence determines the shape of tomorrow's. No great imagination is required to extend our actuality to its logical conclusion in the near future. An Italian film, *La Decima Vittima* (*The Tenth Victim,* 1965) works hard on this principle. In a not-so-distant day (in the twenty-first century), licence to kill will be extended to private citizens—and murderous aggression from the individual will guarantee peace on a larger scale. Unfortunately, after the third reel, it becomes all too clear that the picture is less concerned with the sport of the future than with the battle of the sexes, and all the pretty trimmings of its pop art decor cannot conceal the shallowness of its intentions.

Interpretations cluster around Alfred Hitchcock's *The Birds*

(1963) to such an extent that establishing the director's basic intention has become indispensable to an appreciation of it. The film, as Hitchcock himself stated, bridges a passage from the "fantastic subjective" of his earlier work to the "fantastic objective" offered by science fiction. In *The Birds,* all meaning (inherent or implied) lies in the rapport between reality and fantasy. Since fantasy is a bubble without a real map and a real compass, the more a work's realistic structure is strengthened the more shattering will be the impact of fantasy upon the real. Those who do not grasp this scheme will find the first part of the picture protracted and irrelevant. Hitchcock overwhelms the spectator here with his concern with establishing a milieu, setting up characters, and developing their relationships, before unleashing a cataclysm. A beautiful girl (Tippi Hedren), rich and headstrong, pursues the man she wants, a successful attorney (Rod Taylor), to his home in Bodega Bay on the northern California coast. There she meets his hysterically possessive mother (Jessica Tandy), the schoolteacher (Suzanne Pleshette) who also is in love with him, and other residents of the town. The color is sumptuous, almost through calculation: Tippi's green suit; the landscape of hill, shore, and sky; the upper middle-class California chic of the young man's home. Characteristically, in this long beginning, Hitchcock works threads of the real theme into the story in his best elliptical manner. The over-elegant bird shop and the flock of pigeons flying over San Francisco's Union Square introduce the anxious presence of a bird motif almost immediately. Most of the ensuing moody, low-keyed scenes in the first half end on a jarring note: for no apparent reason, a seagull dives on the heroine, striking a gash on her forehead; the barnyard fowl refuse to eat; a late-evening conversation between Tippi and Suzanne is disrupted by the thud of a suicidal seagull hurtling against the front door.

From this point, in one superb transition, fantasy takes over. The possessive mother drops in at the unnaturally quiet cabin of a neighboring farmer. Her eyes are drawn to the smashed cups in his cupboard—in a previous scene she had nervously dropped and broken one of her best cups—and a few steps farther the farmer's dead body lies, his eyes bloody sockets plucked out by birds. From here on, all the dirty work is done by birds, and the action is all the more terrifying because inexplicable. This is Hitchcock's trump hand: why this sudden reversal of conduct from the birds? Where there is no explanation to offer or solicit, an understanding or communication is no longer possible. As the heroine finds temporary shelter in a town diner, the spectator is treated to a feast of explanations (including witchcraft) and each hypothesis is shattered, point by point, within minutes. When gulls attack the entire area around the diner, we share the feeling of outrage and horror expressed a few minutes before by the bird-watching crone (Ethel Griffies) expounding in her capacity as an ornithologist about man's feathered friends. There are no monsters, no villains, only these "feathered friends" devoid of all the things they might symbolize (the phallus, among others) and soon reduced to an abstraction.

Hitchcock gives these animal antagonists a look of unreality by having many of their scenes processed in (as many as five different exposures for the most elaborate shots), or simply drawn on the film individually while the sound track reverberates with an electronic cawing, chirping, chirring, croaking, and squawking. Or they are kept out of frame as the boarded-up house shakes under the onslaught of a massive winged attack. The final unsettling effect of *The Birds* comes in its inconclusive ending: the birds are not routed, and the principals, stripped of gloss and pretense, are spared. There is a momentary, again inexplicable, truce: the survivors climb into their car and leave Bodega Bay, abandoning the house to the birds. There is no end title.

The plot of *Alphaville* (1965) is replete with references to comic strips, to serials, to cartoons, and to film classics of the past. Out of these vivid contemporary allusions comes a story-line that is clear as glass and simply unsubtle, as if the director (Jean-Luc Godard) were turning the tables on the viewer, offering us beforehand significances and interpretations which we frequently enjoy discovering and belaboring in such films and giving us, in the second place, a movie that constantly stands in the way of our reception of what is offered.

Lemmy Caution—a character originally created in French detective stories and played here by its official movie interpreter, saturnine, pockmarked Eddie Constantine—arrives in Alphaville, city of logic and reason. His mission is to locate Professor von Braun, exiled from our civilization thirty years ago, and induce him to return. Failing to be persuaded, von Braun is to be liquidated. In his search, Caution learns that Alphaville is ruled by a cybernetic monstrosity—Alpha-60, a giant electronic computer that processes, classifies, and programs the life data of its residents. This control has brought about a cult of absolute logical behavior and those who do not conform to it (i.e., those who show some emotion) are ruthlessly destroyed by execution during staged aquacades, or by submitting to the persuasion to commit suicide. To abet this law and order of the Machine, words are kept in place by changing meaning, some being suppressed altogether while new editions of the bible/dictionary are issued daily. Caution eventually finds von Braun and liquidates him when he refuses to return to the Outerlands. By feeding Alpha-60, unclassifiable information (poetry), he causes its autodestruction, and manages to escape from the technocratic metropolis. He takes von Braun's daughter (Anna Karina) along with him after forcing her to remember the meaning of such words as love, tenderness, robin redbreast, autumn light.

Alphaville is the future, but it has a contemporary humor to it, corny and direct. Alphaville is supposed to be a planet, but one you can reach from Earth by car—that is, if you are driving a Ford Galaxie. Nowhere does Lemmy Caution let the highly developed facilities of "this crummy town" impress him. Violence has the casual BANG-POW-ZAP look of the comic book. Caution himself is closer to Dick Tracy than to his origin on the printed page.

As in all Godard pictures, there is in *Alphaville* a fair number of literary and philosophical quotations, though here they are restricted to the sound track, to the loquacious narration by Lemmy, to the *rat-a-tat-tat* dialogue, and to the hoarse expository prose of Alpha-60. (It has an "American" score by Paul Misraki.) Visually, the film belongs purely to the director; every frame is signed by him. Lemmy Caution becomes a Godard hero by sporting a volume of Eluard poems, yet *Alphaville* could not be further away from poetry as a literary craft. Its hall of fame is not peopled by poets, but by Flash Gordon, Heckle and Jeckle, Nosferatu—the deities of new obsessions. Alienating his audience,

Godard inserts negative shots, dazzles the optic organ with sudden bright lights, slurs the messages of his own sound track. One is tempted to ask why? Surely Godard would answer, why not? The spectator accepts private symbols, personal irrelevancies, the psychologically unexplainable from the other visual arts. He can accept them here.

Alphaville is the contrary of *The Birds;* it makes no separation between fantasy and reality. Alphaville the capital is Paris on a wintry night, with her sharp edges, joyless neon lights caught in harsh contrasted glitter by Raoul Coutard's lens. (There is no reconstruction and no distortion of the city, and no need for it, either.) Maybe, in this case, the term science fiction is no longer applicable: *Alphaville* is S-P, science poetry.

APPENDIX

Cast and Credits of Relevant Films Mentioned in the Text

ABBREVIATIONS:

ASST: Assistant
CONSULT: Consultant
COST: Costume Design
DIAL: Dialogue
DIR: Director
LYR: Lyrics
MUS: Music
NARR: Narration
PH: Photographer
PROD: Producer
SCR: Screenplay
SETS: Set Design
SP. EF.: Special Effects
SUP: Supervision

À LA CONQUÊTE DU PÔLE (1912)
Star Films (France)
DIR: Georges Méliès.

ABBOTT AND COSTELLO MEET DR. JEKYLL AND MR. HYDE (1953)
Universal (USA)
DIR: Charles Lamont. SCR: Leo Loeb, John Grant. PH: George Robinson.
WITH Bud Abbott, Lou Costello, Boris Karloff, Helen Westcott, Craig Stevens, John Dierkes, Reginald Denny.

ABBOTT AND COSTELLO MEET FRANKENSTEIN (1948)
Universal (USA)
DIR: Charles Barton. SCR: Robert Lees, Frederic Rinaldo, John Grant. PH: Charles Van Enger.
WITH Bud Abbott, Lou Costello, Lenore Aubert, Lon Chaney, Jr., Bela Lugosi, Glenn Strange, Jane Randolph, Frank Ferguson.

AELITA (1924)
Mezhrabpom (USSR)
DIR: Jacob Protazanov. SCR: Fyodor Otzep, Alexei Falko; from the novel by Alexei Tolstoy. PH: Yuri Zhelyabuzhky, E. Schonemann. SETS: Victor Simov, Isaac Rabinovitch, Alexandra Exter, Sergei Kozlovsky.
WITH Igor Ilinsky, Yulia Solntseva, Nikolai Tseretelly, Nikolai Batalov, V. Orlova, Valentina Kuinzhi.

ALL THAT MONEY CAN BUY (1941)
RKO Radio (USA)
DIR: William Dieterle. SCR: Stephen Vincent Benét, Dan Totheroh; from "The Devil and Daniel Webster" by S. V. Benét. PH: Joseph August. SP. EF.: Van Nest Polglase.
WITH Edward Arnold, Walter Huston, Simone Simon, Anne Shirley, James Craig, Jane Darwell, Gene Lockhart, John Qualen, H. B. Warner, George Cleveland.

ALPHAVILLE (1965)
Chaumiane (France)
DIR–SCR: Jean-Luc Godard. PH: Raoul Coutard. MUS: Paul Mizraki.
WITH Eddie Constantine, Anna Karina, Akim Tamiroff, Howard Vernon, Laszlo Szabo, Michel Delahaye, J.-A. Fieschi, J.-L. Comolli.

ANIMAL WORLD (1956)
Warner Brothers (USA)
PROD–DIR–SCR: Irwin Allen. PH: Harold Wellman. SP. EF.: Willis J. O'Brien, Ray Harryhausen, Arthur S. Rhoades. MUS: Paul Sawtell.

ATAÚD DEL VAMPIRO, EL (1961)
Abel Salazar/Cinematográfica A.B.S.A. (Mexico)
DIR: Fernando Méndez. SCR: Ramon Obón. PH: Rosalio Solano, Kurt Dayton.

WITH Germán Robles, Ariadna Welter, Abel Salazar, Yeire Beirute, Alicia Montoya, Carlos Ancira.

ATTACK OF THE FIFTY FOOT WOMAN (1958)
Allied Artists (USA)
DIR: Nathan Hertz. SCR: Mark Hanna. PH: Jacques R. Marquette. MUS: Ronald Stein.
WITH Allison Hayes, William Hudson, Yvette Vickers, Roy Gordon, George Douglas, Ken Terrell, Otto Waldis, Eileene Stevens, Mike Ross, Frank Chase.

AVENGING CONSCIENCE, The (1914)
Mutual (USA)
DIR: D. W. Griffith; based on writings of Edgar Allan Poe. PH: G. W. Bitzer.
WITH Henry B. Walthall, Blanche Sweet, Spottiswoode Aitken, Ralph Lewis, Mae Marsh, George Seigmann.

BARON MUNCHAUSEN (1911)
Star Films (France)
DIR: Georges Méliès.

BAT, The (1926)
United Artists (USA)
DIR: Roland West. SCR: Roland West; from the play by Mary Roberts Rinehart and Avery Hopwood. PH: Arthur Edeson.
WITH Emily Fitzroy, Louise Fazenda, Eddie Gribbon, Robert McKim, Arthur Houseman, Sojin, Tullio Carminatti, Jack Pickford, Lee Shumway, Jewel Carmen.

BAT WHISPERS, The (1931)
United Artists (USA)
DIR: Roland West. SCR: Roland West; from the play by Mary Roberts Rinehart and Avery Hopwood. PH: Ray June.
WITH Chester Morris, Una Merkel, Grayce Hampton, Maude Eburne, William Bakewell, Gustav von Seyffertitz, Spencer Charters, Ben Bard, Hugh Huntley.

BEAST FROM 20,000 FATHOMS (1953)
Warner Brothers (USA)
DIR: Eugene Lourie. SCR: Lou Morheim, Fred Freiberger from "The Foghorn" by Ray Bradbury. PH: Jack Russell. SP. EF.: Ray Harryhausen.

WITH Paul Christian, Paula Raymond, Cecil Kellaway, Kenneth Tobey, Donald Woods, Jack Pennick, Lee Van Cleef, Ross Elliott, King Donovan, Frank Ferguson, Mary Hill, Michael Fox.

BEAST OF HOLLOW MOUNTAIN (1956)
United Artists (USA) /Películas Rodríguez (Mexico)
DIR: Edward Nassour, Ismael Rodríguez. SCR: Robert Hill; from a story by Willis H. O'Brien. PH: Jorge Stahl, Jr. (DeLuxe Color, CinemaScope).
WITH Guy Madison, Patricia Medina, Eduardo Noriega, Carlos Rivas, Mario Navarro, Julio Villareal, Pascual Garcia Peña, Lupe Carriles.

BEAST WITH FIVE FINGERS, The (1947)
Warner Brothers (USA)
DIR: Robert Florey. SCR: Curt Siodmak. PH: Wesley Anderson. MUS: Max Steiner.
WITH Robert Alda, Andrea King, Peter Lorre, Victor Francen, J. Carroll Naish, Charles Dingle, John Alvin, David Hoffman, Barbara Brown, Patricia White (later Patricia Barry), William Edmunds, Belle Mitchell, Ray Walker, Pedro de Cordoba.

BEAUTY AND THE BEAST——see BELLE ET LA BÊTE, La

BEDLAM (1946)
RKO Radio (USA)
PROD: Val Lewton. DIR: Mark Robson. SCR: Mark Robson, Carlos Keith. PH: Nicholas Musuraca. MUS: Roy Webb.
WITH Boris Karloff, Anna Lee, Billy House, Richard Fraser, Glenn Vernon, Joan Newton, Ian Wolfe, Elizabeth Russell, Robert Clarke, Jason Robards, Leyland Hodgson.

BEFORE I HANG (1940)
Columbia (USA)
DIR: Nick Grinde. SCR: Robert D. Andrews. PH: Benjamin Kline.
WITH Boris Karloff, Evelyn Keyes, Bruce Bennett, Pedro de Cordoba, Edward Van Sloan, Don Beddoe, Robert Fiske, Kenneth MacDonald, Frank Richards, Ben Taggart, Wright Kramer, Bertram Marbrugh.

BELLE ET LA BÊTE, La (1946)
Andre Paulve Production (France)
DIR:–SCR: Jean Cocteau. PH: Henri Alekan. SETS: Christian Bérard. COST: Escoffier. MUS: Georges Auric.
WITH Jean Marais, Josette Day, Marcel André, Mila Parély, Nane Germon, Michel Auclair.

BELLS, The (1926)
Chadwick (USA)
DIR: James Young. SCR: James Young; from the play by Erckmann-Chatrian. PH: L. William O'Connell.
WITH Lionel Barrymore, Eddie Phillips, Lola Todd, Gustav von Seyffertitz, Otto Lederer, Lorimer Johnston, Boris Karloff, Fred Warren.

BETWEEN WORLDS——see MÜDE TOD, Der

BIRDS, The (1963)
Universal (USA)
DIR: Alfred Hitchcock. SCR: Evan Hunter; from the story by Daphne Du Maurier. PH: Robert Burks (Technicolor). SP. EF.: Lawrence A. Hampton. SOUND CONSULT: Bernard Herrmann.
WITH Rod Taylor, Tippi Hedren, Jessica Tandy, Suzanne Pleshette, Veronica Cartwright, Ethel Griffies, Charles McGraw, Doreen Lang, Ruth McDevitt, Joe Mantell, Malcolm Atterbury, Elizabeth Wilson, Karl Swenson, Lonny Chapman, Doodles Weaver, John McGovern.

BLACK CAT, The (1934)
Universal (USA)
DIR: Edgar G. Ulmer. SCR: Peter Ruric; from the story by Edgar Allan Poe. PH: John Mescall.
WITH Boris Karloff, Bela Lugosi, David Manners, Jacqueline Wells (later Julie Bishop), Lucille Lund, Egon Brecher, Ann Duncan, Henry Armetta, Albert Conti, Harry Cording, Andre Cheron, George Davis, Alphonse Martell, Tony Marlow, Paul Weigel.

BLACK CAT, The (1941)
Universal (USA)
DIR: Albert S. Rogell. SCR: Robert Lees, Fred Rinaldo, Eric Taylor, Robert Neville. PH: Stanley Cortez.
WITH Basil Rathbone, Hugh Herbert, Broderick Crawford, Bela Lugosi, Gale Sondergaard, Anne Gwynne, Gladys Cooper, Cecilia Loftus, Claire Dodd, John Eldredge, Alan Ladd.

BLACK ORCHIDS (1916)
Bluebird (USA)
DIR: Rex Ingram. SCR: R. Ingram. PH: Duke Hayward.
WITH Cleo Madison, Wedgewood Nowell, Howard Crampton, Francis McDonald.

BLACK ROOM, The (1935)
Columbia (USA)
DIR: Roy William Neill. SCR: Henry Myers; based on the writings of Arthur Strawn. PH: Al Siegler.
WITH Boris Karloff, Marian Marsh, Katherine De Mille, Robert Allen, John Buckler, Thurston Hall, Frederick Vogeding, Torben Meyer, Egon Brecher, Edward Van Sloan, Lois Lindsey, Colin Tapley, Henry Kolker, John Bleifer, Herbert Evans.

BLACK SABBATH——see TRE VOLTI DELLA PAURA, I

BLACK SCORPION, The (1957)
Warner Brothers (USA)
DIR: Edward Ludwig. SCR: David Duncan, Robert Blees. PH: Lionel Lindon. SP. EF.: Willis O'Brien. MUS: Paul Sawtell.
WITH Richard Denning, Mara Corday, Carlos Rivas, Mario Navarro, Carlos Muzquiz, Pascual Pena, Fanny Schiller, Pedro Galvan, Arturo Martinez.

BLACK SUNDAY——see MASCHERA DEL DEMONIO, La

BLACK ZOO (1963)
Allied Artists (USA)
DIR: Richard Gordon. PROD–SCR: Herman Cohen. PH: Floyd Crosby (Panavision Eastmancolor) . MUS: Paul Dunlap.
WITH Michael Gough, Jeanne Cooper, Virginia Grey, Rod Lauren, Jerome Cowan, Elisha Cook, Marianna Hill, Warene Ott, Eilene Janssen, Edward Platt, Oren Curtis, Eric Stone, Dani Lynn, Susan Slavin.

BLADE AM SATANS BOG (1921)
Nordisk Films Kompagni (Denmark)
DIR: Carl Dreyer. SCR: Edgar Hoyer; from the novel by Marie Corelli. PH: George Schneevoight. SETS: Carl Dreyer, Axel Bruun, Jens G. Lind.
WITH Helge Nissen, Halvard Hoff, Jacob Texiere, Erling Hansson, Ebon Strandin, Tenna Kraft, Clara Pontoppidan, Karina Bell, Elith Pio.

BLIND BARGAIN, A (1922)
Goldwyn (USA)
DIR: Wallace Worsley. SCR: J. G. Hawks; from "The Octave of Claudius" by Barry Pain. PH: Norbert Brodin.

WITH Raymond McKee, Lon Chaney, Virginia True Boardman, Jacqueline Logan, Fontaine La Rue.

BLOB, The (1958)
Paramount (USA)
DIR: Irvin S. Yeaworth, Jr. SCR: Theodore Simonson, Kate Phillips. PH: Thomas Spalding (DeLuxe Color)
WITH Steve McQueen, Aneta Corseaut, Earl Rowe, Olin Howland, Stephen Chase, John Benson, George Karis, Elbert Smith, Robert Fields, James Bonnet, Anthony Franke.

BLOOD AND BLACK LACE——see SEI DONNE PER L'ASSASSINO

BLOOD AND ROSES——see ET MOURIR DE PLAISIR

BLOOD FEAST (1963)
Boxoffice Spectaculars (USA)
DIR: Herschell G. Lewis. PROD: David F. Friedman. SCR: A. Louis Downe. PH: Herschell G. Lewis (in Bloodcolor).
WITH Thomas Wood, Mal Arnold, Connie Mason, Scott H. Hall, Lyn Bolton.

BLOOD OF DRACULA (1957)
American International (USA)
DIR: Herbert L. Strock. PROD: Herman Cohen. SCR: Ralph Thornton. PH: Monroe Askins. MUS: Paul Dunlap.
WITH Sandra Harrison, Louise Lewis, Gail Ganley, Jerry Blaine, Heather Ames, Malcolm Atterbury, Mary Adams, Don Devlin, Jeanne Dean, Richard Devon, Paul Maxwell, Michael Hall.

BODY SNATCHER, The (1945)
RKO Radio (USA)
PROD: Val Lewton. DIR: Robert Wise. SCR: Philip MacDonald, Carlos Keith; from the novel by Robert Louis Stevenson. PH: Robert de Grasse.
WITH Boris Karloff, Bela Lugosi, Henry Daniell, Edith Atwater, Russell Wade, Rita Corday (later Paule Crosset), Sharyn Moffett, Donna Lee.

BRIDE OF FRANKENSTEIN, The (1935)
Universal (USA)
DIR: James Whale. SCR: John L. Balderston, William Hurlbut; based on characters created by Mary Shelley. PH: John D. Mescall. MUS: Franz Waxman.

WITH Boris Karloff, Colin Clive, Valerie Hobson, Elsa Lanchester, Ernest Thesiger, O. P. Heggie, Dwight Frye, E. E. Clive, Una O'Conner, Anne Darling, Douglas Walton, Gavin Gordon, Neil Fitzgerald, Reginald Barlow, Mary Gordon, Tempe Piggott, Ted Billings, Lucien Prival, Grace Cunard, Rollo Lloyd, Walter Brennan, John Carradine.

BRIDES OF DRACULA (1960)
Hammer Films (G. B.)
DIR: Terence Fisher. SCR: Jimmy Sangster, Peter Bryan, Edward Percy. PH: Jack Asher (Technicolor). MUS: Malcolm Williamson.
WITH Peter Cushing, Martita Hunt, Yvonne Monlaur, Freda Jackson, David Peel, Miles Malleson, Mona Washbourne, Andree Melly, Henry Oscar, Michael Ripper, Vera Cook, Marie Devereaux, Henry Scott.

BUCK ROGERS (1939)
Universal Serial in 12 Chapters. (USA)
DIR: Ford Beebe, Saul Goodkind. SCR: Norman Hall, Ray Trampe; from the cartoon strip by Dick Calkinds and Phil Nolan. PH: Jerry Ash.
WITH Larry Crabbe, Constance Moore, Jackie Moran, Henry Brandon, Wheeler Oakman, Philson Ahn, Jack Mulhall, Carleton Young, Reed Howes.

BUCKET OF BLOOD (1959)
American International (USA)
DIR–PROD: Roger Corman. SCR: Charles B. Griffith. PH: Jack Marquette. MUS: Fred Katz.
WITH Dick Miller, Barboura Morris, Anthony Carbone, Julian Burton, Ed Nelson, John Brinkley, John Shaner, Judy Bamber, Myrtle Domerel, Bert Convy, Jhean Burton.

BURN WITCH BURN——see NIGHT OF THE EAGLE
CABINET OF DR. CALIGARI, The——see KABINETT des DR. CALIGARI, Das

CALLING DR. DEATH (1943)
Universal (USA)
DIR: Reginald LeBorg. SCR: Edward Dein. PH: Virgil Miller. MUS: Paul Sawtell.
WITH Lon Chaney, Jr., Patricia Morison, Ramsay Ames, David Bruce, Fay Helm, J. Carroll Naish, Lisa Golm, Holmes Herbert, Alec Craig, Mary Hale, John Elliott.

CALTIKI, IL MOSTRO IMMORTALE (1959)
Galatea Film/Bruno Vailati (Italy/USA)
DIR: Robert Hampton (Riccardo Freda). SCR: Philip Just (Filippo Sanjust). PH: John Foam (Mario Bava). MUS: Robert Nicholas (Roman Vlad).
WITH John Merivale, Didi Perego, Daniela Rocca, Gerard Herter, Daniele Vargas, Victor Andree, Arturo Dominici, Giacomo Rossi-Stuart.

CAPTIVE WILD WOMAN (1943)
Universal (USA)
DIR: Edward Dmytryk. SCR: Griffin Jay, Henry Sucher. PH: George Robinson. MUS: H. J. Salter.
WITH Acquanetta, John Carradine, Evelyn Ankers, Milburn Stone, Fay Helm, Lloyd Corrigan, Martha MacVicar (later Martha Vickers), Paul Fix, Vince Barnett.

CARNIVAL OF SINNERS——see MAIN DU DIABLE, La
CASTLE OF DOOM——see VAMPYR

CAT AND THE CANARY, The (1927)
Universal (USA)
DIR: Paul Leni. SCR: Robert F. Hill, Alfreda Cohn; from the play by John Willard. PH: Gilbert Warrenton.
WITH Laura La Plante, Creighton Hale, Forrest Stanley, Gertrude Astor, Tully Marshall, Flora Finch, Arthur Edmund Carewe, Martha Mattox, George Siegmann, Lucien Littlefield, Joe Murphy, Billy Engle.

CAT AND THE CANARY, The (1939)
Paramount (USA)
DIR: Elliott Nugent. SCR: Walter De Leon, Lynn Starling; from the play by John Willard. PH: Charles Lang. MUS: Prof. Ernst Toch.
WITH Bob Hope, Paulette Goddard, John Beal, Douglass Montgomery, Gale Sondergaard, Elizabeth Patterson, Nydia Westman, George Zucco, John Wray, George Regas.

CAT CREEPS, The (1930)
Universal (USA)
DIR: Rupert Julian. SCR: Gladys Lehman; from the play by John Willard. PH: Jerry Ash, Hal Mohr.
WITH Helen Twelvetrees, Raymond Hackett, Lilyan Tashman, Jean Hersholt, Montague Love, Lawrence Grant, Theodore von Eltz, Blanche Frederici, Elizabeth Patterson.

CAT PEOPLE, The (1942)
RKO: Radio (USA)
PROD: Val Lewton. DIR: Jacques Tourneur. SCR: DeWitt Bodeen. PH: Nicholas Musuraca. MUS: Roy Webb.
WITH Simone Simon, Kent Smith, Tom Conway, Jane Randolph, Jack Holt, Elizabeth Russell, Alan Napier, Mary Jane Halsey, Elizabeth Dunne.

CHIKYU BOEIGUN (1957)
Toho (Japan)
DIR: Inoshiro Honda. SCR: Takeshi Kimura; from the original story by Jojiro Okami as adapted by Shigeru Kayama. PH: Hajime Koizumi (Eastmancolor). SP. EF: Eiji Tsuburuya.
WITH Kenji Sahara, Yumi Shirakawa, Momoko Kochi, Akihiko Hirata, Takashi Shimura, Susumu Fujita.

CHINESE PARROT, The (1927)
Universal (USA)
DIR: Paul Leni. SCR: J. Grubb Alexander; from the story by Earl Derr Biggers. PH: Ben Klein.
WITH Marion Nixon, Florence Turner, Hobart Bosworth, Edmund Burns, Albert Conti, K. Sojin, George Kuwa, Slim Summerville, Anna May Wong, Etta Lee, Jack Trent, Dan Maxon, Edgar Kennedy.

CHRONICLE OF THE GRAY HOUSE, The——see
CHRONIK VON GRIESHUUS

CHRONIK VON GRIESHUUS (1923)
Union-UFA (Germany)
DIR: Arthur von Gerlach. SCR: Thea von Harbou; from a story by Theodor Storm. PH: Karl Drews, Fritz Arno Wagner, Eric Nitzchmann. SETS: Hans Poelzig, Robert Herlth, Walter Röhrig.
WITH Paul Hartmann, Lil Dagover, Gertrud Arnold, Rudolph Forster, Gertrud Welcker, Arthur Kraussneck.

CÍSAŘŮV PEKAŘ, PEKAŘŮV CÍSAŘ (1951)
State Film Studios (Czechoslovakia)
DIR: Martin (Mac) Fric. SCR: Jan Werich, M. Fric, Jiří Brdečka. PH: Jan Stallich, Bohumil Haba (color).
WITH: Jan Werich, František Černý, Nataša Gollová, Marie Vášová, Jiří Plachý, Zdeněk Stěpánek.

CLIMAX, The (1944)
Universal (USA)
DIR: George Waggner. SCR: Curt Siodmak, Lynn Starling; from a play by Edward Locke. PH: Hal Mohr (Technicolor). MUS: Edward Ward.
WITH Susanna Foster, Turhan Bey, Boris Karloff, Gale Sondergaard, June Vincent, Jane Farrar, Thomas Gomez, George Dolenz, Ludwig Stossel, Erno Verebes, Lotte Stein, Scotty Beckett, William Edmunds, Maxwell Hayes, Dorothy Lawrence.

CONQUERING POWER, The (1922)
Metro-Goldwyn (USA)
DIR: Rex Ingram. SCR: June Mathis; based on the novel "Eugenie Grandet" by Honoré de Balzac. PH: John F. Seitz.
WITH Alice Terry, Rudolph Valentino, Eric Mayne, Ralph Lewis, Carrie Daumery, Edward Connelly, George Atkinson, Ward Wing, Willard Lee Hall, Mark Fenton.

CONQUEST OF SPACE (1955)
Paramount (USA)
PROD: George Pal. DIR: Byron Haskin. SCR: James O'Hanlon, Philip Yordan, Barre Lyndon, George Worthington Yates; adapted from the writings of Chesley Bonestell and Willy Ley. PH: Lionel Lindon (Technicolor). MUS: Van Cleave.
WITH Walter Brooke, Eric Fleming, William Hopper, Ross Martin, Joan Shawlee, William Redfield, Phil Foster, Mickey Shaughnessy, Benson Fong, Vito Scotti, Michael Fox, Iphigenie Castiglioni.

CONQUEST OF THE POLE——see À LA CONQUÊTE DU PÔLE

CREATION OF THE HUMANOIDS (1963)
Genie Productions (USA)
DIR: Wesley E. Barry. SCR: Jay Simms. PH: Hal Mohr.
WITH Don Megowan, Erica Elliot, Frances McCann, Don Doolittle, David Cross, George Milan.

CREATURE FROM THE BLACK LAGOON (1954)
Universal (USA)
DIR: Jack Arnold. SCR: Harry Essex, Arthur Ross. PH: William E. Snyder (3-D).
WITH Richard Carlson, Julia Adams, Richard Denning, Antonio Moreno, Nestor Paiva, Ricou Browning, Whit Bissell, Ben Chapman, Rodd Redwing, Julio Lopez.

CURSE OF FRANKENSTEIN, The (1957)
Hammer Films (G.B.)
DIR: Terence Fisher. SCR: Jimmy Sangster. PH: Jack Asher (Warnercolor).
WITH Peter Cushing, Christopher Lee, Hazel Court, Robert Urquhart, Valerie Gaunt, Noel Hood, Marjorie Hume, Sally Walsh, Hugh Dempster, Ann Blake.

CURSE OF THE CAT PEOPLE, The (1944)
RKO Radio (USA)
PROD: Val Lewton. DIR: Robert Wise, Gunther Fritsch. SCR: DeWitt Bodeen. PH: Nicholas Musuraca. MUS: Roy Webb.
WITH: Simone Simon, Kent Smith, Jane Randolph, Ann Carter, Elizabeth Russell, Eve March, Julia Dean, Erford Gage, Sir Lancelot, Joel Davis, Juanita Alvarez.

CURSE OF THE DEMON——see NIGHT OF THE DEMON

CURSE OF THE FLY, The (1965)
20th Century-Fox/Lippert (USA)
DIR: Don Sharp. SCR: Harry Spalding. PH: Basil Emmett (CinemaScope). MUS: Bert Shefter.
WITH Brian Donlevy, Carole Gray, George Baker, Michael Graham, Jeremy Wilkins, Charles Carson, Burt Kwouk, Yvette Rees, Rachel Kempson, Mary Manson, Warren Stanhope, Arnold Bell, Stan Simmons.

CURSE OF THE MUMMY'S TOMB, The (1964)
Hammer-Swallow Films (G.B.)
DIR: Michael Carreras. SCR: Henry Younger. PH: Otto Heller. (Techniscope/Technicolor).
WITH Ronald Howard, Terence Morgan, Fred Clark, Jeanne Roland, George Pastell, Jack Gwillim, Marianne Stone, Michael Ripper.

CURSE OF THE WEREWOLF, The (1961)
Hammer Films (G.B.)
DIR: Terence Fisher. SCR: John Elder; from the novel "The Werewolf of Paris" by Guy Endore. PH: Arthur Grant (Eastmancolor).
WITH Oliver Reed, Clifford Evans, Yvonne Romain, Catherine Feller, Anthony Dawson, Josephine Llewellyn, Richard Wordsworth, Hira Talfrey, John Gabriel, Warren Mitchell, Ann Blake, George Woodbridge, Michael Ripper, Dennis Shaw, Sheila Brennan, Joy Webster, Renny Lester, Justin Walters.

DAMNED, The (1961)
Hammer Films (G.B.)
DIR: Joseph Losey. SCR: Evan Jones; from the novel "Children of Light" by H. L. Lawrence. PH: Arthur Grant.
WITH Macdonald Carey, Shirley Ann Field, Viveca Lindfors, Oliver Reed, Alexander Knox, James Villiers, Barbara Everest, Walter Gotell, Brian Oulton, Kenneth Cope, Caroline Sheldon, David Palmer, Rebecca Dignam, Thomas Kempinski, Siobhan Taylor.

DANTE'S INFERNO (1924)
Fox (USA)
DIR: Henry Otto. SCR: Edmund Goulding, Cyrus Wood. PH: Joseph August.
WITH Pauline Starke, Ralph Lewis, Lawson Butt, Gloria Grey, Diana Miller, Josef Swickard, Howard Gaye, William Scott, Robert Klein, Winifred Landis, Lorimer Johnston, Lon Poff, Bud Jamison.

DANTE'S INFERNO (1935)
Fox (USA)
DIR: Harry Lachman. SCR: Philip Klein, Robert M. Yost. PH: Rudolph Mate.
WITH Spencer Tracy, Claire Trevor, Henry B. Walthall, Alan Dinehart, Scott Beckett, Robert Gleckler, Rita Cansino (later Hayworth), Gary Leon, Willard Robertson, Morgan Wallace, Ray Corrigan.

DARK EYES OF LONDON (1940)
Associated British (G.B.)
DIR: Walter Summers. SCR: Patrick Kirwin, Walter Summers, J. F. Argyle; from the novel by Edgar Wallace. PH: Bryan Langly.
WITH Bela Lugosi, Hugh Williams, Greta Gynt, Edmon Ryan, Wilfred Walter, Alexander Field, A. E. Owne, Julie Suedo, Gerald Pring, B. Herbert, May Hallett.

DAY MARS INVADED THE EARTH, The (1963)
20th Century-Fox/API (USA)
DIR–PROD: Maury Dexter. SCR: Harry Spaulding. MUS: Richard LaSalle.
WITH Kent Taylor, Marie Windsor, William Mims, Betty Beall, Lowell Brown, Gregg Shank.

DAY OF WRATH——see VREDENS DAG

DAY THE EARTH STOOD STILL, The (1951)
20th Century-Fox (USA)
DIR: Robert Wise. SCR: Edmund H. North. PH: Leo Tover. MUS: Bernard Herrmann.
WITH Michael Rennie, Patricia Neal, Hugh Marlowe, Sam Jaffe, Billy Gray, Frances Bavier, Frank Conroy, Lock Martin, Carleton Young, Fay Roope, Edith Evanson, Robert Osterloh, Tyler McVey, James Seay.

DEAD MAN'S EYES (1944)
Universal (USA)
DIR: Reginald LeBorg. SCR: Dwight V. Babcock. PH: Paul Ivano. MUS: Paul Sawtell.
WITH Lon Chaney, Jr., Jean Parker, Paul Kelly, Thomas Gomez, Acquanetta, Jonathan Hale, Edward Fielding, George Meeker, Eddie Dunn, Pierre Watkin.

DEAD OF NIGHT (1945)
Ealing (G.B.)
DIR: Cavalcanti–"Christmas Party" and "Ventriloquist" sequences; Charles Crichton–"Golfing" sequence; Basil Dearden–"Hearse" sequence; Robert Hamer–"Mirror" sequence. SCR: John Baines, Angus MacPhail, T. E. B. Clarke; from stories by J. Baines, A. MacPhail, E. F. Benson, and H. G. Wells. PH: Jack Parker, H. Julius. MUS: Georges Auric.
WITH Mervyn Johns, Roland Culver, Mary Merrall, Googie Withers, Frederick Valk, Antony Baird, Sally Ann Howes, Robert Wyndham, Judy Kelly, Miles Malleson, Michael Allan, Barbara Leake, Ralph Michael, Esme Percy, Basil Radford, Naunton Wayne, Peggy Bryan, Allan Jeayes, Michael Redgrave, Elizabeth Welch, Hartley Power, Magda Kun, Garry Marsh, Renee Gadd.

DEADLY MANTIS, The (1957)
Universal (USA)
DIR: Nathan Juran. SCR: Martin Berkeley; from the writings of William Alland. PH: Ellis W. Carter. MUS: Joseph Gershenson.
WITH Craig Stevens, Alix Talton, William Hopper, Donald Randolph, Pat Conway, Florenz Ames, Paul Smith, Floyd Simmons, Paul Campbell.

DEATH KISS, The (1932)
World-Wide (USA)
DIR: Edwin L. Marin. SCR: Barry Barringer, Gordon Kahn.
PH: Norbert Brodine.

WITH David Manners, Adrienne Ames, Bela Lugosi, John Wray, Mona Maris, Barbara Bedford, Vince Barnett, Alexander Carr, Edward Van Sloan, Harold Minjir, Wade Boteler, Alan Roscoe, Edmund Burns, Al Hill, Jimmy Donlin, Lee Moran.

DEATH TAKES A HOLIDAY (1934)
Paramount (USA)
DIR: Mitchell Leisen. SCR: Maxwell Anderson, Gladys Lehman, Walter Ferris; from the play by Alberto Casella. PH: Charles Lang.
WITH Fredric March, Evelyn Venable, Katherine Alexander, Gail Patrick, Sir Guy Standing, Helen Westley, Kathleen Howard, Kent Taylor, Henry Travers, G. P. Huntley, Jr., Edward Van Sloan, Otto Hoffman, Frank Yaconelli, Anna Delinsky.

DECIMA VITTIMA, La (1965)
Carlo Ponti (Italy)
DIR: Elio Petri. SCR: E. Petri, Ennio Flaiano, Tonino Guerra, Giorgio Salvione; from a novel by Robert Sheckley. PH: Gianni Di Venanzo (Eastmancolor). MUS: Piero Piccioni.
WITH Marcello Mastroianni, Ursula Andress, Elsa Martinelli, Salvo Randone, Massimo Serato, Evi Rigano, Milo Quesada, Luce Bonifassy, Anita Sanders, Mickey Knox, Richard Armstrong, Walter Williams, George Wang.

DELUGE (1933)
RKO Radio (USA)
DIR: Felix Feist, Jr. SCR: John Goodrich, Warren B. Duff; from a story by S. Fowler Wright. PH: Norbert Brodine, William B. Williams.
WITH Peggy Shannon, Lois Wilson, Sidney Blackmer, Matt Moore, Fred Kohler, Ralf Harolde, Samuel S. Hinds, Edward Van Sloan.

DESTINATION MOON (1950)
Eagle-Lion (USA)
PROD: George Pal. DIR: Irving Pichel. SCR: Robert Heinlein, Rip Van Ronkel, James O'Hanlon; from a story by R. Heinlein. PH: Lionel Lindon (Technicolor). MUS: Leith Stevens.
WITH John Archer, Warner Anderson, Erin O'Brien-Moore, Tom Powers, Dick Wesson.

DESTINY——see MÜDE TOD, Der

DEVIL COMMANDS, The (1941)
Columbia (USA)
DIR: Edward Dmytryk. SCR: Robert D. Andrews, Milton Gunzburg; from a story by William Stone. PH: Allen G. Siegler.

WITH Boris Karloff, Amanda Duff, Anne Revere, Richard Fiske Dorothy Adams, Shirley Warde, Ralph Penney, Walter Baldwin, Kenneth MacDonald.

DEVIL DOLL, The (1936)
Metro-Goldwyn-Mayer (USA)
DIR: Tod Browning. SCR: Tod Browning, Garrett Fort, Guy Endore Erich von Stroheim; based on "Burn Witch Burn" by A. A. Merritt PH: Leonard Smith.
WITH Lionel Barrymore, Maureen O'Sullivan, Frank Lawton, Henry B. Walthall, Rafaela Ottiano, Grace Ford, Arthur Hohl, Juanita Quigley, Lucy Beaumont, Robert Greig, Pedro de Cordoba.

DEVIL'S ASSISTANT, The (1917)
Mutual (USA)
DIR: Harry Pollard. SCR: H. Pollard; from a story by F. Edward Hungerford.
WITH Margarita Fisher, Jack Mower.

DEVIL'S COMMANDMENT, The——see VAMPIRI, I
DIE DIE MY DARLING——see FANATIC

DIE, MONSTER, DIE (1965)
American-International (USA/G.B.)
DIR: Daniel Haller. SCR: Jerry Sohl; from the story "The Color Out of Space" by H. P. Lovecraft. PH: Paul Beeson (color).
WITH Boris Karloff, Nick Adams, Freda Jackson, Suzan Farmer, Terence DeMarney, Patrick Magee, Leslie Dwyer, Sheila Raynor, Billy Milton.

DINOSAUR AND THE MISSING LINK, The (1917)
Edison Co. (USA)
CONCEIVED, EXECUTED: Willis H. O'Brien.

DR. CYCLOPS (1940)
Paramount (USA)
DIR: Ernest B. Schoedsack. SCR: Tom Kilpatrick. PH: Ellsworth Hoagland (Technicolor). MUS: Ernst Toch, Gerard Carbonara, Albert Hay Malotte. SP. EF.: Farciot Edouart, Wallace Kelly.
WITH Albert Dekker, Janice Logan, Thomas Coley, Charles Halton, Victor Kilian, Frank Yaconelli, Bill Wilkerson, Allen Fox.

DR. JEKYLL AND MR. HYDE (1908)
Selig Polyscope (USA)

DR. JEKYLL AND MR. HYDE (1910)
Nordisk (Danish)
WITH Alwin Neuss.

DR. JEKYLL AND MR. HYDE (1912)
Thanhauser (USA)
DIR: Lucius Henderson.
WITH James Cruze, Marguerite Snow, Harry Benham.

DR. JEKYLL AND MR. HYDE (1913)
Kineto-Kinemacolor (G.B.)

DR. JEKYLL AND MR. HYDE (1913)
IMP (USA)
WITH King Baggot, Jane Gail.

DR. JEKYLL AND MR. HYDE (1920)
Pioneer Film Corp. (USA)
PROD: Louis B. Mayer.
WITH Sheldon Lewis.

DR. JEKYLL AND MR. HYDE (1920)
Paramount (USA)
DIR: John S. Robertson. SCR: Clara S. Berenger; from the novel by Robert Louis Stevenson.
WITH John Barrymore, Martha Mansfield, Nita Naldi, Brandon Hurst, Charles Lane, Louis Wolheim.

DR. JEKYLL AND MR. HYDE (1932)
Paramount (USA)
DIR: Rouben Mamoulian. SCR: Samuel Hoffenstein, Percy Heath; from the novel by Robert Louis Stevenson. PH: Karl Struss.
WITH Fredric March, Miriam Hopkins, Rose Hobart, Holmes Herbert, Halliwell Hobbes, Arnold Lucy, Tempe Piggott.

DR. JEKYLL AND MR. HYDE (1941)
Metro-Goldwyn-Mayer (USA)
DIR–PROD: Victor Fleming. SCR: John Lee Mahin; from the novel by Robert Louis Stevenson. PH: Joseph Ruttenberg. SP. EF.: Warren Newcombe. MUS: Franz Waxman.
WITH Spencer Tracy, Ingrid Bergman, Lana Turner, Ian Hunter, Donald Crisp, Barton MacLane, C. Aubrey Smith, Sara Allgood, Frances Robinson, Billy Bevan, Lumsden Hare, Peter Godfrey.

DOCTOR MABUSE (1922)
In Two Parts: I–DER SPIELER (THE GREAT GAMBLER). II–MENSCHEN DER ZEIT (INFERNO).
Ullstein-UCO Films/UFA (Germany)
DIR: Fritz Lang. SCR: Fritz Lang, Thea von Harbou; from the novel by Norbert Jacques. PH: Carl Hoffmann. SETS: Otto Hunte, Stahl-Urach.
WITH Rudolph Klein-Rogge, Alfred Abel, Aud Egede Nissen, Gertrud Welcker, Bernhard Goetzke, Paul Richter, Forster Larinaga, Hans Adalbert von Schlettow, Georg John, Karl Huszar, Greta Berger, Julius Falkenstein, Lydia Potechina, Anita Berber, Adele Sandrock, Max Adalbert, Paul Biensfeldt, Hans J. Junkermann, Auguste Prasch-Grevenberg, Karl Platen.

DR. RENAULT'S SECRET (1942)
20th Century-Fox (USA)
DIR: Henry Lachman. SCR: William Bruckner, Robert F. Metzler. PH: Virgil Miller.
WITH J. Carroll Naish, John Shepperd (later Shepherd Strudwick), Lynne Roberts, George Zucco, Bert Roach, Eugene Borden, Jack Norton.

DR. TERROR'S HOUSE OF HORRORS (1964)
Amicus (G.B.)
DIR: Freddie Francis, SCR: Milton Subotsky. PH: Alan Hume (Technicolor/Techniscope). MUS: Elizabeth Lutyens.
WITH Peter Cushing, Neils McCallum, Ursula Howells, Peter Madden, Katy Wild, Edward Underdown, Ann Bell, Alan Freeman, Bernard Lee, Jeremy Kemp, Roy Castle, Thomas Baptiste, Christopher Lee, Michael Gough, Isla Blair, Donald Sutherland, Max Adrian, Jennifer Jayne, Irene Richmond, Kenny Lynch, Harold Lang.

DR. X (1932)
First National/Warner (USA)
DIR: Michael Curtiz. SCR: Earl Baldwin, Robert Tasker; from the story by Howard W. Comstock and Allen C. Miller. PH: Richard Tower, Ray Ranahan (Technicolor).
WITH Lionel Atwill, Fay Wray, Lee Tracy, Preston Foster, George Rosener, Mae Busch, Leila Bennett, Arthur Edmund Carewe, John Wray, Harry Beresford, Robert Warwick, Tom Dugan, Willard Robertson, Harry Holman.

DRACULA (1931)
Universal (USA)
DIR: Tod Browning. SCR: Garrett Fort; from the novel by Bram Stoker and the play by Hamilton Deane and John L. Balderston. PH: Karl Freund.
WITH Bela Lugosi, Helen Chandler, David Manners, Dwight Frye, Edward Van Sloan, Frances Dade, Herbert Bunston, Charles Gerrard. (A Spanish language version was filmed simultaneously. DIR: George Melford. WITH Carlos Villarías, Lupita Tovar, and Barry Norton.)

DRACULA (1958)
Hammer Films (G.B.)
DIR: Terence Fisher. SCR: Jimmy Sangster; from the novel by Bram Stoker. PH: Jack Asher (Technicolor). MUS: James Bernard.
WITH Peter Cushing, Michael Gough, Melissa Stribling, Christopher Lee, Carol Marsh, John Van Eyssen, Miles Malleson, Valerie Gaunt.

DRACULA PRINCE OF DARKNESS (1965)
Hammer Films (G.B.)
DIR: Terence Fisher. SCR: John Samson; based on characters from the novel by Bram Stoker. PH: Michael Reed (Technicolor/Techniscope). MUS: James Bernard.
WITH Christopher Lee, Barbara Shelley, Andrew Keir, Francis Matthews, Suzan Farmer, Charles Tingwell, Thorley Walters, Philip Latham, Joyce Hemson.

DRACULA'S DAUGHTER (1936)
Universal (USA)
DIR: Lambert Hillyer. SCR: Garrett Fort, based on his story. PH: George Robinson.
WITH Gloria Holden, Otto Kruger, Marguerite Churchill, Irving Pichel, Edward Van Sloan, Nan Gray, Hedda Hopper, Gilbert Emery, Eily Malyon, Claude Allister, E. E. Clive, Halliwell Hobbes, Billy Bevan, Douglas Wood.

DRUMS OF JEOPARDY (1931)
Tiffany (USA)
DIR: George B. Seitz. SCR: Florence Ryerson; from the play by Harold MacGrath. PH: Arthur Reed.
WITH Warner Oland, June Collyer, Lloyd Hughes, George Fawcett, Ernest Hilliard, Florence Lake, Wallace MacDonald, Clara Blandick, Mischa Auer, Hale Hamilton, Ann Brody.

EMPEROR AND THE GOLEM, The——see
CISARŮV PEKAR, PEKARŮV CISAR

ET MOURIR DE PLAISIR (1960)
Films E.G.E./Documento Films (France/Italy)
DIR: Roger Vadim. SCR: Claude Brule, Claude Martin, Roger Vadim; from "Carmilla" by Sheridan Le Fanu. PH: Claude Renoir (Technirama/Eastmancolor). MUS: Jean Prodromides.
WITH Annette Stroyberg, Mel Ferrer, Elsa Martinelli, Serge Marquand, R. J. Chauffard, Marc Allegret, Camilla Stroyberg, Nathalie LeForet, Gabrielle Farinon, Alberto Bonucci.

EVIL OF FRANKSTEIN, The (1964)
Hammer Films (G.B.)
DIR: Freddie Francis. SCR: John Elder; based on characters from the novel by Mary Shelley. PH: John Wilcox (Eastmancolor). MUS: Don Banks.
WITH Peter Cushing, Peter Woodthorpe, Sandor Eles, Duncan Lamont, Katy Wild, James Maxwell, David Hutcheson, Kiwi Kingston.

F.P.1 (1933)
Fox/Gaumont/UFA (G.B./France/Germany)
DIR: Karl Hartl. PROD: Erich Pommer. SCR: Walter Reisch, Curt Siodmak. PH: Gunther Rittau, Konstantin Tschet.
WITH Leslie Fenton, Conrad Veidt, Jill Esmond, George Merritt, Donald Calthrop, Alexander Field, Francis L. Sullivan, Warwick Ward, Nicholas Hannen, William Freshman, Dr. Philip Manning. (There were German, French, and British versions filmed simultaneously).

FACE OF FU MANCHU, The (1965)
Anglo-Amalgamated (G.B.)
DIR: Don Sharp. SCR: Peter Welbeck; based on characters from the novels by Sax Rohmer. PH: Ernest Steward (Technicolor/Techniscope). MUS: Christopher Whelen.
WITH Christopher Lee, Nigel Green, Joachim Fuchsberger, Karin Dor, Tsai Chin, Howard Marion Crawford, Walter Rilla, James Robertson Justice, Poulet Tu.

FAHRENHEIT 451 (1966)
Anglo-Enterprise-Vineyard (G.B./France)

DIR: François Truffaut. SCR: François Truffaut, Jean-Louis Richard; from the novel by Ray Bradbury. PH: Nicholas Roeg (Technicolor). MUS: Bernard Herrmann.
WITH Julie Christie, Oskar Warner, Cyril Cusack, Anton Diffring, Jeremy Spenser, Bee Duffell.

FANATIC (1965)
Hammer Films (G.B.)
DIR: Silvio Narizzano. SCR: Richard Matheson; based on the novel "Nightmare" by Anne Blaisdell. PH: Arthur Ibbetson (Technicolor). MUS: Wilfred Josephs.
WITH Tallulah Bankhead, Stefanie Powers, Peter Vaughan, Yootha Joyce, Donald Sutherland, Maurice Kaufman, Gwendolyn Watts, Diane King.

FANTASTIC VOYAGE (1966)
20th Century-Fox (USA)
DIR: Richard Fleischer. SCR: Harry Kleiner, from a story by Otto Klement and Jay Lewis Bixby, adapted by David Duncan. PH: Ernest Laszlo (DeLuxe Color). SETS: Jack Martin Smith, Dale Mennesy. SP. EF.: L. B. Abbott, Art Cruickshank, and Emil Kosa, Jr.
WITH Stephen Boyd, Raquel Welch, Edmond O'Brien, Donald Pleasance, Arthur O'Connell, William Redfield, Arthur Kennedy, Jean Del Val, Barry Coe, Ken Scott.

FAUST (1926)
UFA (Germany)
DIR: F. W. Murnau. SCR: Hans Kyser, from German folk sagas. TITLES: Gerhard Hauptmann. PH: Carl Hoffmann. SETS: Walter Röhrig and Robert Herlth.
WITH Emil Jannings, Gosta Ekman, Camilla Horn, Yvette Guilbert, Frieda Richard, William Dieterle, Hanna Ralph, Werner Fütterer, Eric Barclay.

FIRST MAN INTO SPACE (1959)
Amalgamated/MGM (G.B.)
DIR: Robert Day. SCR: John Croydon and Lance Z. Hargreaves, from a story by Wyott Ordung. PH: Geoffrey Faithful.
WITH Marshall Thompson, Marla Landi, Bill Edwards, Robert Ayres, Bill Nagy, Carl Jaffe, Roger Delgado, John McLaren, Richard Shaw, Bill Nick.

FIRST MEN IN THE MOON (1964)
British Lion/Columbia (G.B.)
DIR: Nathan Juran. SCR: Nigel Kneale, Ian Read; based on the novel by H. G. Wells. PH: Wilkie Cooper, (Panavision/Technicolor). SP. EF.: Ray Harryhausen.
WITH Edward Judd, Martha Hyer, Lionel Jeffries, Erik Chitty, Betty McDowall, Miles Malleson, Lawrence Herder, Gladys Henson, Marne Maitland, Paul Carpenter, Sean Kelly.

FLASH GORDON (1936)
Universal Serial in 13 Chapters. (USA)
DIR: Frederick Stephani. SCR: Frederick Stephani, George Plympton, Basil Dickey, Ella O'Neill; based on the comic strip by Alex Raymond. PH: Jerry Ash, Richard Fryer.
WITH Larry "Buster" Crabbe, Jean Rogers, Priscilla Lawson, Charles Middleton, John Lipson, Richard Alexander, Frank Shannon, Duke York, Jr., Earl Askam, Theodore Lorch, James Pierce, Muriel Goodspeed, Richard Tucker.

FLIGHT TO MARS (1951)
Monogram (USA)
DIR: Lesley Selander. PROD: Walter Mirisch. SCR: Arthur Strawn. PH: Harry Neumann.
WITH Marguerite Chapman, Cameron Mitchell, Virginia Huston, Arthur Franz, John Litel, Richard Gaines, Morris Ankrum, Lucille Barkley, Robert Barrat, Edward Earle.

FLY, The (1958)
20th Century-Fox (USA)
DIR: Kurt Neumann. SCR: James Clavell; from the story by George Langelaan. PH: Karl Struss (DeLuxe Color/CinemaScope). MUS: Paul Sawtell.
WITH Al Hedison (later David Hedison), Patricia Owens, Vincent Price, Herbert Marshall, Kathleen Freeman, Betty Lou Gerson, Charles Herbert, Eugene Borden, Torben Meyer.

FLYING SAUCER, The (1950)
Film Classics (USA)
DIR–PROD: Mikel Conrad. SCR: Mikel Conrad, based on his story. PH: Philip Tannura. MUS: Darrel Calker.
WITH Mikel Conrad, Pat Garrison, Virginia Hewitt, Hatz von Teuffen, Lester Sharpe, Russell Hicks, Frank Darien, Denver Pyle, Roy Engle, Gerry Owen, Phillip Morris.

FOLIE DU DOCTEUR TUBE, La (1916)
Louis Nalpas-Les Films d'Art (France)
DIR–SCR: Abel Gance. PH: Wentzel.
WITH Albert Dieudonné.

FORBIDDEN PLANET (1956)
Metro-Goldwyn-Mayer (USA)
DIR: Fred McLeod Wilcox. SCR: Cyril Hume. PH: George J. Folsey (Eastmancolor/CinemaScope).
WITH Walter Pidgeon, Anne Francis, Leslie Nielsen, Warren Stevens, Jack Kelly, Bob Dix, Richard Anderson, Earl Holliman, James Drury, George Wallace, Jimmy Thompson, Harry Harvey, Jr.

FOUR-SIDED TRIANGLE (1952)
Hammer Films (G.B.)
DIR: Terence Fisher, SCR: Terence Fisher, Paul Tabori; from the novel by William F. Temple. PH: Reginald Wyer. MUS: Malcolm Arnold.
WITH Barbara Payton, Stephen Murray, James Hayter, John van Eyssen, Percy Marmont, Kynaston Reeves.

FRANKENSTEIN (1910)
Edison (USA)
From the novel by Mary Shelley.
WITH (?) Charles Ogle.

FRANKENSTEIN (1931)
Universal (USA)
DIR: James Whale. SCR: Garrett Fort, Francis Edward Faragoh; from the novel by Mary Shelley. PH: Arthur Edeson.
WITH Colin Clive, Mae Clarke, John Boles, Boris Karloff, Edward Van Sloan, Dwight Frye, Lionel Belmore, Marilyn Harris, Otis Harlan, Frederick Kerr.

FRANKENSTEIN MEETS THE WOLF MAN (1943)
Universal (USA)
DIR: Roy William Neill. SCR: Curt Siodmak. PH: George Robinson. MUS: H. J. Salter.
WITH Ilona Massey, Patric Knowles, Lon Chaney, Jr., Lionel Atwill, Bela Lugosi, Maria Ouspenskaya, Dennis Hoey, Dwight Frye, Rex Evans, Don Barclay, Harry Stubbs.

FRAU IM MOND (1928)
Fritz Lang Film/G.M.B.H.–UFA (Germany).
DIR: Fritz Lang. SCR: Fritz Lang, Thea von Harbou. PH: Kurt Kourant, Oskar Fishinger, Otto Kanturek. SETS: Otto Hunte, Emil Hasler, Karl Vollbrecht.
WITH Gerda Maurus, Willy Fritsch, Fritz Rasp, Gustav von Wangenheim, Klaus Pohl, Gustl Stark-Gesettenbaur.

FREAKS (1932)
Metro-Goldwyn-Mayer (USA)
DIR: Tod Browning. SCR: Willis Goldbeck, Leon Gordon; from the story "Spurs" by Tod Robbins. PH: Merritt B. Gerstad.
WITH Wallace Ford, Leila Hyams, Olga Baclanova, Roscoe Ates, Henry Victor, Harry and Daisy Earles, Daisy and Violet Hilton, Rose Dione, Edward Brophy, Matt McHugh, Randian, Johnny Eck, Martha the Armless Wonder.

FROZEN GHOST, The (1945)
Universal (USA)
DIR: Harold Young. SCR: Bernard Schubert, Luci Ward. PH: Paul Ivano.
WITH Lon Chaney, Jr., Evelyn Ankers, Wilburn Stone, Tala Birell, Elena Verdugo, Martin Kosleck, Arthur Hohl, Douglass Dumbrille.

FRUSTA E IL CORPO, La (1964)
Vox/Leone (Italy)
DIR: John M. Old (Mario Bava). SCR: Julian Berry, Robert Hugo, Martin Hardy. PH: David Hamilton (Ubaldo Terzano) (Technicolor).
WITH Daliah Lavi, Christopher Lee, Tony Kendall, Harriet White, Isli Oberon, Jacques Herlin.

GAME OF DEATH, A (1945)
RKO Radio (USA)
DIR: Robert Wise. SCR: Norman Houston; from the story "The Most Dangerous Game" by Richard Connell. PH: J. Roy Hunt. MUS: Paul Sawtell.
WITH John Loder, Audrey Long, Edgar Barrier, Russell Wade, Russell Hicks, Jason Robards, Gene Stutenroth, Noble Johnson, Robert Clarke.

GENUINE (1920)
Decla-Bioscop (Germany)
DIR: Robert Wiene. SCR: Carl Mayer. PH: Willy Hameister. SETS: Cesar Klein.
WITH Fern Andra, Harald Paulsen, Ernst Gronau, John Gottowt, H. H. von Twardowski.

GHOST, The——see SPETTRO, Lo

GHOST BREAKERS, The (1940)
Paramount (USA)
DIR: George Marshall. SCR: Walter DeLeon. PH: Charles Lang.
WITH Bob Hope, Paulette Goddard, Richard Carlson, Paul Lukas, Anthony Quinn, Willie Best, Virginia Brissac, Pedro de Cordoba, Noble Johnson, Tom Dugan, Paul Fix, Lloyd Corrigan.

GHOST OF FRANKENSTEIN, The (1942)
Universal (USA)
DIR: Erle C. Kenton. SCR: W. Scott Darling. PH: Milton Krasner, Woody Bredell. MUS: Charles Previn.
WITH Sir Cedric Hardwicke, Lon Chaney, Jr., Ralph Bellamy, Evelyn Ankers, Lionel Atwill, Bela Lugosi, Janet Ann Gallow.

GHOST OF SLUMBER MOUNTAIN, The (1919)
World-Cinema Distributing Corp. (USA)
SP. EF.: Willis H. O'Brien. PROD: Herbert M. Dawley.

GHOST TALKS, The (1929)
Fox (USA)
DIR: Lew Seiler. SCR: Frederick H. Brennan, Harlan Thompson. PH: George Meehan.
WITH Helen Twelvetrees, Charles Easton, Stepin Fetchit, Carmel Myers, Earle Fox, Joe Brown, Baby Mack, Arnold Lucy, Bess Flowers, Dorothy McGowan, Mickey Bennett, Henry Sedley, Clifford Dempsey.

GHOUL, The (1933)
Gaumont British (G.B.)
DIR: T. Hayes Hunter. SCR: Rupert Downing; adapted from a story by Dr. Frank King and Leonard Hines. PH: Gunther Krampf.
WITH Boris Karloff, Anthony Bushell, Dorothy Hyson, Cedric Hardwicke, Ernest Thesiger, Kathleen Harrison, Harold Huth, D. A. Clarke-Smith, Ralph Richardson.

GIANT BEHEMOTH, The (1959)
Artistes Alliance (G.B.)
DIR: Douglas Hickox, Eugene Lourie. SCR: Eugene Lourie. PH: Ken Hodges. SP. EF. SUPERV.: Willis H. O'Brien.
WITH Gene Evans, Andre Morell, Leigh Madison, Henry Vidon, John Turner, Jack McGowran, Maurice Kaufmann, Leonard Sachs.

GLORY OF LOVE, The——see WHILE PARIS SLEEPS

GODZILLA, KING OF THE MONSTERS (1955)
Toho (Japan)
DIR: Inoshiro Honda. SCR: Takeo Murata, I. Honda. PH: Masao Tamai, Guy Roe. SP. EF.: Eiji Tsuburuya.
WITH Raymond Burr, Takaski Shimura, Momoko Kochi, Akira Takarada, Akihiko Hirata, Sachio Sakai, Fuyuki Murakami, Ren Yamamoto, Toyoaki Suzuki, Tadashi Okabe, Toranosuke Ogawa, Frank Iwanaga.

GOLD (1934)
UFA (Germany)
DIR: Karl Hartl. SCR: Rolf E. Vanloo. PH: Gunther Rittau. SETS: Otto Hunte.
WITH Brigitte Helm, Michael Bohnen, Hans Albers, Lien Dyers, Frederich Kayssler.
(There was a version in the French language filmed simultaneously, directed by Serge de Poligny, with Pierre Blanchar, Brigitte Helm, Line Noro, and Jacques Dumesnil.)

GOLEM, Der (1915)
Bioscop (Germany)
DIR: Paul Wegener, Henrik Galeen. PH: Guido Seeber. SETS: R. A. Dietrich, Rochus Gliese.
WITH Paul Wegener, Lyda Salmonova, Henrik Galeen, Carl Ebert.

GOLEM, Der (1920)
UFA (Germany)
DIR: Paul Wegener, Carl Boese. SCR: Paul Wegener, Henrik Galeen. PH: Karl Freund. SETS: Hans Poelzig. COST: Rochus Gliese.
WITH Paul Wegener, Albert Steinrück, Ernst Deutsch, Lyda Salmonova, Hans Sturm, Grete Schroeder, Lothar Meuthel, Otto Gebuhr, Max Kronert, Dore Paetzold.

GOLEM, Le (1936)
Metropolis Pictures (France)
DIR: Julien Duvivier. SCR: Andre-Paul Antoine. PH: Vich, Stalich.
WITH Harry Baur, Roger Karl, Gaston Jacquet, Germaine Aussey, Roger Duchesne, Aimos, Charles Dorat, Jany Holt, Ferdinand Hart.

GOLEM UND DIE TÄNZERIN, Der (1917)
Bioscop (Germany)
DIR: Paul Wegener.
WITH Paul Wegener.

GORGON, The (1964)
Hammer Films (G.B.)
DIR: Terence Fisher. SCR: John Gilling. PH: Michael Reed (Technicolor) . MUS: James Bernard.
WITH Peter Cushing, Richard Pasco, Barbara Shelley, Christopher Lee, Michael Goodliffe, Joyce Hemson, Sally Nesbitt, Michael Peake, Prudence Hyman, Toni Gilpin, Jack Watson, Jeremy Longhurst.

GORILLA, The (1927)
First National (USA)
DIR: Alfred Santell. SCR: Alfred A. Cohen, James T. O'Donahue, Henry McCarthy; from the play by Ralph Spence. PH: Arthur Edeson.
WITH Charlie Murray, Frank Kelsey, Alice Day, Tully Marshall, Claude Gillingwater, Walter Pidgeon, Gaston Glass.

GORILLA, The (1931)
Warner Brothers (USA)
DIR: Bryan Foy. SCR: B. Harrison Orkow; from the play by R. Spence. PH: Sid Hickox.
WITH Lila Lee, Joe Frisco, Harry Gribbon, Walter Pidgeon, Purnell Pratt, Edwin Maxwell, Roscoe Karns, Lauder Stevens.

GORILLA, The (1939)
20th Century-Fox (USA)
DIR: Allan Dwan. SCR: Rian James, Sid Silvers; from the play by R. Spence. PH: Edward Cronjager. MUS: David Buttolph.
WITH The Ritz Brothers, Anita Louise, Patsy Kelly, Lionel Atwill, Bela Lugosi, Joseph Calleia, Edward Norris, Wally Vernon, Paul Harvey, Art Miles.

HANDS OF ORLAC, The——see ORLACS HAENDE
HAUNTED CASTLE, The——see SCHLOSS VOGELOD

HAUNTED HOUSE, The (1929)
First National (USA)
DIR: Benjamin Christensen. SCR: Richard Bee, Lajos Biro; from the play by Owen Davis. PH: Sol Polito.
WITH Larry Kent, Thelma Todd, Edmund Breese, Barbara Bedford, Eve Southern, Flora Finch, Sidney Bracy, Chester Conklin, William V. Mong, Montagu Love, Johnnie Gough.

HAUNTED PALACE, The (1963)
American-International (USA)
DIR–PROD: Roger Corman. SCR: Charles Beaumont; from stories by H. P. Lovecraft and Edgar Allan Poe. PH: Floyd Crosby (Panavision/Pathecolor). MUS: Ronald Stein.
WITH Vincent Price, Debra Paget, Lon Chaney, Jr., Frank Maxwell, Leo Gordon, Elisha Cook, John Dierkes, Milton Parsons, Cathy Merchant, Guy Wilkerson, Harry Ellerbe, Darlene Lucht, Barboura Morris, Bruno Ve Sota.

HAUNTING, The (1963)
Argyle-MGM (G.B.)
DIR: Robert Wise. SCR: Nelson Gidding; from the novel "The Haunting of Hill House" by Shirley Jackson. PH: David Boulton (Panavision). SP. EF.: Tom Howard. MUS: Humphrey Searle.
WITH Julie Harris, Claire Bloom, Richard Johnson, Russ Tamblyn, Lois Maxwell, Fay Compton, Rosalie Crutchley, Diane Clare, Ronald Adam, Freda Knorr, Janet Mansell, Amy Dalby, Rosemary Dorken, Pamela Buckley, Howard Lang, Mavis Villiers, Verina Greenlaw, Paul Maxwell, Susan Richards, Claud Jones, Connie Tilton.

HÄXAN (1920)
Svenska (Sweden)
DIR: Benjamin Christensen. SCR: Benjamin Christensen. PH: Johan Ankerstjerne.
WITH Maren Pedersen, Clara Pontoppidan, Elith Pio, Oscar Stribolt, Tora Teje, Benjamin Christensen, John Andersen, Astrid Holm, Poul Reumert, Alice O'Fredericks.

HOMUNCULUS (1916)
Bioscop (Germany) Serial in 6 Chapters.
DIR: Otto Rippert. SCR: Otto Rippert, Robert Neuss. PH: Carl Hoffmann.
WITH Olaf Fønss, Frederich Kuhn, Theodor Loos, Mechtild Their, Maria Carmi, Gustav Kühne, Egede Nissen.

HORRIBLE DR. HITCHCOCK, The——see RAPTUS

HORROR CHAMBER OF DR. FAUSTUS, The——see YEUX SANS VISAGE, Les

HORROR OF DRACULA——see DRACULA (1958)

HORRORS OF THE BLACK MUSEUM (1959)
Anglo-Amalgamated (G.B.)
DIR: Arthur Crabtree. PROD: Herman Cohen. SCR: Aben Kandel, Herman Cohen. PH: Desmond Dickinson (CinemaScope/Eastmancolor).
WITH Michael Gough, June Cunningham, Shirley Ann Field, Geoffrey Keen, Beatrice Varley, Austin Trevor, Malou Pantera, Dorinda Stevens, Hilda Barry, Nora Gordon.

HOUND OF THE BASKERVILLES, The (1939)
20th Century-Fox (USA)
DIR: Sidney Lanfield. SCR: Ernest Pascal; from the novel by Arthur Conan Doyle. PH: J. Peverell Marley.
WITH Basil Rathbone, Richard Greene, Wendy Barrie, Nigel Bruce, Lionel Atwill, John Carradine, Barlowe Borland, Beryl Mercer, Morton Lowry, Ralph Forbes, Eily Malyon, E. E. Clive, Nigel De Brulier, Mary Gordon, Peter Willes, Ivan Simpson, Ivan MacLaren, John Burton, Dennis Green, Evan Thomas.

HOUND OF THE BASKERVILLES, The (1959)
Hammer Films (G.B.)
DIR: Terence Fisher. SCR: Peter Bryan; from the novel by Arthur Conan Doyle. PH: Jack Asher (Technicolor). MUS: James Bernard.
WITH Peter Cushing, Andre Morell, David Oxley, Christopher Lee, Marla Landi, Francis deWolf, Miles Malleson, John Le Mesurier.

HOUSE OF DRACULA (1945)
Universal (USA)
DIR: Erle C. Kenton. SCR: Edward T. Lowe. PH: George Robinson. MUS: Edgar Fairchild.
WITH Lon Chaney, Jr., Martha O'Driscoll, Jane Adams, John Carradine, Lionel Atwill, Onslow Stevens, Glenn Strange, Skelton Knaggs, Ludwig Stossel, Beatrice Gray, Joseph E. Bernard, Harry Lamont.

HOUSE OF FRANKENSTEIN (1944)
Universal (USA)
DIR: Erle C. Kenton. SCR: Edward T. Lowe; based on an original story by Curt Siodmak. PH: George Robinson. MUS: H. J. Salter.

WITH Boris Karloff, Lon Chaney, Jr., Anne Gwynne, J. Carroll Naish, Elena Verdugo, John Carradine, Peter Coe, Lionel Atwill, George Zucco, Sig Rumann, William Edmunds, Philip van Zandt, Julius Tannen, Olaf Hytten, Frank Reicher, Brandon Hurst, Glenn Strange.

HOUSE OF FRIGHT——see TWO FACES OF DR. JEKYLL, The

HOUSE OF HORROR (1929)
First National (USA)
DIR: Benjamin Christensen. SCR: Richard Bee; with dialogue by William Irish. PH: Ernest Haller, Sol Polito.
WITH Thelma Todd, Louise Fazenda, Chester Conklin, James Ford, Dale Fuller, William V. Mong, William Orlamond, Emile Chautard, Tenen Holtz, Michael Visaroff, Yola d'Avril.

HOUSE OF USHER, The (1960)
American-International (USA)
DIR–PROD: Roger Corman. SCR: Richard Matheson; from the story "The Fall of the House of Usher" by Edgar Allan Poe. PH: Floyd Crosby (Pathecolor/CinemaScope). MUS: Les Baxter.
WITH Vincent Price, Mark Damon, Myrna Fahey, Harry Ellerbe.

HOUSE OF WAX (1953)
Warner Brothers (USA)
DIR: Andre deToth. SCR: Crane Wilbur; from the story by Charles Belden. PH: Bert Glennon (3-D/Warnercolor).
WITH Vincent Price, Frank Lovejoy, Phyllis Kirk, Carolyn Jones, Paul Picerni, Roy Roberts, Angela Clarke, Charles Buchinski (later Bronson), Paul Cavanaugh, Dabbs Greer, Philip Tonge.

HOUSE ON HAUNTED HILL, The (1958)
Allied Artists (USA)
DIR–PROD: William Castle. SCR: Robb White. PH: Carl E. Guthrie. MUS: Von Dexter.
WITH Vincent Price, Carol Ohmart, Richard Long, Alan Marshall, Carolyn Craig, Elisha Cook, Julie Mitchum, Leona Anderson.

HOW TO MAKE A MONSTER (1958)
American-International (USA)
DIR: Herbert L. Strock. PROD: Herman Cohen. SCR: Kenneth Langtry, Herman Cohen. MUS: Paul Dunlap.

WITH Robert H. Harris, Paul Brinegar, Gary Conway, Gary Clarke, John Ashley, Malcolm Atterbury, Dennis Cross, Heather Ames, Walter Reed, Joan Chandler, Pauline Myers, Morris Ankrum, Paul Maxwell, Eddie Marr, Robert Shayne, Rod Dana, Jacqueline Ebeier, Thomas B. Henry, John Phillips.

HUNCHBACK OF NOTRE DAME, The (1923)
Universal (USA)
DIR: Wallace Worsley. SCR: Percy Poore Sheehan, Edward T. Lowe, Jr.; based on the novel "Notre Dame de Paris" by Victor Hugo. PH: Robert S. Newhard, Tony Kornman.
WITH Lon Chaney, Patsy Ruth Miller, Norman Kerry, Ernest Torrence, Gladys Brockwell, Kate Lester, Winifred Bryson, Eulalie Jensen, Brandon Hurst, Tully Marshall, Raymond Hatton, Nigel de Brulier, Nick de Ruiz.

HUNCHBACK OF NOTRE DAME, The (1939)
RKO Radio (USA)
DIR: William Dieterle. PROD: Pandro S. Berman. SCR: Sonya Levien, Bruno Frank; based on the novel by Victor Hugo. PH: Joseph August. SETS: Van Nest Polglase. SP. EF.: Vernon Walker. MUS: Alfred Newman.
WITH Charles Laughton, Sir Cedric Hardwicke, Maureen O'Hara, Thomas Mitchell, Edmond O'Brien, Alan Marshall, Walter Hampden, Katherine Alexander, Minna Gombell, Arthur Hohl, George Tobias, George Zucco, Harry Davenport, Helene Whitney, Fritz Leiber, Etienne Girardot, Rod La Rocque, Spencer Charters.

HUNCHBACK OF NOTRE DAME, The (1957)
Robert and Raymond Hakim (France)
DIR: Jean Delannoy. SCR: Jean Aurenche, Jacques Prévert; based on the novel by Victor Hugo. PH: Michel Kelber (Technicolor/CinemaScope). MUS: Georges Auric.
WITH Anthony Quinn, Gina Lollobrigida, Jean Danet, Alain Cuny, Danielle Dumont, Jean Tissier, Maurice Sarfati, Robert Hirsch, Philippe Clay.

I WALKED WITH A ZOMBIE (1943)
RKO Radio (USA)
DIR: Jacques Tourneur. PROD: Val Lewton. SCR: Curt Siodmak, Ardel Wray. PH: J. Roy Hunt. MUS: Roy Webb.

WITH James Ellison, Frances Dee, Tom Conway, Edith Barrett, Christine Gordon, James Bell, Theresa Harris, Sir Lancelot, Darby Jones, Jeni LeGon.

I WAS A TEENAGE FRANKENSTEIN (1957)
American-International (USA)
DIR: Herbert L. Strock. PROD: Herman Cohen. SCR: Kenneth Langtry. PH: Lathrop Worth. MUS: Paul Dunlap.
WITH Whit Bissell, Phyllis Coates, Robert Burton, Gary Conway, George Lynn, John Cliff, Marshall Bradford, Claudia Bryar, Angela Blake, Russ Whiteman, Gretchen Thomas, Joy Stoner, Larry Carr.

I WAS A TEENAGE WEREWOLF (1957)
American-International (USA)
DIR: Gene Fowler, Jr. PROD: Herman Cohen. SCR: Ralph Thornton. PH: Joseph LaShelle.
WITH Michael Landon, Yvonne Lime, Whit Bissell, Tony Marshall, Dawn Richard, Barney Phillips, Ken Miller, Cindy Robbins, Michael Rougas, Malcolm Atterbury, Eddie Marr, Vladimir Sokoloff, Louise Lewis, Guy Williams.

IKARIA XB1 (1963)
Barrandov (Czecho.)
DIR: Jindrich Polak. SCR: Pavel Juracek, Jindrich Polak. PH: Van Kalis (AGFAcolor). MUS: Zdenek Liska.
WITH Zdenek Stepanek, Radovan Lukavsky, Dana Medricka. Irena Kacirkova, Jiri Vrstala, Ludek Munzar, Emilie Vasayova.

INCREDIBLE SHRINKING MAN, The (1957)
Universal (USA)
DIR: Jack Arnold. PROD: Albert Zugsmith. SCR: Richard Matheson; from his original story. PH: Ellis W. Carter. SP. EF.: Clifford Stine. MUS: Joseph Gershenson.
WITH Grant Williams, Randy Stuart, April Kent, Paul Langton, Raymond Bailey, William Schallert, Diana Darrin, Frank Scannell, Helene Marshall, Billy Curtis.

INNOCENTS, The (1961)
20th Century-Fox (G.B.)
DIR:-PROD: Jack Clayton. SCR: William Archibald, Truman Capote, John Mortimer; adapted from the novella "Turn of the Screw" by Henry James. PH: Freddie Francis (CinemaScope).
MUS: Georges Auric.

WITH Deborah Kerr, Martin Stephens, Pamela Franklin, Megs Jenkins, Michael Redgrave, Peter Wyngarde, Clytie Jessop, Isla Cameron, Eric Woodburn.

INVADERS FROM MARS (1953)
20th Century-Fox (USA)
DIR: William Cameron Menzies. SCR: Richard Blake. PH: John Seitz (Cinecolor)
WITH Helena Carter, Arthur Franz, Jimmy Hunt, Leif Erickson, Hillary Brooke, Morris Ankrum, Max Wagner, Janine Perreau.

INVASION OF THE BODY SNATCHERS (1956)
Allied Artists (USA)
DIR: Don Siegel. PROD: Walter Wanger. SCR: Daniel Mainwaring; from a story by Jack Finney. PH: Ellsworth Fredericks. MUS: Carmen Dragon.
WITH Kevin McCarthy, Dana Wynter, Carolyn Jones, King Donovan, Larry Gates, Jean Willes, Virginia Christine, Ralph Dumke, Tom Fadden, Whit Bissell, Kenneth Patterson, Guy Way, Eileen Stevens, Beatrice Maude, Dabbs Greer, Pat O'Malley.

INVISIBLE MAN, The (1933)
Universal (USA)
DIR: James Whale. SCR: R. C. Sherriff (with Philip Wylie: uncredited). PH: Arthur Edeson.
WITH Claude Rains, Gloria Stuart, William Harrigan, Henry Travers, Una O'Connor, Forrester Harvey, Holmes Herbert, E. E. Clive, Dudley Digges, Harry Stubbs, Donald Stuart, Merle Tottenham.

INVISIBLE MAN RETURNS, The (1940)
Universal (USA)
DIR: Joe May. SCR: Curt Siodmak, Lester Cole; from an original story by Joe May and C. Siodmak. PH: Milton Krasner.
WITH Sir Cedric Hardwicke, Vincent Price, Nan Gray, John Sutton, Cecil Kellaway, Alan Napier, Forrester Harvey, Frances Robinson, Ivan Simpson, Edward Fielding, Harry Stubbs.

INVISIBLE RAY, The (1936)
Universal (USA)
DIR: Lambert Hillyer. SCR: John Colton. PH: George Robinson, John P. Fulton.
WITH Boris Karloff, Bela Lugosi, Frances Drake, Frank Lawton, Walter Kingsford, Beulah Bondi, Violet Kemble Cooper, Nydia West-

man, Daniel Haines, George Renavent, Paul Weigel, Adele St. Maur, Frank Reicher, Lawrence Stewart, Etta McDaniel, Inez Seabury, Winter Hall.

ISLAND OF LOST SOULS (1933)
Paramount (USA)
DIR: Erle Kenton. SCR: Waldemar Young, Philip Wylie; from the H. G. Wells story "The Island of Dr. Moreau." PH: Karl Struss.
WITH Charles Laughton, Bela Lugosi, Richard Arlen, Leila Hyams, Kathleen Burke, Arthur Hohl, Stanley Fields, Tetsu Komai, Rosemary Grimes, Paul Hurst, Joe Bonomo, Duke Yorke, George Irving, John George, Hans Steinke.

ISLE OF THE DEAD (1945)
RKO Radio (USA)
DIR: Mark Robson. PROD: Val Lewton. SCR: Ardel Wray. PH: Jack Mackenzie. MUS: Leigh Harline.
WITH Boris Karloff, Ellen Drew, Marc Cramer, Katherine Emery, Helene Thimig, Alan Napier, Jason Robards, Ernst Dorian, Skelton Knaggs, Sherry Hall.

IT CAME FROM BENEATH THE SEA (1955)
Columbia (USA)
DIR: Robert Gordon. SCR: George Worthington Yates, Hal Smith. PH: Henry Freulich. MUS: Mischa Bakaleinikoff.
WITH Kenneth Tobey, Faith Domergue, Ian Keith, Donald Curtis, Harry Lauter, Del Courtney, Dean Maddox, Jr., Ed Fisher.

IT CAME FROM OUTER SPACE (1953)
Universal (USA)
DIR: Jack Arnold. SCR: Harry Essex; from a story by Ray Bradbury. PH: Clifford Stine (3-D).
WITH Richard Carlson, Barbara Rush, Charles Drake, Russell Johnson, Kathleen Hughes, Joseph Sawyer, Dave Willock, Alan Dexter.

JANUSKOPF, DER (1920)
Lippow/Decla-Bioscop (Germany)
DIR: F. W. Murnau. SCR: Hans Janowitz; from the novel "Dr. Jekyll and Mr. Hyde" by Robert Louis Stevenson. PH: Carl Hoffmann, Karl Freund.

WITH Conrad Veidt, Margarete Schlegel, Willy Keyser-Heyl, Margarete Kupfer, Gustav Botz, Jaro Fürth, Magnus Stifter, Marga Reuter, Lansa Rudolph, Danny Gurtler.

JASON AND THE ARGONAUTS (1963)
BLC/Columbia (USA/G.B.)
DIR: Don Chaffey. SCR: Jan Read, Beverley Cross. PH: Wilkie Cooper (Technicolor). SP. EF.: Ray Harryhausen (SuperDynamation). MUS: Bernard Herrmann.
WITH Todd Armstrong, Nancy Kovack, Gary Raymond, Laurence Naismith, Niall MacGinnis, Michael Gwynn, Douglas Wilmer, Jack Gwillim, Honor Blackman, Andrew Faulds, Nigel Green, John Crawford, John Cairney, Patrick Troughton.

JETÉE, La (1963)
Argos Films (France)
DIR: Chris Marker. SCR: C. Marker. PH: Jean Ravel. MUS: Trevor Duncan.
WITH Helène Chatelain, Davos Hanich, Jacques Ledoux, André Heinrich, Jacques Branchu, Pierre Joffray.

JOURNEY TO THE SEVENTH PLANET (1961)
American-International (USA/Sweden)
DIR–PROD: Sidney Pink. SCR: S. Pink, Ib Melchior. PH: Age Wiltrup (sequences in Eastmancolor).
WITH John Agar, Greta Thyssen, Ann Smyrner, Mimi Heinrich, Carl Ottosen, Ove Sproge, Louis Miehe Renard, Peter Monch, Ulla Moritz, Annie Birgit Garde, Bente Juel.

JUNGLE CAPTIVE (1945)
Universal (USA)
DIR: Harold Young. SCR: M. Coates Webster, Dwight V. Babcock. PH: Maury Gertsman. MUS: Paul Sawtell.
WITH Otto Kruger, Amelita Ward, Vicky Lane, Phil Brown, Jerome Cowan, Rondo Hatton, Eddie Acuff, Ernie Adams.

JUNGLE WOMAN (1944)
Universal (USA)
DIR: Reginald LeBorg. SCR: Bernard Schubert, Henry Sucher, Edward Dein. PH: Jack Mackenzie.
WITH Evelyn Ankers, Acquanetta, J. Carroll Naish, Lois Collier, Samuel S. Hinds, Milburn Stone, Douglass Dumbrille, Nana Bryant, Richard Powers, Alex Craig, Pierre Watkin, Christian Rub.

JUST IMAGINE (1930)
Fox (USA)
DIR: David Butler. SCR: D. Butler; from an original story by DeSylva, Brown, and Henderson. DIAL–MUS–LYR: DeSylva, Brown, and Henderson. PH: Ernest Palmer.
WITH El Brendel, Maureen O'Sullivan, John Garrick, Marjorie White, Frank Albertson, Hobart Bosworth, Kenneth Thompson, Mischa Auer, Sidney De Gray, Wilfred Lucas, Ivan Linow, Joyzelle, J. W. Girard.

KABINETT DES DR. CALIGARI, Das (1920)
Decla-Bioscop (Germany)
DIR: Robert Wiene. SCR: Carl Mayer, Hans Janowitz. DES: Hermann Warm, Walter Reimann, Walter Röhrig. PH: Willie Hameister.
WITH Werner Krauss, Conrad Veidt, Friedrich Feher, Lil Dagover, Hans Heinz von Twardowski, Rudolf Klein-Rogge, Rudolf Lettinger.

KILLERS FROM SPACE (1954)
RKO Radio (USA)
DIR: W. Lee Wilder. SCR: Bill Raynor. PH: William Clothier.
WITH Peter Graves, Barbara Bestar, James Seay, Frank Gerstle, Steve Pendleton, Shep Menken, John Merrick, Jack Daly, Ruth Bennett, Ben Welden, Ron Kennedy, Leslie Dorr.

KING KONG (1933)
RKO Radio (USA)
DIR: Merian C. Cooper, Ernest B. Schoedsack. SCR: James Creelman, Ruth Rose; from an original story by Edgar Wallace and M. C. Cooper. PH: Edward Linden. MUS: Max Steiner. SP. EF.: Willis H. O'Brien.
WITH Fay Wray, Robert Armstrong, Bruce Cabot, Frank Reicher, Sam Hardy, Noble Johnson, James Flavin, Steve Clemento, Victor Wong.

KONGA (1961)
American-International (USA/G.B.)
DIR: John Lemont. PROD: Herman Cohen. SCR: Aben Kandel, Herman Cohen. PH: Desmond Dickinson (Eastmancolor and Spectamation). MUS: Gerard Schurmann.
WITH Michael Gough, Margo Johns, Jess Conrad, Claire Gordon, Austin Trevor, Vanda Godsell, Kim Tracy, Stanley Morgan, Jack Watson.

LADRÓN DE CADÁVERES (1958)
Internacional Cinematográfica (Mexico)
DIR: Fernando Méndez. SCR: Fernando Méndez, Alejandro Verbitzky. PH: Victor Herrera.
WITH Columba Domínguez, Crox Alvarado, Wolf Rubinski, Carlos Riquelme, Arturo Martínez, Eduardo Alcaraz, Guillermo Hernández, Alejandro Cruz, Yerye Berute.

LAST WARNING, The (1929)
Universal (USA)
DIR: Paul Leni. SCR: Alfred A. Cohn. PH: Hal Mohr.
WITH Laura LaPlante, Montagu Love, Roy D'Arcy, Margaret Livingston, John Boles, Bert Roach, Carrie Daumery, Burr McIntosh, Mack Swain, Slim Summerville, Torben Meyer, D'Arcy Corrigan, Bud Phelps, Charles K. French, Fred Kelsey, Tom O'Brien, Harry Northrup.

LEAVES FROM SATAN'S BOOK——see BLADE AM SATANS BOG

LEOPARD MAN (1943)
RKO Radio (USA)
DIR: Jacques Tourneur. PROD: Val Lewton. SCR: Ardel Wray, Edward Dein; from the novel "Black Alibi" by Cornell Woolrich. PH: Robert de Grasse. ED: Mark Robson. MUS: Roy Webb.
WITH Dennis O'Keefe, Jean Brooks, Margo, Isabel Jewell, James Bell, Margaret Landry, Abner Biberman, Richard Martin, Tula Parma, Ben Bard, Ariel Heath, Fely Franquelli.

LIFE WITHOUT SOUL (1915)
Ocean Film Corp. (USA)
DIR: Joseph W. Smiley. SCR: from the novel "Frankenstein" by Mary Shelley.
WITH Percy Darrell Standing, Lucy Cotton, Pauline Curley, Jack Hopkins, George DeCarlton, William W. Cohill.

LIGHT WITHIN, The——MÜDE TOD, Der

LILIOM (1930)
Fox (USA)
DIR: Frank Borzage. SCR: S. N. Behrman, Sonya Levien; from the play by Ferenc Molnar. PH: Chester Lyons.
WITH Charles Farrell, Rose Hobart, Estelle Taylor, Lee Tracy, James Marcus, Walter Abel, Mildred Van Dorn, Bert Roach, H. B. Warner.

LILIOM (1933)
S. A. F. Fox Film (France)
DIR: Fritz Lang. PROD: Erich Pommer. SCR: F. Lang, Robert Liebmann; from the play by Ferenc Molnar. PH: Rudolph Maté, Louis Née. SETS: Paul Colin, René Renoux. MUS: Jean Lenoir, Franz Waxman.
WITH Charles Boyer, Madeleine Ozeray, Florelle, Robert Arnoux, Antonin Artaud, Vivienne Romance, Mila Parély.

LODGER, The (1944)
20th Century-Fox (USA)
DIR: John Brahm. SCR: Barre Lyndon; from the story by Marie Belloc-Lowndes. MUS: Hugo Friedhofer.
WITH Merle Oberon, George Sanders, Laird Cregar, Sir Cedric Hardwicke, Sarah Allgood, Aubrey Mather, Queenie Leonard, Doris Lloyd, David Clyde, Helena Pickard, Lumsden Hare, Frederick Worlock, Olaf Hitten, Anita Bolster, Billy Bevan, Skelton Knaggs, Forrester Harvey, Edmund Breon.

LONDON AFTER MIDNIGHT (1927)
Metro-Goldwyn-Mayer (USA)
DIR: Tod Browning. SCR: Tod Browning, Waldemar Young. PH: Merritt B. Gerstad.
WITH Lon Chaney, Marceline Day, Henry B. Walthall, Percy Williams, Conrad Nagel, Polly Moran, Edna Tichenor, Claude King.

LOST WORLD, The (1925)
First National-Watterson R. Rothacker (USA)
DIR: Harry Hoyt. SCR: Marion Fairfax; from the novel by Arthur Conan Doyle. PH: Arthur Edeson. SP. EF.: Willis H. O'Brien.
WITH Bessie Love, Wallace Beery, Lewis Stone, Lloyd Hughes, Alma Bennett, Arthur Hoyt, Virginia Brown Faire, Bull Montana, Margaret McWade, George Bunny.

LOST WORLD, The (1960)
20th Century-Fox (USA)
DIR: Irwin Allen. SCR: Irwin Allen, Charles Bennett; from the novel by Arthur Conan Doyle. PH: Winton Hoch (DeLuxe Color/CinemaScope). MUS: Paul Sawtell, Bert Shefter.
WITH Michael Rennie, Jill St. John, David Hedison, Claude Rains, Fernando Lamas, Richard Haydn, Ray Stricklyn, Jay Novello, Ian Wolfe, Colin Campbell.

MAD GENIUS, The (1931)
Warner Brothers (USA)
DIR: Michael Curtiz. SCR: J. Grubb Alexander, Harvey Thew; from the story "The Idol" by Martin Brown. PH: Barney McGill.
WITH John Barrymore, Marian Marsh, Donald Cook, Carmel Myers, Charles Buttersworth, Mae Madison, Luis Alberni, Andre Luget, Boris Karloff, Frankie Darro.

MAD LOVE (1935)
Metro-Goldwyn-Mayer (USA)
DIR: Karl Freund. SCR: Guy Endore, P. J. Wolfson, John L. Balderston; from the novel "Les Mains d'Orlac" by Maurice Renard. PH: Chester Lyons, Gregg Toland.
WITH Peter Lorre, Frances Drake, Colin Clive, Ted Healy, Sara Haden, Isabel Jewell, Edward Brophy, Cora Sue Collins, Keye Luke, Henry Kolker, Harold Huber, Charles Trowbridge, May Beatie, Ian Wolfe, Rollo Lloyd, Murray Kinnell.

MAGICIAN, The (1926)
Metro-Goldwyn-Mayer (USA)
DIR: Rex Ingram. SCR: Rex Ingram; from the novel by Somerset Maugham. PH: John F. Seitz.
WITH Alice Terry, Paul Wegener, Ivan Petrovich, Firmin Gemier, Gladys Haner, Stowitts.

MAGNETIC MONSTER, The (1953)
United Artists (USA)
DIR: Curt Siodmak. PROD: Ivan Tors. SCR: Ivan Tors, Curt Siodmak. PH: Charles van Enger.
WITH Richard Carlson, King Donovan, Jean Byron, Jarma Lewis, Harry Ellerbe, Leo Britt, Leonard Mudie, Byron Foulger, Michael Fox, John Zaremba, Frank Gerstle, John Vosper.

MAIN DU DIABLE, La (1942)
Tobis-Continental (France)
DIR: Maurice Tourneur. SCR: Jean-Paul Le Chanois. PH: Armand Thirard. MUS: Roger Dumas.
WITH Pierre Fresnay, Josseline Gaël, Palau, Noel Roquevert, Guillaume de Sax, Andre Varennes, Pierre Larquey.

MAN FROM PLANET X, The (1951)
United Artists-Wisberg-Pollexfen (USA)

DIR: Edgar Ulmer. PROD: Aubrey Wisberg, Jack Pollexfen. SCR: A. Wisberg, J. Pollexfen; from their original story. PH: John L. Russell. MUS: Charles Koff.
WITH Robert Clarke, Margaret Field, Raymond Bond, William Schalert, Roy Engel, Charles Davis, Gilbert Fallman, David Ormont.

MAN THEY COULD NOT HANG, The (1939)
Columbia (USA)
DIR: Nick Grinde. SCR: Karl Brown. PH: Benjamin Kline. MUS: M. W. Stoloff.
WITH Boris Karloff, Lorna Gray, Robert Wilcox, Roger Pryor, Ann Doran, Don Beddoe, Byron Foulger, Joseph deSteffani, Charles Trowbridge, Dick Curtis, James Craig, John Tyrrell.

MAN WHO CHANGED HIS MIND, The (1936)
Gaumont-British (G.B.)
DIR: Robert Stevenson. SCR: L. DuGarde Peach, Sidney Gilliat. PH: Jack Cox.
WITH Boris Karloff, Anna Lee, John Loder, Frank Cellier, Lyn Harding, Cecil Parker, Donald Calthrop.

MAN WHO LAUGHS, The (1928)
Universal (USA)
DIR: Paul Leni. SCR: J. Grubb Alexander; from the novel by Victor Hugo. PH: Gilbert Warrenton.
WITH Conrad Veidt, Mary Philbin, Olga Baclanova, George Siegmann, Brandon Hurst, Cesare Gravina, Stuart Holmes, Josephine Crowell, Sam de Grasse, Edgard Norton, Torben Meyer, Nick de Ruiz, Julius Molner, Zimbo the Dog.

MAN WITH NINE LIVES, The (1940)
Columbia (USA)
DIR: Nick Grinde. SCR: Karl Brown. PH: Benjamin Kline.
WITH Boris Karloff, Jo Ann Sayers, Roger Pryor, Stanley Brown, John Dilson, Byron Foulger, Hal Taliaferro, Charles Trowbridge, Ernie Adams.

MAN-MADE MONSTER (1941)
Universal (USA)
DIR: George Waggner. SCR: Joseph West. PH: Elwood Bredell. MUS: Charles Previn.
WITH Lionel Atwill, Lon Chaney, Jr., Anne Nagel, Frank Albertson, Samuel S. Hinds, William Davidson, Connie Bergen, Ben Taggart,

Ivan Miller, Chester Gan, George Meader, Byron Foulger, Russell Hicks, Frank O'Connor, John Dilson.

MARK OF THE VAMPIRE, The (1935)
Metro-Goldwyn-Mayer (USA)
DIR: Tod Browning. SCR: Guy Endore, Bernard Schubert; from the story by Tod Browning. PH: James Wong Howe.
WITH Lionel Barrymore, Elizabeth Allan, Bela Lugosi, Lionel Atwill, Jean Hersholt, Henry Wadsworth, Donald Meek, Jessie Ralph, Ivan Simpson, Leila Bennett, Carol Borland, Holmes Herbert, June Gittelson, Michael Visaroff.

MASCHERA DEL DEMONIO, La (1960)
Galatea-Jolly Films (Italy)
DIR: Mario Bava. SCR: Ennio DeConcini, Mario Serandrei; from the story "The Vij" by Nikolai Gogol. PH: Ubaldo Terzano. MUS: Les Baxter (for American version), Roberto Nicolosi (for Italian version).
WITH Barbara Steele, John Richardson, Ivo Garrani, Andrea Checci, Arturo Dominici, Enrico Olivieri, Antonio Pierfederici, Clara Bindi, Germana Dominici.

MASK, The (1961)
Julian Roffman (Canada)
DIR: Julian Roffman. SCR: Frank Taubes, Sandy Haber. PH: Herbert S. Alpert. SP.EF.: James B. Gordon (sequences in 3–D). MUS: Louis Applebaum.
WITH Paul Stevens, Claudette Nevins, Bill Walker, Anne Collings, Eleanor Beecroft, William Bryden, Ray Lawlor, Jim Moran, Nancy Island.

MASK OF FU MANCHU, The (1932)
Metro-Goldwyn-Mayer (USA)
DIR: Charles Brabin. SCR: Irene Kuhn, Edgar Woolf, John Willard; from a story by Sax Rohmer. PH: Gaetano Gaudio.
WITH Boris Karloff, Lewis Stone, Karen Morley, Charles Starrett, Myrna Loy, Jean Hersholt, Lawrence Grant, David Torrence.

MASQUE OF THE RED DEATH (1964)
Anglo-Amalgamated/American International (USA/G.B.)
DIR: Roger Corman. SCR: Charles Beaumont, R. Wright Campbell; from the story by Edgar Allan Poe. PH: Nicolas Roeg (Technicolor). MUS: David Lee.
WITH Vincent Price, Hazel Court, Jane Asher, David Weston, Patrick MaGee, Nigel Green, Skip Marten, John Westbrook, Gay Brown,

Julian Burton, Doreen Dawn, Jean Lodge, Verina Greenlaw, Paul Whitsun-Jones, Brian Hewlett.

MAZE, The (1953)
Allied Artists (USA)
DIR: William Cameron Menzies. PROD: Walter Mirisch. SCR: Dan Ullman; from the story by Maurice Sandoz. PH: Harry Neumann (3–D).
WITH Richard Carlson, Veronica Hurst, Katherine Emery, Michael Pate, Lilian Bond, Hillary Brooke, John Dodsworth, Stanley Fraser, Owen McGiveney, Robin Hughes.

METROPOLIS (1926)
UFA (Germany)
DIR: Fritz Lang. SCR: Fritz Lang, Thea von Harbou. PH: Karl Freund, Gunther Rittau. SETS: Otto Hunte, Erich Kettelhut, Karl Vollbrecht.
WITH Brigitte Helm, Alfred Abel, Gustave Froehlich, Rudolf Klein-Rogge, Heinrich George, Fritz Rasp.

MIGHTY JOE YOUNG (1949)
RKO Radio (USA)
DIR: Ernest B. Schoedsack. SCR: Ruth Rose. PH: J. Roy Hunt. SP. EF.: Willis H. O'Brien, assisted by Ray Harryhausen.
WITH Terry Moore, Ben Johnson, Robert Armstrong, Frank McHugh, Douglas Fowley, Dennis Green, Paul Guilfoyle, Nestor Paiva, Regis Toomey, Lora Lee Michel, James Flavin.

MIRACLES FOR SALE (1939)
Metro-Goldwyn-Mayer (USA)
DIR: Tod Browning. SCR: Harry Ruskin, Marion Parsonnet, James E. Grant. PH: Charles Lawton.
WITH Robert Young, Florence Rice, Henry Hull, Astrid Allwyn, Gloria Holden, Frank Craven, Lee Bowman, Cliff Clark, Water Kingsford, Frederic Worlock, William Demarest.

MONOLITH MONSTERS, The (1957)
Universal (USA)
DIR: John Sherwood. SCR: Norman Jolley, Robert M. Fresco; from a story by Jack Arnold, Robert M. Fresco. PH: Ellis W. Carter. SP. PH: Clifford Stine. MUS: Joseph Gershenson.
WITH Grant Williams, Lola Albright, Phil Harvey, Les Tremayne, Trevor Bardette, William Flaherty, Harry Jackson, Richard Cutting, Steve Darrell, Linda Scheley, Dean Cromer.

MONSTER OF FATE, The——see GOLEM, Der (1915)

MONSTER THAT CHALLENGED THE WORLD, The (1957)
United Artists (USA)
DIR: Arnold Laven. SCR: Pat Fielder. PH: Lester White. UNDERWATER PH: Scotty Welbourne. MUS: Heinz Roemheld.
WITH Tim Holt, Audrey Dalton, Hans Conried, Casey Adams, Mimi Gibson, Gordon Jones, Marjorie Stapp, Barbara Darrow, Jody McCrea, William Swan, Charles Tannen, Hal Taggert, Milton Parsons.

MONSTER WALKS, The (1932)
Mayfair (USA)
DIR: Frank Strayer. SCR: Robert Ellis. PH: Jules Cronjager.
WITH Rex Lease, Vera Reynolds, Mischa Auer, Sheldon Lewis, Martha Mattox, Sidney Bracy, Sleep 'n 'Eat (later Willie Best).

MOST DANGEROUS GAME, The (1932)
RKO Radio (USA)
DIR: Irving Pichel, Ernest B. Schoedsack. SCR: James Creelman; from the short story by Richard Connell. PH: Henry Gerrard. MUS: Max Steiner.
WITH Joel McCrea, Fay Wray, Robert Armstrong, Leslie Banks, Hale Hamilton, Noble Johnson.

MOTHRA (1962)
Toho (Japan)
DIR: Inoshiro Honda. SCR: Shinichi Sekizawa. PH: Hajime Koizumi (Eastmancolor/Tohoscope). SP. EF.: Eiji Tsuburuya.
WITH Franky Sakai, Hiroshi Koizumi, Kyoko Kagawa, Emi Itoh, Yumi Itoh, Jelly Itoh, Ken Uehara.

MÜDE TOD, Der (1921)
Decla-Bioscop (Germany)
DIR: Fritz Lang. SCR: Fritz Lang, Thea von Harbou. PH: Erich Nietzchmann, Fritz Arno Wagner, Herman Salfrank. SETS: Hermann Warm, Robert Herlth, Walter Röhrig.
WITH Bernhard Goetzke, Lil Dagover, Walter Janssen, Rudolf Klein-Rogge.

MUMMY, The (1932)
Universal (USA)
DIR: Karl Freund. SCR: John L. Balderston; based on a story by Nina Wilcox Putnam and Richard Schayer. PH: Charles Stumar.
WITH Boris Karloff, Zita Johann, David Manners, Arthur Byron,

Edward Van Sloan, Bramwell Fletcher, Noble Johnson, Leonard Mudie, Henry Victor.

MUMMY, The (1959)
Hammer Films (G.B.)
DIR: Terence Fisher. SCR: Jimmy Sangster. PH: Jack Asher (Technicolor).
WITH Peter Cushing, Christopher Lee, Yvonne Furneaux, Eddie Byrne, Felix Aylmer, Raymond Huntley, John Stuart, Dennis Shaw.

MUMMY'S CURSE, The (1944)
Universal (USA)
DIR: Leslie Goodwins. SCR: Bernard Schubert. PH: Virgil Miller. MUS: Paul Sawtell.
WITH Lon Chaney, Jr., Virginia Christine, Peter Coe, Kay Harding, Dennis Moore, Martin Kosleck, Kurt Katch, Addison Richards, Holmes Herbert, Charles Stevens, William Farnum, Napoleon Simpson.

MUMMY'S GHOST, The (1944)
Universal (USA)
DIR: Reginald LeBorg. SCR: Griffin Jay, Henry Sucher, Brenda Weisberg. PH: William Sickner.
WITH John Carradine, Lon Chaney, Jr., Ramsey Ames, Robert Lowery, Barton MacLane, Claire Whitney, George Zucco, Frank Reicher, Harry Shannon, Emmett Vogan, Lester Sharpe, Oscar O'Shea.

MUMMY'S HAND, The (1940)
Universal (USA)
DIR: Christy Cabanne. SCR: Griffin Jay, Maxwell Shane. PH: Elwood Bredell.
WITH Dick Foran, Peggy Moran, Wallace Ford, Eduardo Ciannelli, George Zucco, Cecil Kellaway, Charles Trowbridge, Tom Tyler, Sigfried Arno, Eddie Foster, Harry Stubbs, Michael Mark, Mara Tarta, Leon Belasco.

MUMMY'S TOMB, The (1942)
Universal (USA)
DIR: Harold Young. SCR: Griffin Jay, Henry Sucher. PH: George Robinson. MUS: H. J. Salter.
WITH Lon Chaney, Jr., Dick Foran, Elyse Knox, John Hubbard, George Zucco, Wallace Ford, Turhan Bey, Virginia Brissac, Cliff Clark, Mary Gordon, Paul Burns, Frank Reicher, Emmett Vogan.

MURDERS IN THE RUE MORGUE (1932)
Universal (USA)
DIR: Robert Florey. SCR: Tom Reed, Dale van Avery; from the story by Edgar Allan Poe.
DIAL: John Huston. PH: Karl Freund.
WITH Bela Lugosi, Sidney Fox, Leon Waycoff (later Ames), Bert Roach, Brandon Hurst, Noble Johnson, D'Arcy Corrigan, Betty Ross Clarke, Arlene Francis.

MY WORLD DIES SCREAMING (1958)
Mowco Int. (USA)
DIR: Harold Daniels. SCR: Robert C. Dennis. PH: Frederick West. MUS: Darrell Calker.
WITH Gerald Mohr, Cathy O'Donnell, William Ching, John Qualen, Barry Bernard.

MYSTERIANS, The——see CHIKYU BOEIGUN

MYSTERIOUS ISLAND (1929)
Metro-Goldwyn-Mayer (USA)
DIR: Lucien Hubbard. SCR: L. Hubbard, Carl L. Pierson; from a novel by Jules Verne. PH: Percy Hilburn (Technicolor).
WITH Lionel Barrymore, Jane Daly, Harry Gribbon, Montague Love, Snitz Edwards, Dolores Brinkman, Gibson Gowland, Lloyd Hughes.

MYSTERIOUS ISLAND (1961)
Columbia (G.B.)
DIR: Cy Endfield. SCR: John Prebble, Daniel Ullman, Crane Wilbur; from a novel by Jules Verne. PH: Wilkie Cooper (Eastmancolor/SuperDynamation). SP. EF.: Ray Harryhausen. MUS: Bernard Herrmann.
WITH Michael Craig, Joan Greenwood, Michael Callan, Gary Merrill, Herbert Lom, Beth Rogan, Percy Herbert, Dan Jackson, Nigel Green.

MYSTERY OF THE WAX MUSEUM (1933)
Warner Brothers (USA)
DIR: Michael Curtiz. SCR: Don Mullaly, Carl Erickson. PH: Ray Ranahan (Technicolor).
WITH Lionel Atwill, Fay Wray, Glenda Farrell, Allen Vincent, Monica Bannister, Gavin Gordon, Frank McHugh, Edwin Maxwell, Arthur Edmund Carewe, DeWitt Jennings, Holmes Herbert, Pat O'Malley.

NANNY, The (1965)
Hammer Films (G.B.)
DIR: Seth Holt. SCR: Jimmy Sangster; based on a novel by Evelyn Piper. PH: Harry Waxman. MUS: Richard Rodney Bennett.
WITH Bette Davis, Wendy Craig, Jill Bennett, James Villiers, William Dix, Pamela Franklin, Jack Watling, Maurice Denham, Nora Gordon, Harry Fowler, Angharad Aubrey.

NIBELUNGEN, DER (1924)
UFA (Germany)
In Two Parts: I–SIEGFRIEDS TOD (SIEGFRIED). II–KRIEMHILDS RACHE (KRIEMHILD'S REVENGE).
DIR: Fritz Lang. SCR: Fritz Lang, Thea von Harbou; adapted from the Germanic saga. PH: Carl Hoffmann, Günther Rittau, Walter Ruttmann. SETS: Otto Hunte, Erich Kettelhut, Karl Vollbrecht; based on paintings of Arnold Böcklin.
WITH Paul Richter, Margaret Schön, Hanna Ralph, Bernhard Goetzke, Theodor Loos, Hans Adalbert von Schlettow, Georg John, Gertrude Arnold, Rudolf Klein-Rogge.

NIGHT IS THE PHANTOM——see FRUSTA E IL CORPO, La

NIGHT OF TERROR (1933)
Columbia (USA)
DIR: Benjamin Stoloff. SCR: Beatrice Van, William Jacobs; from a story by Willard Mack. PH: Joseph Hilton.
WITH Bela Lugosi, Sally Blaine, Wallace Ford, Gertrude Michael, Tully Marshall, George Meeker, Edwin Maxwell, Mary Frey, Oscar Smith, Matt McHugh, Bryant Washburn.

NIGHT OF THE DEMON (1958)
Columbia (G.B.)
DIR: Jacques Tourneur. SCR: Charles Bennett, Hal E. Chester; based on the story "Casting the Runes" by Montague R. James. PH: Ted Scaife. MUS: Clifton Parker.
WITH Dana Andrews, Peggy Cummins, Niall MacGinnis, Maurice Denham, Athene Seyler, Liam Redmond, Reginald Beckwith, Rosamund Greenwood.

NIGHT OF THE EAGLE (1962)
Anglo-Amalgamated (G.B.)
DIR: Sidney Hayers. SCR: Charles Beaumont, Richard Matheson, George Baxt; based on the story "Conjure Wife" by Fritz Lieber. PH: Reginald Wyer.

WITH Janet Blair, Peter Wyngarde, Margaret Johnston, Kathleen Byron, Anthony Nicholls, Colin Gordon, Reginald Beckwith, Jessica Dunning, Norman Bird, Judith Stott, Bill Mitchell.

NOSFERATU, EINE SYMPHONIE DES GRAUENS (1922)
Prana Co. (Germany)
DIR: F. W. Murnau. SCR: Henrik Galeen; from the novel "Dracula" by Bram Stoker. PH: Fritz Arno Wagner. SETS: Albin Grau.
WITH Max Schreck, Alexander Granach, Gustav von Wangenheim, Greta Schroeder, Ruth Landshoff.

OLD DARK HOUSE (1932)
Universal (USA)
DIR: James Whale. SCR: Benn W. Levy; from the novel "Benighted" by J. B. Priestley; DIAL: R. C. Sherriff. PH: Arthur Edeson.
WITH Boris Karloff, Melvyn Douglas, Charles Laughton, Gloria Stuart, Lilian Bond, Ernest Thesiger, Eva Moore, Raymond Massey, Brember Wells, John Dudgeon.

ON BORROWED TIME (1939)
Metro-Goldwyn-Mayer (USA)
DIR: Harold S. Bucquet. SCR: Alice Duer Miller, Frank O'Neill, Claudine West; from the play by Paul Osborne and Lawrence Watkin. PH: Joseph Ruttenberg.
WITH Lionel Barrymore, Sir Cedric Hardwicke, Beulah Bondi, Una Merkel, Bobs Watson, Henry Travers, Nat Pendleton, Eily Malyon, Grant Mitchell, Ian Wolfe, Philip Terry, Charles Waldron, Truman Bradley.

ONE EXCITING NIGHT (1922)
United Artists (USA)
DIR: D. W. Griffith. SCR: from a story by Irene Sinclair. PH: Hendrick Sartov.
WITH Carol Dempster, Henry Hull, Morgan Wallace, Porter Strong, Margaret Dale, Grace Griswold, Irma Harrison.

ONE MILLION B.C. (1940)
United Artists (USA)
DIR: Hal Roach, Hal Roach, Jr., D. W. Griffith. SCR: Mickell Novak, George Baker, Joseph Frickert. PH: Norbert Brodine. SP. EF.: Roy Seawright. MUS: Werner R. Heymann. NARR: Conrad Nagel.

WITH Victor Mature, Carole Landis, Lon Chaney, Jr., Mamo Clarke, Nigel deBrulier, Inez Palange, John Hubbard, Jean Porter, Norman Budd, Mary Gale Fisher, Jacqueline Dalya, Edgar Edwards.

ORLACS HAENDE (1925)
Pan-film (Austria)
DIR: Robert Wiene. PH: Günter Krampf. SCR: Ludwig Kerzt; from the novel by Maurice Renard. SETS: Stefan Wessely.
WITH Conrad Veidt, Alexandra Sorina, Carmen Cartellieri, Fritz Kortner.

ORPHÉE (1950)
Andre Paulve-Films du Palais Royal (France)
DIR–SCR: Jean Cocteau. PH: Nicholas Hayer. SETS: D'Eaubonne. COST: Marcel Escoffier. MUS: Georges Auric.
WITH Jean Marais, François Perier, Maria Casarés, Marie Déa, Henri Cremiux, Jacques Varennes, Pierre Bertin, Juliette Gréco, Roger Blin, Edouard Dermithe.

ORPHEUS——see ORPHÉE

PEEPING TOM (1960)
Anglo-Amalgamated/Archers (G.B.)
DIR–PROD: Michael Powell. SCR: Leo Marks. PH: Otto Heller (Technicolor). MUS: Brian Easdale.
WITH Carl Boehm, Moira Shearer, Anna Massey, Maxine Audley, Esmond Knight, Bartlett Mullins, Shirley Ann Field, Michael Goodliffe, Brenda Bruce.

PETER IBBETSON (1935)
Paramount (USA)
DIR: Henry Hathaway. SCR: Vincent Lawrence, Waldemar Young, Constance Collier, John Meehan, Edwin Justus Mayer; taken from the play by John Nathaniel Raphael based on the novel by George Du Maurier. PH: Charles Lang, Gordon Jennings.
WITH Gary Cooper, Ann Harding, Ida Lupino, John Halliday, Douglas Dumbrille, Virginia Weidler, Dickie Moore, Doris Lloyd, Elsa Buchanan, Christian Rub, Donald Meek, Gilbert Emery, Elsa Prescott, Marcelle Corday, Colin Tapley, Adrienne d'Ambricourt, Theresa Maxwell Conover, Olive Morgan, Ambrose Barker, Thomas Monk, Blanche Craig.

PHANTOM FROM SPACE (1953)
United Artists (USA)
DIR: W. Lee Wilder. SCR: Bill Raynor, Miles Wilder. PH: William Clothier.
WITH Ted Cooper, Noreen Nash, James Seay, Rudolph Anders, Harry Landers, Jack Daly.

PHANTOM OF THE OPERA, The (1925)
Universal (USA)
DIR: Rupert Julian. PROD: Carl Laemmle. SCR: Raymond Shrock, Elliot Clawson; based on the novel by Gaston Leroux. PH: Charles van Enger, Virgil Miller, Milton Bridenbecker (Technicolor seq.). ASST. DIR.: Edward Sedgwick.
WITH Lon Chaney, Mary Philbin, Norman Kerry, Snitz Edwards, Gibson Gowland, John St. Polis, Virginia Pearson, Arthur Edmund Carewe, Edith Yorke, Anton Vaverka, Bernard Siegel, John Miljan, Olive Ann Alcorn, Edward Cecil, Alexander Bevani, Grace Marvin, George B. Williams, Bruce Covington, Cesare Gravina.

PHANTOM OF THE OPERA, The (1943)
Universal (USA)
DIR: Arthur Lubin. PROD: George Waggner. SCR: Erich Taylor, Samuel Hoffenstein. PH: Hal Mohr, W. Howard Greene (Technicolor). MUS: Edward Ward.
WITH Nelson Eddy, Susanna Foster, Claude Rains, Edgar Barrier, Leo Carillo, Jane Farrar, J. Edward Bromberg, Hume Cronyn, Barbara Everest, Gladys Blake, Miles Mander, Kate Lawson, Fritz Leiber, Paul Marion, Rosina Galli.

PHANTOM OF THE OPERA, The (1962)
Hammer Films (G.B.)
DIR: Terence Fisher. PROD: Anthony Hinds. SCR: John Elder. PH: Arthur Grant (Eastmancolor). MUS: Edwin Astley.
WITH Herbert Lom, Heather Sears, Thorley Walters, Edward de Souza, Michael Gough, Miriam Karlin, Marne Maitland, Michael Ripper, Renee Houston, Harold Goodwin, Sonya Cordeau, Patrick Throughton, Liane Aukin, Leila Forde.

PHANTOM OF THE RUE MORGUE (1954)
Warner Brothers (USA)
DIR: Roy del Ruth. SCR: Harold Medford, James R. Webb; based on the story "Murders in the Rue Morgue" by Edgar Allan Poe. PH: J. Peverell Marley (3-D; Warnercolor).

WITH Karl Malden, Claude Dauphin, Patricia Medina, Steve Forrest, Allyn McLerie, Veola Vonn, Dolores Dorn, Anthony Caruso, Merv Griffin, Erin O'Brien-Moore, Paul Richards, The Flying Zacchinis.

PICTURE OF DORIAN GRAY, The (1945)
Metro-Goldwyn-Mayer (USA)
DIR: Albert Lewin. SCR: A. Lewin; from the novel by Oscar Wilde. PH: Harry Stradling (Technicolor seq.).
WITH George Sanders, Hurd Hatfield, Donna Reed, Angela Lansbury, Peter Lawford, Lowell Gilmore, Richard Fraser, Douglas Walton, Morton Lowry, Miles Mander, Lilian Bond, Mary Forbes, Billy Bevan, Lydia Bilbrook, Moyna MacGill, Robert Greig.

PILLOW OF DEATH (1946)
Universal (USA)
DIR: Wallace Fox. SCR: George Bricker. PH: Jerome Ash. MUS: Frank Skinner.
WITH Lon Chaney, Jr., Brenda Joyce, Rosalind Ivan, J. Edward Bromberg, Clara Blandick, Wilton Graff, Victoria Horne, George Cleveland, Fern Emmett, J. Farrell MacDonald, Bernard B. Thomas.

PIT AND THE PENDULUM, The (1961)
American-International (USA)
DIR–PROD: Roger Corman. SCR: Richard Matheson; from the story by Edgar Allan Poe. PH: Floyd Crosby (Technicolor; CinemaScope). MUS: Les Baxter.
WITH Vincent Price, John Kerr, Barbara Steele, Luana Anders, Anthony Carbone, Patrick Westwood, Lynne Bernay, Larry Turner, Mary Menzies, Charles Victor.

PLAGUE OF THE ZOMBIES (1966)
Hammer Films (G.B.)
DIR: John Gilling. SCR: Peter Bryan. PH: Arthur Grant (Technicolor). MUS: James Bernard.
WITH Andre Morell, Diane Clare, Jacqueline Pearce, Brook Williams, John Carson, Alex Davion, Michael Ripper, Tim Condron, Bernard Egan, Normann Mann, Francis Wiley.

PLANET OF THE VAMPIRES——see TERRORE NELLO SPAZIO

PLANET BURA (1962)
New Realm (U.S.S.R.)
DIR: Pavel Klushantsev. SCR: P. Klushantsev, Alexander Kazantsev. PH: Arkady Klimov (Sovcolor).

WITH Kyunna Ignatova, Gennadi Vernov, Vladimir Yemelianov, Yurie Sarantsev, Georgi Zhonov.

PREMATURE BURIAL, The (1962)
American-International (USA)
DIR–PROD: Roger Corman. SCR: Charles Beaumont, Ray Russell; from the story by Edgar Allan Poe. PH: Floyd Crosby (Pathecolor/ Panavision). MUS: Ronald Stein.
WITH Ray Milland, Hazel Court, Richard Ney, Heather Angel, Alan Napier, John Dierkes, Richard Miller.

PSYCHO (1960)
Paramount (USA)
DIR–PROD: Alfred Hitchcock. SCR: Joseph Stefano; from the novel by Robert Bloch. PH: John L. Russell. MUS: Bernard Herrmann.
WITH Anthony Perkins, Janet Leigh, Vera Miles, John Gavin, Martin Balsam, John McIntyre, Simon Oakland, Frank Albertson, Pat Hitchcock, Vaughn Taylor, Lurene Tuttle, John Anderson, Mort Mills.

PURITAN PASSIONS (1923)
Film Guild-Hodkinson (USA)
DIR: Frank Tuttle. SCR: Frank Tuttle, A. Cleelman; from "The Scarecrow" by Percy MacKaye. PH: Fred Waller.
WITH Glenn Hunter, Mary Astor, Osgood Perkins, Frank Tweed, Maude Hill.

QUATERMASS EXPERIMENT, The (1955)
Hammer Films (G.B.)
DIR: Val Guest. SCR: Richard Landau, Val Guest; based on a TV play by Nigel Kneale. PH: Jimmy Harvey. SP. EF.: Leslie Bowie.
WITH Brian Donlevy, Jack Warner, Margia Dean, Richard Wordsworth, Thora Hird, David King Wood, Harold Lang, Gordon Jackson, Lionel Jeffries, Maurice Kauffman.

RAPTUS (1962)
Panda (Italy)
DIR: Robert Hampton (Riccardo Freda). SCR: Julyan Perry. PH: Donald Green (Raffaele Masciocchi) - (Technicolor/Panavision).

WITH Barbara Steele, Robert Flemyng, Montgomery Glenn, Maria Teresa Vianello, Harriet White, Spencer William.

RAVEN, The (1935)
Universal (USA)
DIR: Louis Friedlander (Lew Landers). SCR: David Boehm; inspired by the story by Edgar Allan Poe. PH: Charles Stumar.
WITH Boris Karloff, Bela Lugosi, Irene Ware, Lester Matthews, Inez Courtney, Samuel S. Hinds, Ian Wolfe, Spencer Charters, Maidel Turner, Arthur Hoyt.

RAVEN, The (1963)
American-International (USA)
DIR–PROD: Roger Corman. SCR: Richard Matheson; from the story by Edgar Allan Poe. PH: Floyd Crosby (Panavision/Pathecolor). MUS: Les Baxter.
WITH Vincent Price, Peter Lorre, Boris Karloff, Hazel Court, Olive Sturgess, Jack Nicholson, Connie Wallace.

RED PLANET MARS (1952)
United Artists-Veiller-Hyde (USA)
DIR: Harry Horner. SCR: John L. Balderston, Anthony Veiller. PH: Joseph Biroc. MUS: David Chudnow.
WITH Peter Graves, Andrea King, Orley Lindgren, Bayard Veiller, Walter Sande, Marvin Miller, Herbert Berghof, Willis Bouchey, Richard Powers, Morris Ankrum, House Peters, Vince Barnett, Gene Roth, Grace Leonard, Bill Kennedy.

REPTILE, The (1966)
Hammer Films (G.B.)
DIR: John Gilling. SCR: John Elder. PH: Arthur Grant (Technicolor). MUS: Don Banks.
WITH Noel Willman, Jennifer Daniel, Jacqueline Pearce, Ray Barrett, Michael Ripper, John Laurie, Marne Maitland, David Baron, Charles Lloyd Pack.

REPULSION (1965)
Royal Films International (G.B.)
DIR: Roman Polanski. SCR: Roman Polanski, Gerard Brach. PH: Gil Taylor. MUS: Chico Hamilton.
WITH Catherine Deneuve, Ian Hendry, John Fraser, Yvonne Furneaux, Patrick Wymark, Renee Houston, Helen Fraser, Valerie Taylor,

James Villiers, Hugh Futcher, Mike Pratt, Monica Merlin, Imogen Graham.

RETURN OF DR. X, The (1939)
Warner Brothers (USA)
DIR: Vincent Sherman. SCR: Lee Katz. PH: Sid Hickox.
WITH Humphrey Bogart, Rosemary Lane, Dennis Morgan, Wayne Morris, Lya Lys, John Litel, Olin Howland, Huntz Hall, Vera Lewis, Charles Wilson, Howard Hickman, Arthur Aylsworth, Creighton Hale, Joseph Crehan, Jack Mower.

RETURN OF THE FLY, The (1959)
20th Century-Fox (USA)
DIR–SCR: Edward L. Bernds. PH: Brydon Baker (Cinemascope). MUS: Paul Sawtell.
WITH Vincent Price, Brett Halsey, David Frankham, John Sutton, Dan Seymour, Danielle de Metz, Florence Strom, Janine Grandel, Richard Flato, Pat O'Hara.

RETURN OF THE VAMPIRE, The (1944)
Columbia (USA)
DIR: Lew Landers. SCR: Griffin Jay. PH: John Stumar. L. W. O'Connell. MUS: M. W. Stoloff.
WITH Bela Lugosi, Nina Foch, Frieda Inescort, Miles Mander, Roland Varno, Matt Willis, Ottola Nesmith, Gilbert Emery, Leslie Denison.

REVENGE OF FRANKENSTEIN, The (1958)
Hammer Films (G.B.)
DIR: Terence Fisher. SCR: Jimmy Sangster. PH: Jack Asher (Technicolor). MUS: Leonard Salzedo.
WITH Peter Cushing, Francis Mathews, Eunice Gayson, Michael Gwynn, John Welsh, Lionel Jeffries, Oscar Quitak, John Stuart, Arnold Diamond, Charles Lloyd Pack.

REVOLT OF THE ZOMBIES (1936)
Halperin Pictures (USA)
DIR: Victor Halperin. SCR: Howard Higgin, Rollo Lloyd, V. Halperin. PH: J. Arthur Feindel.
WITH Dorothy Stone, Dean Jagger, Roy D'Arcy, Robert Noland, George Cleveland, Fred Warren, Carl Stockdale, Teru Shimada, William Crowell.

ROBINSON CRUSOE ON MARS (1964)
Paramount (USA)
DIR: Byron Haskin. SCR: Ib Melchior, John Higgins. PH: Winton C. Hoch (Techniscope/Technicolor). MUS: Van Cleave.
WITH Paul Mantee, Vic Lundin, Adam West.

ROCKET SHIP XM (1950)
Lippert (USA)
DIR–PROD: Kurt Neumann. SCR: Kurt Neumann, from his original story. PH: Karl Struss. MUS: Ferde Grofé.
WITH Lloyd Bridges, Osa Massen, John Emery, Noah Beery, Jr., Hugh O'Brien, Morris Ankrum.

RUN FOR THE SUN (1956)
United Artists (USA)
DIR: Roy Boulting. SCR: Dudley Nichols, Roy Boulting; from the story "The Most Dangerous Game" by Richard Connell. PH: Joe LaShelle (Technicolor/Superscope).
WITH Richard Widmark, Jane Greer, Trevor Howard, Peter Van Eyck, Carlos Henning.

SANTO CONTRA LAS MUJERES VAMPIRO (1962)
Tele/Cine/Radio (Mexico)
DIR–SCR: Alfonso Corona Blake. PH: Manuel Gonzalez. MUS: Raul Lavista.
WITH "Santo," Lorena Velazquez, Maria Duval, Jaime Fernandez, Ofelia Montesco, Laura Marquetti, Ray Mendoza, Black Shadow, Cavernario Galindo.

SCHLOSS VOGELÖD (1921)
Decla-Bioscop (Germany)
DIR: F. W. Murnau. PH: Fritz Arno Wagner. SCR: Carl Mayer, Berthold Viertel; from the novel by Rudolf Stratz.
WITH Paul Hartmann, Olga Tschechowa, Arnold Korff, Paul Bildt.

SEI DONNE PER L'ASSASSINO (1964)
Emmepi/de Beauregard/Monachia (Italy)
DIR: Mario Bava. SCR: Mario Bava, Marcello Fondato, Giuseppe Barilla. PH: Ubaldo Terzano (Eastmancolor). MUS: Carlo Rustichelli.
WITH Eva Bartok, Cameron Mitchell, Mary Arden, Arianna Gorini, Claude Dantes, Harriet White, Francesca Ungaro, Lea Kruger, Nadia Anty, Mara Carminoso, Heidi Stroh.

SEVEN FOOTPRINTS TO SATAN (1929)
First National (USA)
DIR: Benjamin Christensen. SCR: Richard Bee; TITLES: William Irish; from a story by Abraham Merritt. PH: Sol Polito.
WITH Thelma Todd, Creighton Hale, William V. Mong, Sheldon Lewis, Sojin, Laska Winters, Ivan Christy, DeWitt Jennings, Nora Cecil, Kalla Pasha, Harry Tenbrooke, Cissy Fitzgerald, Alonzo Rositto, Thelma McNeil.

SEVENTH VICTIM, The (1943)
RKO Radio (USA)
PROD: Val Lewton. DIR: Mark Robson. SCR: DeWitt Bodeen, Charles O'Neal. PH: Nicholas Musuraca. MUS: Roy Webb.
WITH Tom Conway, Jean Brooks, Isabel Jewell, Kim Hunter, Evelyn Brent, Erford Gage, Ben Bard, Hugh Beaumont, Chef Milani, Marguerita Sylva, Mary Newton, Wally Brown, Feodor Chaliapin, Elizabeth Russell.

SEVENTH VOYAGE OF SINBAD, The (1958)
Columbia (USA)
DIR: Nathan Juran. SCR: Kenneth Kolb. PH: Wilkie Cooper (Technicolor/Dynamation). SP. EF.: Ray Harryhausen. MUS: Bernard Herrmann.
WITH Kerwin Mathews, Kathryn Grant, Richard Eyer, Torin Thatcher, Alec Mango, Virgilio Teixeira, Nino Falanga, Luis Guedes, Harold Kasket, Nana de Herrera.

SHAPE OF THINGS TO COME (1936)
London Films (G.B.)
PROD: Alexander Korda. DIR: William Cameron Menzies. SCR: H. G. Wells; from his writings. PH: George Perinal. SP. EF.: Harry Zech. MUS: Arthur Bliss.
WITH Raymond Massey, Ralph Richardson, Sophie Stewart, Margareta Scott, Maurice Braddell, Edward Chapman, Pearl Argyle, Sir Cedric Hardwicke, Derrick de Marney, Allan Jeayes, Patricia Hilliard.

SKULL, The (1965)
Amicus (G.B.)
DIR: Freddie Francis. SCR: Milton Subotsky. PH: John Wilcox (Techniscope/Technicolor). MUS: Elizabeth Lutyens.
WITH Peter Cushing, Patrick Wymark, Jill Bennett, Christopher Lee, Nigel Green, April Olrich, Michael Gough, George Coulouris,

Patrick Magee, Peter Woodthorpe, Maurice Good, Frank Forsyth, Anna Palic.

SNIPER, The (1952)
Columbia-Kramer (USA)
DIR: Edward Dmytryk. SCR: Edward and Edna Anhalt. PH: Burnett Guffey. MUS: Morris Stoloff.
WITH Adolphe Menjou, Arthur Franz, Marie Windsor, Frank Faylen, Richard Kiley, Mabel Paige, Marlo Dwyer, Geraldine Carr, Jay Novello, Ralph Peters, Max Palmer, Sidney Miller, Dani Sue Nolan, Cliff Clark.

SON OF DRACULA (1943)
Universal (USA)
DIR: Robert Siodmak. SCR: Eric Taylor; from an original idea by Curt Siodmak. PH: George Robinson. MUS: H. J. Salter.
WITH Lon Chaney, Jr., Robert Paige, Louise Allbritton, Evelyn Ankers, Frank Craven, J. Edward Bromberg, Samuel S. Hinds, Adeline DeWalt Reynolds, Patrick Moriarity, Etta McDaniel, George Irving.

SON OF FRANKENSTEIN (1939)
Universal (USA)
DIR: Rowland V. Lee. SCR: Willis Cooper; based on characters created by Mary Shelley. PH: George Robinson.
WITH Basil Rathbone, Boris Karloff, Bela Lugosi, Josephine Hutchinson, Lionel Atwill, Emma Dunn, Donnie Dunnagan, Gustav von Seyffertitz, Edgar Norton.

SON OF KONG (1933)
RKO Radio (USA)
DIR: Ernest B. Schoedsack. SCR: from a story by Ruth Rose. PH: Eddie Linden, Vernon Walker, J. O. Taylor. Sp. EF.: Willis H. O'Brien. MUS: Max Steiner.
WITH Robert Armstrong, Helen Mack, Frank Reicher, John Marston, Victor Wong, Ed Brady, Katherine Ward, Lee Kohlmar, Gertrude Sutton, Gertrude Short, Noble Johnson, Clarence Wilson.

SORROWS OF SATAN, The (1925)
Paramount (USA)
DIR: D. W. Griffith. SCR: Forrest Halsey; from the novel by Marie Corelli. PH: Harry Fischbeck.

WITH Adolphe Menjou, Carol Dempster, Lya de Putti, Ricardo Cortez, Ivan Lebedeff, Marcia Harris, Nellie Savage, Dorothy Hughes, Lawrence D'Orsay.

SPACE CHILDREN, The (1958)
Paramount (USA)
DIR: Jack Arnold. SCR: Bernard C. Schoenfeld. MUS: Van Cleave. PH: Ernest Laszlo.
WITH Michael Ray, Adam Williams, Peggy Weber, Johnny Washbrook, Jackie Coogan, Richard Shannon, Raymond Bailey, Sandy Descher, Larry Pennell, John Crawford, Russell Johnson.

SPACEWAYS (1953)
Hammer Films (G.B.)
DIR: Terence Fisher. SCR: Paul Tabori, Richard Landau; from a radio play by Charles Eric Maine. PH: Reginald Wyer. MUS: Ivor Slanfy.
WITH Howard Duff, Eva Bartok, Andrew Osborn, Alan Weatley, Phillip Leaver, Michael Medwin, Cecile Chevreau, Anthony Ireland, David Horne.

SPETTRO, Lo (1963)
Panda (Italy)
DIR: Robert Hampton (Riccardo Freda). SCR: Riccardo Freda, Robert Davidson (Oreste Biancoli). PH: Donald Green (Raffaele Masciocchi) - (Technicolor/Panavision). MUS: Frank Wallace (Franco Mannino), Roman Vlad.
WITH Barbara Steele, Peter Baldwin, Leonard Elliott (Elio Jotta), Harriet White, Umberto Raho, Charles Kechler, Reginald Price Anderson, Carol Bennet.

SPHINX, The (1933)
Monogram (USA)
DIR: Phil Rosen. SCR: Albert de Mond. PH: Gilbert Warrenton.
WITH Lionel Atwill, Sheila Terry, Theodore Newton, Paul Hurst, Luis Alberni, Robert Ellis, Lucien Prival, Paul Fix, Lillian Leighton, Hooper Atchley, Wilfred Lucas, George Hayes.

SPIDERS, The——see SPINNEN, Die

SPINNEN, Die (1919)
In Two Parts: I–DER GOLDENE SEE (THE GOLDEN LAKE). II–DAS BRILLANTEN SCHIFF (THE DIAMOND SHIP).
Decla-Bioscop (Germany)

DIR–SCR: Fritz Lang. PH: (I) Emile Schünemann; (II) Karl Freund. SETS: Otto Hunte, Carl Kirmse.
WITH Lil Dagover, Carl de Vogt, Ressel Orla, Georg John, Paul Morgan, Bruno Lettinger.

SPIONE (1927)
Fritz Lang Film G.M.B.H.-UFA (Germany)
DIR: Fritz Lang. SCR: Fritz Lang, Thea von Harbou. PH: Fritz Arno Wagner. SETS: Otto Hunte, Karl Vollbrecht.
WITH Rudolf Klein-Rogge, Gerda Maurus, Willy Fritsch, Lupu Pick, Fritz Rasp, Hertha von Walther, Craighall Sherry, Paul Hoerbiger, Grete Berger, Lien Dyers.

STEINERNE REITER, Der (1923)
Decla-Bioscop (Germany)
DIR: Fritz Wendhausen. SCR: Thea von Harbou. PH: Karl Hoffmann. SETS: Heinrich Heuser.
WITH Rudolf Klein-Rogge, Lucie Mannheim, Georg John, Fritz Kampers, Gustav von Wangenheim, Paul Biensfeldt, Otto Framer.

STONE RIDER——see STEINERNE REITER, Der

STORM PLANET——see PLANETA BURA

STRANGE CONFESSION (1945)
Universal (USA)
DIR: John Hoffman. SCR: M. Coates Webster. PH: Maury Gertsman. MUS: Frank Skinner.
WITH Lon Chaney, Jr., Brenda Joyce, Milburn Stone, Lloyd Bridges, Addison Richards, Mary Gordon, George Chandler, Wilton Graff, Francis McDonald, Jack Norton, Christian Rub.

STUDENT VON PRAG (1913)
Bioscop (Germany)
DIR: Stellan Rye. SCR: Hanns Heinz Ewers. PH: Guido Seeber. SETS: Robert A. Dietrich, K. Richter.
WITH Paul Wegener, John Gottowt, Greta Berger, Lyda Salmonova, Lothar Körner.

STUDENT VON PRAG (1926)
Sokal (Germany)
DIR: Henrik Galeen. SCR: Henrik Galeen; from a novel by H. H. Ewers. PH: Günther Krampf, Erich Nitzschmann. SETS: Hermann Warm.

WITH Conrad Veidt, Agnes Esterhazy, Eliza La Porta, Werner Krauss, Ferdinand von Alten.

SUPERNATURAL (1933)
Paramount (USA)
DIR: Victor Halperin. SCR: Harvey Thew, Brian Marlowe; from a story by Garnett Weston. PH: Arthur Martinelli.
WITH Carole Lombard, Randolph Scott, Vivienne Osborne, Allan Dinehart, H. B. Warner, Beryl Mercer, William Farnum, Willard Robertson, George Burr McAnnan, Lyman Williams.

SVENGALI (1931)
Warner Brothers (USA)
DIR: Archie Mayo. SCR: J. Grubb Alexander; from the novel "Trilby" by George Du Maurier. PH: Barney McGill.
WITH John Barrymore, Marian Marsh, Carmel Myers, Luis Alberni, Donald Crisp, Lumsden Hare, Bramwell Fletcher, Paul Porcasi.

TALES OF TERROR (1962)
American-International (USA)
DIR–PROD: Roger Corman. SCR: Richard Matheson; from stories by Edgar Allan Poe. PH: Floyd Crosby (Pathecolor).
WITH Vincent Price, Basil Rathbone, Peter Lorre, Debra Paget, Joyce Jameson, David Frankham, Maggie Pierce, Leona Gage.

TARANTULA (1955)
Universal (USA)
DIR: Jack Arnold. SCR: Martin Berkeley. PH: George Robinson. MUS: Joseph Gershenson.
WITH John Agar, Mara Corday, Leo G. Carroll, Nestor Paiva, Ross Elliott, Ed Rand.

TENTH VICTIM, The—see DECIMA VITTIMA, La

TERROR, The (1928)
Warner Brothers (USA)
DIR: Roy del Ruth. SCR: Harvey Gates; from a play by Edgar Wallace. PH: Barney McGill.
WITH May McAvoy, Louise Fazenda, Edward Everett Horton, Alec B. Francis, Matthew Betz, Holmes Herbert, John Miljan, Otto Hoffman, Joseph Girard, Frank Austin.

TERROR, The (1963)
American-International (USA)
DIR–PROD: Roger Corman. SCR: Leo Gordon, Jack Hill. PH: John Nicholaus (Vistascope/Pathecolor). MUS: Arnold Stein.
WITH Boris Karloff, Jack Nicholson, Sandra Knight, Richard Miller, Dorothy Neumann, Jonathan Haze.

TERROR FROM THE YEAR 5000 (1958)
American-International (USA)
DIR–PROD–SCR: Robert J. Gurney, Jr. PH: Arthur Florman.
WITH Ward Costello, Joyce Holden, John Stratton, Frederic Downs.

TERRORE NELLO SPAZIO (1965)
American-International (USA/Italy)
DIR: Mario Bava. SCR: Ib Melchior, Louis M. Heyward. PH: Antonio Rinaldi (ColorScope).
WITH Barry Sullivan, Norma Bengell, Angel Aranda, Evi Marandi, Fernando Villena, Mario Morales, Franco Andrei.

TESTAMENT DES DR. MABUSE, Das (1932)
Nero Filmgesellschaft (Germany)
DIR: Fritz Lang. SCR: Fritz Lang, Thea von Harbou. PH: Fritz Arno Wagner. SETS: Karl Vollbrecht, Emil Hasler.
WITH Rudolf Klein-Rogge, Otto Wernicke, Gustav Diesl, Oscar Beregi, Vera Liessem, Camilla Spira.
(There was a version filmed simultaneously in the French language.)

TESTAMENT DU DR. CORDELIER, Le (1961)
Jean Renoir-Sofirad (France)
DIR: Jean Renoir. SCR: J Renoir; based on the novel "Dr. Jekyll and Mr. Hyde" by Robert Louis Stevenson. PH: Georges Leclerc. MUS: Joseph Kosma.
WITH Jean-Louis Barrault, Michel Vitold, Teddy Bilis, Jean Topart, Micheline Gary, Jacques Dannouville, André Certes, Jean-Pierre Granval, Jacqueline Morane, Gaston Modot.

THEM! (1954)
Warner Brothers (USA)
DIR: Gordon Douglas. SCR: Ted Sherdeman. PH: Sid Hickox.
WITH James Whitmore, Edmund Gwenn, Joan Weldon, James Arness, Onslow Stevens, Sandy Descher, Mary Ann Hokanson, Chris Drake, Sean McClory, Don Shelton, Fess Parker, Olin Howlin.

THESE ARE THE DAMNED——see DAMNED, The

THIEF OF BAGDAD, The (1940)
London Films (G.B.)
DIRS: Ludwig Berger, Michael Powell, Tim Whelan, SCR: Lajos Biro, Miles Malleson. SP. EF.: Lawrence Butler. PH: George Perinal, Osmond Borradaile (Technicolor). MUS: Miklos Rozsa.
WITH Conrad Veidt, Sabu, June Duprez, Mary Morris, John Justin, Rex Ingram, Miles Malleson, Hay Petrie, Adelaide Hall, Morton Selten, Bruce Winston, Roy Emerton, Allan Jeayes.

THING, The (1951)
RKO Radio (USA)
PROD: Howard Hawks. DIR: Christian Nyby. SCR: Charles Lederer; from the story "Who Goes There?" by John W. Campbell, Jr. PH: Russell Harlan. MUS: Dimitri Tiomkin.
WITH Margaret Sheridan, Kenneth Tobey, Robert Cornthwaite, Douglas Spencer, James Young, Dewey Martin, Robert Nichols, William Self, Eduard Franz, Sally Creighton, James Arness.

THINGS TO COME——see SHAPE OF THINGS TO COME

THIRTEEN GHOSTS (1960)
Columbia (USA)
DIR–PROD: William Castle. SCR: Robb White. PH: Joseph Biroc (Stereoscopic seq.). MUS: Von Dexter.
WITH Charles Herbert, Jo Morrow, Martin Milner, Rosemary De Camp, Donald Woods, Margaret Hamilton, John van Dreelen.

THIRTEENTH CHAIR, The (1929)
Metro-Goldwyn-Mayer (USA)
DIR: Tod Browning. SCR: Elliot Clawson; from a play by Bayard Veiller. PH: Merritt B. Gerstad.
WITH Conrad Nagel, Leila Hyams, Margaret Wycherly, Helene Millard, Holmes Herbert, Mary Forbes, Bela Lugosi, John Davidson, Charles Quartermaine, Moon Carroll, Cyril Chadwick, Bertram Johns, Gretchen Holland, Frank Leigh, Clarence Geldert, Lal Chand Mehra.

THIS ISLAND EARTH (1955)
Universal (USA)
DIR: Joseph Newman. SCR: Franklin Coen, Edward O'Callaghan. PH: Clifford Stine (Technicolor). MUS: Herman Stein.
WITH Jeff Morrow, Faith Domergue, Rex Reason, Lance Fuller, Russell Johnson, Robert Nichols, Douglas Spencer, Karl Lindt, Regis Parton.

THREE LIGHTS, The——see MÜDE TOD, Der

THREE WORLDS OF GULLIVER, The (1960)
Columbia (G.B.)
DIR: Jack Sher. SCR: Arthur Ross, Jack Sher; from the novel "Gulliver's Travels" by Jonathan Swift. PH: Wilkie Cooper (Eastmancolor/Superdynamation). SP. EF.: Ray Harryhausen. MUS: Bernard Herrmann.
WITH Kerwin Mathews, Jo Morrow, June Thorburn, Lee Patterson, Gregoire Aslan, Basil Sydney, Martin Benson, Marian Spencer, Peter Bull, Alec Mango, Sherry Alberoni.

TINGLER, The (1959)
Columbia (USA)
DIR–PROD: William Castle. SCR: Robb White. PH: Wilfrid M. Cline. MUS: Von Dexter.
WITH Judith Evelyn, Vincent Price, Darryl Hickman, Patricia Cutts, Philip Coolidge.

TOMB OF LIGEIA, The (1964)
Anglo-Amalgamated/American-International (G.B.)
DIR: Roger Corman. SCR: Robert Towne; from the tale "Ligeia" by Edgar Allan Poe. PH: Arthur Grant (Scope/Color). MUS: Kenneth V. Jones.
WITH Vincent Price, Elizabeth Shepherd, John Westbrook, Oliver Johnston, Derek Francis, Richard Vernon, Ronald Adam, Frank Adam, Frank Thornton, Denis Gilmore.

TOWER OF LONDON (1939)
Universal (USA)
DIR: Rowland V. Lee. SCR: Robert N. Lee. PH: George Robinson. MUS: Charles Previn.
WITH Basil Rathbone, Boris Karloff, Barbara O'Neil, Ian Hunter, Vincent Price, Nan Gray, Ernest Cossart, John Sutton, Leo G. Carroll, Rose Hobart, Miles Mander, Lionel Belmore, Ronald Sinclair, Ralph Forbes, Frances Robinson, G. P. Huntley, John Rodion, Donnie Dunnagan, John Herbert-Bond, Walter Tetley.

TRANSATLANTIC TUNNEL (1935)
Gaumont-British (G.B.)
DIR: Maurice Elvey. SCR: Curt Siodmak; DIAL: L. DuGarde Peach, Clemence Dane; from a story by B. Kellermann. PH: G. Krampf.

WITH Richard Dix, Leslie Banks, Helen Vinson, Madge Evans, C. Aubrey Smith, Basil Sydney, Henry Oscar, Hilda Trevelyan, Jimmy Hanley, Cyril Raymond, Walter Huston, George Arliss.

TRE VOLTI DELLA PAURA, I (1963)
Emmepi/Galatea/Lyre (Italy)
DIR: Mario Bava. SCR: Mario Bava, Marcello Fondato, Alberto Bevilacqua. PH: Ubaldo Terzano (Eastmancolor). MUS: Roberto Nicolosi.
WITH Boris Karloff, Michele Mercier, Mark Damon, Susy Andersen, Jacqueline Pierreux, Milly Monti, Lidia Alfonsi, Rika Dialina.

TRIFLING WOMEN (1922)
Metro (USA)
DIR–SCR: Rex Ingram. PH: John Seitz.
WITH Barbara LaMarr, Ramon Novarro, Lewis Stone, Edward Connelly.

TRILBY (1915)
Equitable-World (USA)
DIR: Maurice Tourneur. SCR: from the novel by George Du Maurier.
WITH Clara Kimball Young, Wilton Lackaye, Chester Barnett, Paul McAllister, James Young.

TRILBY (1923)
First National (USA)
DIR: James Young. SCR: Richard Walton Tully, from the novel by George Du Maurier. PH: George Benoit.
WITH Andree Lafayette, Arthur Edmund Carewe, Creighton Hale, Philo McCullough, Wilfred Lucas, Francis McDonald, Maurice Cannon.

TRIP TO THE MOON, A——see VOYAGE DANS LA LUNE, Le

TWENTY MILLION MILES TO EARTH (1957)
Columbia (USA)
DIR: Nathan Juran. SCR: Charlott Knight, Ray Harryhausen. PH: Irving Lippman, Carlos Ventimiglia. SP. EF.: Ray Harryhausen.
WITH William Hopper, Joan Taylor, Frank Puglia, John Zaremba, Tito Vuolo, Arthur Space, Jan Arvan.

TWENTY-SEVENTH DAY, The (1957)
Columbia (USA)
DIR: William Asher. SCR: John Mantley. PH: Henry Freulich. MUS: Mischa Bakaleinikoff.

WITH Gene Barry, Valerie French, George Voskovec, Arnold Moss, Stefan Schnabel, Ralph Clanton, Friedrich Ledebur, Paul Birch.

TWO FACES OF DR. JEKYLL, The (1960)
Hammer Films (G.B.)
DIR: Terence Fisher. SCR: Wolf Mankowitz, from the novel, "Dr. Jekyll and Mr. Hyde" by Robert Louis Stevenson. PH: Jack Asher (Eastmancolor).
WITH Paul Massie, Dawn Addams, Christopher Lee, David Kossoff, Francis de Wolff, Norma Marla, Magda Miller.

UNDERWATER CITY, The (1962)
Columbia (USA)
DIR: Frank McDonald. SCR: Owen Harris. PH: Gordon Avil (Eastmancolor). MUS: Ronald Stein.
WITH William Lundigan, Julie Adams, Roy Roberts, Carl Benton Reid, Chet Douglas, Paul Dubov, Karen Norris, Kathie Browne.

UNDYING MONSTER, The (1942)
20th Century-Fox (USA)
DIR: John Brahm. SCR: Lillie Hayward, Michel Jacoby, from a novel by Jessie D. Kerruish. PH: Lucien Ballard. MUS: Emil Newman and David Raksin.
WITH James Ellison, Heather Angel, John Howard, Bramwell Fletcher, Heather Thatcher, Eily Malyon, Aubrey Mather, Halliwell Hobbes, Heather Wilde, Alec Craig, Holmes Herbert, Dave Thursby, Donald Stuart, John Rogers, Matthew Boulton.

UNEARTHLY STRANGER, The (1963)
Anglo-Amalgamated (G.B.)
DIR: John Krish. SCR: Rex Carlton. PH: Reg Wyler. MUS: Edward Williams.
WITH John Neville, Gabriella Licudi, Philip Stone, Patrick Newell, Jean Marsh, Warren Mitchell.

UNHOLY NIGHT, The (1929)
Metro-Goldwyn-Mayer (USA)
DIR: Lionel Barrymore. SCR: Dorothy Farnum, Edwin Justus Mayer; from a story by Ben Hecht. PH: Ira Morgan.
WITH Ernest Torrence, Dorothy Sebastian, Roland Young, Nathalie Moorehead, Polly Moran, Sojin, Sidney Jarvis, George Cooper, John

Miljan, Boris Karloff, John Loder, Lionel Belmore, John Roche, Richard Tucker, Philip Strange, Claude Fleming, Gerard Barry, Clarence Geldert.

UNHOLY THREE, The (1925)
Metro-Goldwyn-Mayer (USA)
DIR: Tod Browning. SCR: Waldemar Young; from a story by C. A. Robbins. PH: David Kesson.
WITH Lon Chaney, Mae Busch, Matt Moore, Victor McLaglen, Harry Earles, Matthew Betz, Walter Perry, John Merkyl, Percy Williams, Marjorie Morton, Violet Crane, Lou Morrison, Edward Connelly, William Humphreys, A. E. Warren.

UNHOLY THREE, The (1930)
Metro-Goldwyn-Mayer (USA)
DIR: Jack Conway. SCR: J. C. Nugent and Elliott Nugent; from a story by Clarence Aaron Robbins. PH: Percy Hillburn.
WITH Lon Chaney, Jr., Lila Lee, Elliott Nugent, Harry Earles, John Miljan, Ivan Linow, Clarence Burton, Crauford Kent.

UNINVITED, The (1944)
Paramount (USA)
DIR: Lewis Allen. SCR: Dodie Smith, Frank Partos; from a novel by Dorothy Macardle. MUS: Victor Young.
WITH Ray Milland, Ruth Hussey, Gail Russell, Cornelia Otis Skinner, Donald Crisp, Dorothy Stickney, Barbara Everest, Alan Napier.

UNKNOWN, The (1927)
Metro-Goldwyn-Mayer (USA)
DIR: Tod Browning. SCR: Waldemar Young; from a story by Tod Browning. PH: Merritt B. Gerstad.
WITH Lon Chaney, Joan Crawford, Norman Kerry, Nick de Ruiz, John George, Frank Lanning.

VAMPIRE BAT, The (1933)
Majestic (USA)
DIR: Frank Strayer. SCR: Edward Lowe. PH: Ira Morgan.
WITH Lionel Atwill, Fay Wray, Melvyn Douglas, George E. Stone, Maude Eburne, Dwight Frye, Robert Fraser, Rita Carlisle, Lionel Belmore, William V. Mong. Stella Adams, Paul Weigel, Fern Emmett, Harrison Greene, Carl Stockdale.

VAMPIRI, I (1957)
Titanus/Athena (Italy)
DIR: Riccardo Freda. SCR: Piero Regnoli, Rik Sjöström. PH: Mario Bava (CinemaScope). SETS: Beni Montresor. MUS: Roman Vlad, Franco Mannino.
WITH Gianna Maria Canale, Antoine Balpêtré, Paul Müller, Carlo D'Angelo, Wandisa Guida, Dario Michaelis, Renato Tontini, Charles Fawcett.

VAMPIRO, El (1959)
Abel Salazar/Cinematográfica A.B.S.A. (Mexico)
DIR: Fernando Méndez. SCR: Henrich Rodríguez, Ramon Obón. PH: Rosario Solano. MUS: Gustavo Carrion.
WITH Germán Robles, Ariadna Welter, Abel Salazar, José Luis Siménez, July Danery, Joseph Chávez, Mercedes Soler, Lydia Mellón, Carmen Montejo.

VAMPYR (1932)
Les Films Carl Dreyer (France)
DIR: Carl Dreyer. SCR: Carl Dreyer, Christen Jul; from the story "Carmilla" by Sheridan Le Fanu. PH: Rudolf Maté. MUS: Wolfgang Zeller.
WITH Julian West (Baron Nicolas de Gunzburg), Sybille Schmitz, Henriette Gerard, Jan Hieronimko, Albert Bras, N. Babanini, Rena Mandel, Maurice Schutz.

VILLAGE OF THE DAMNED, The (1960)
Metro-Goldwyn-Mayer (G.B.)
DIR: Wolf Rilla. SCR: Sterling Silliphant, Wolf Rilla, George Barclay; from the novel "The Midwich Cuckoos" by John Wyndham. PH: Geoffrey Faithfull (Metroscope). SP. EF.: Tom Howard. MUS: Ron Goodwin.
WITH George Sanders, Barbara Shelley, Michael Gwynne, Laurence Naismith, Jenny Laird, Martin Stephens, Charlotte Mitchell, Rosamund Greenwood, John Phillips, Richard Vernon, Richard Warner.

VOYAGE DANS LA LUNE, Le (1902)
Star Films (France)
DIR: Georges Méliès.

VOYAGE TO THE END OF THE UNIVERSE——see IKARIA XB1

VREDENS DAG (1943)
Palladium-Copenhagen (Denmark)
DIR: Carl Dreyer. SCR: Carl Dreyer, Mogens Skot-Hansen, Poul Knudsen; from the play "Anne Pedersdotter" by Wiers Jensen. PH: Carl Andersson. MUS: Poul Schierbeck.
WITH Thorkild Roose, Lisbeth Movin, Sigrid Neeiendam, Preben Lerdorff, Anna Svierkier, Albert Hoeberg, Olaf Ussing.

WACHSFIGURENKABINETT (1924)
Neptun-Films (Germany)
DIR: Paul Leni. SCR: Henrik Galeen. PH: Helmar Lerski. SETS: P. Leni, Ernst Stern.
WITH Emil Jannings, Conrad Veidt, Werner Krauss, Wilhelm Dieterle, Olga von Balieff, John Gottowt.

WALKING DEAD, The (1936)
Warner Brothers (USA)
DIR: Michael Curtiz. SCR: Ewart Adamson, Peter Milne, Robert Adams, Lillie Hayward. PH: Hal Mohr.
WITH Boris Karloff, Marguerite Churchill, Ricardo Cortez, Barton MacLane, Warren Hull, Henry O'Neill, Ruth Robinson, Addison Richards, Miki Morita, Eddie Acuff, Edmund Gwenn, Kenneth Harlan, Adrian Rosley, Paul Joseph King.

WAR OF THE SATELLITES (1958)
Allied Artists (USA)
DIR: Roger Corman. SCR: Lawrence Louis Goldman. PH: Floyd Crosby. MUS: Walter Greene.
WITH Dick Miller, Susan Cabot, Richard Devon, Eric Sinclair, Michael Fox, Robert Shayne, Jerry Barclay, Jay Sayer, Mitzi McCall, John Brinkley, Beech Dickerson.

WAR OF THE WORLDS, The (1953)
Paramount (USA)
PROD: George Pal. DIR: Byron Haskin. SCR: Barre Lyndon; from the novel by H. G. Wells. PH: George Barnes (Technicolor).
WITH Gene Barry, Ann Robinson, Henry Brandon, Les Tremayne, Bob Cornthwaite, Sandro Giglio, Lewis Martin, Jack Kruschen, Bill Phipps.

WEIRD WOMAN (1944)
Universal (USA)
DIR: Reginald LeBorg. SCR: Brenda Weisberg; from a story by Fritz Leiber, Jr. PH: Virgil Miller. MUS: Paul Sawtell.
WITH Lon Chaney, Jr., Anne Gwynne, Evelyn Ankers, Elizabeth Russell, Ralph Morgan, Lois Collier, Elizabeth Risdon, Phil Brown, Manna Kaapa, Jackie Lou Harding.

WEREWOLF OF LONDON, The (1935)
Universal (USA)
DIR: Stuart Walker. SCR: Robert Harris. PH: Charles Stumar.
WITH Henry Hull, Warner Oland, Valerie Hobson, Spring Byington, Lester Matthews, Zeffie Tilbury, Ethel Griffies, J. M. Kerrigan, Charlotte Granville, Lawrence Grant, Reginald Barlow, Clark Williams.

WHAT EVER HAPPENED TO BABY JANE? (1962)
Seven Arts/Aldrich (USA)
DIR: Robert Aldrich. SCR: Lukas Heller, based on the novel by Henry Farrell. PH: Ernest Haller. MUS: Frank DeVol.
WITH Bette Davis, Joan Crawford, Victor Buono, Anna Lee, Maidie Norman, Marjorie Bennett, Barbara Merrill, Dave Willock, Ann Barton, Julie Allred, Gina Gillespie, Ernest Anderson.

WHEN WORLDS COLLIDE (1951)
Paramount (USA)
PROD: George Pal. DIR: Rudolph Maté. SCR: Sydney Boehm, from the original story by Edwin Balmer and Philip Wylie. PH: John F. Seitz (Technicolor). MUS: Leith Stevens.
WITH Richard Derr, Barbara Rush, Peter Hanson, Judith Ames, John Hoyt, Mary Murphy, Laura Elliott, Stephen Chase, Sandro Giglio, Frank Cady, Hayden Rorke.

WHILE PARIS SLEEPS (1923)
Paramount/W. W. Hodkinson (USA)
DIR: Maurice Tourneur. SCR: from "The Glory of Love" by Pan (pseudonym for Leslie Beresford). PH: Rene Guissart.

WITH Lon Chaney, Mildred Manning, Jack Gilbert, J. Farrell MacDonald, Harden Kirtland.

WHITE ZOMBIE (1932)
Amusement Securities (USA)
DIR: Victor Halperin. SCR: Garnett Weston, from his original story. PH: Arthur Martinelli. MUS: arranged by Abe Meyer.

WITH Bela Lugosi, Madge Bellamy, John Harron, Joseph Cawthorn, Robert Frazer, Clarence Muse, Brandon Hurst, Dan Crimmins, John Peters, George Burr McAnnan.

WITCHCRAFT THROUGH THE AGES——see HÄXAN

WIZARD, The (1927)
Fox (USA)
DIR: Richard Rosson. SCR: Harry O. Hoyt, based on the play "Balaoo" by Gaston Leroux. PH: Frank B. Good.
WITH Edmund Lowe, Leila Hyams, Gustav von Seyffertitz, Barry Norton, George Kotsonaros, Norman Trevor.

WOLF MAN, The (1941)
Universal (USA)
DIR: George Waggner. SCR: Curt Siodmak. PH: Joseph Valentine.
WITH Claude Rains, Ralph Bellamy, Evelyn Ankers, Warren William, Patric Knowles, Bela Lugosi, Lon Chaney, Jr., Maria Ouspenskaya, Fay Helm.

WOMAN IN THE MOON——see FRAU IM MOND

X, THE MAN WITH THE X-RAY EYES (1963)
American-International (USA)
DIR–PROD: Roger Corman. SCR: Ray Russell, Robert Dillon. PH: Floyd Crosby (Pathecolor). MUS: Les Baxter.
WITH Ray Milland, Diana Van Der Vlis, Harold J. Stone, John Hoyt, Don Rickles, John Dierkes, Lorrie Summers, Vickie Lee, Kathryn Hart, Carol Irey.

YEUX SANS VISAGE, Les (1960)
Champs-Elysées Productions (France)
DIR: Georges Franju. SCR: Pierre Boileau, Thomas Narcejac, Jean Redon, Claude Sautet. DIAL: Pierre Gascar. PH: Eugen Shuftan. MUS: Maurice Jarre.
WITH Pierre Brasseur, Alida Valli, Edith Scob, Juliette Mayniel, Beatrice Altariba, François Guérin, René Genin.

YOUNG DIANA (1922)
Cosmopolitan-Paramount (USA)
DIR: Albert Capellani, Robert Vignola. SCR: Luther Reed, from a novel by Marie Corelli. PH: Harold Wenstrom. SETS: Joseph Urban.
WITH Marion Davies, Forest Stanley, Gypsy O'Brien, Maclyn Arbuckle, Pedro de Cordoba.

INDEX

Abbott and Costello Meet Dr. Jekyll and Mr. Hyde, 100; cast and credits, 173
Abbott and Costello Meet Frankenstein, 103; cast and credits, 174
Abel, Alfred, 31
Academy Awards, 82, 95, 102, 121
Adams, Julia, 138
Aelita, 19; cast and credits, 174
Agate, James, 81
Agee, James, 114
Aitken, Spottiswoode, 43
À la Conquête du Pôle, 6; cast and credits, 173
Alberni, Luis, 80
Aldrich, Robert, 144
Alice in Wonderland, xiv
Allen, Lewis, 116
All That Money Can Buy, 45; cast and credits, 174
Alphaville, 163, 169–71; cast and credits, 174
America (1900–1928), 37–58
Ames, Leon, 73
Amicus, 144
Anderson, Poul, 119
Andra, Fern, 18
Andrews, Dana, 144, 145
Angelico, Fra, xii
Anglo-Amalgamated, 144
Animal World, The, 96; cast and credits, 174
Ankers, Evelyn, 103
Antoine, André, 41
Applause, 81
Arlen, Richard, 85
Arliss, George, 7
Armstrong, Robert, 93, 95
Arness, James, 123
Arnold, Jack, 133
Asimov, Isaac, 119
Astor, Mary, 45
Ataúd del Vampiro, El, 159; cast and credits, 174–75
Attack of the Fifty Foot Woman, 119; cast and credits, 175
Atwill, Lionel, 80, 81, 87, 98, 99, 101, 103, 133
Auric, Georges, 117
Avenging Conscience, The, 39, 42–43; cast and credits, 175

Baclanova, Olga, 56, 70, 71
Baggot, King, 41
Baird, Antony, 117
Balderston, John L., 61, 64, 67, 128
Balmer, Edwin, 121
Balzac, Honoré, 42
Bara, Theda, 61
Baron Munchausen, 7; cast and credits, 175
Barrault, Jean-Louis, 84
Barry, Gene, 125
Barrymore, John, 11, 40–41, 71, 79, 80, 83
Barrymore, Lionel, 72
Bat, The, 38, 43, 45, 55, 56; cast and credits, 175
Battleship Maine, 3–4
Battleship Potemkin, 17
Bat Whispers, The, 175
Baum, L. Frank, 37
Bava, Mario, 156, 157, 158
Beast from 20,000 Fathoms, The, 131; cast and credits, 175–76

Beast of Hollow Mountain, The, 96; cast and credits, 176
Beast with Five Fingers, The, 103–04; cast and credits, 176
Beaumont, Charles, 119, 145, 148
Beauty and the Beast. See *Belle et la Bête, La.*
Bedlam, 115; cast and credits, 176
Beery, Wallace, 52
Before I Hang, 99; cast and credits, 176
Bellamy, Madge, 88
Belle et la Bête, La, 50; cast and credits, 176
Bells, The, 43, 63; cast and credits, 177
Benét, Stephen Vincent, 45
Berger, Ludwig, 54
Bergerac, Cyrano de, 119
Berghof, Herbert, 127
Bergman, Ingmar, 149
Bergman, Ingrid, 83
Bergson, Henri, 166
Between Worlds. See *Müde Tod, Der.*
Bierce, Ambrose, 37
Biggers, Earl Derr, 38, 56
Big Heat, The, 25
Biograph Company, 7
Birds, The, 163, 167–69, 171; cast and credits, 177
Birth of a Nation, 17, 43
Bishop Murder Case, The, 60
Bissell, Whit, 140
Black Cat, The (1934), 62, 74–75; cast and credits, 177
Black Cat, The (1941), 43, 128; cast and credits, 177
Black Orchids, 53; cast and credits, 177
Black Room, The, 76; cast and credits, 178
Black Sabbath. See *Tre Volti della Paura, I.*
Black Scorpion, The, 95; cast and credits, 178
Black Sunday. See *Maschera del Demonio, La.*
Black Zoo, The, 140; cast and credits, 178
Blade am Satans Bog, 44; cast and credits, 178
Blake, Alfonso Corona, 158, 159
Blake, William, xiii
Blind Bargain, 46, 47; cast and credits, 178–79
Blish, James, 119
Blob, The, 122, 125, 156; cast and credits, 179
Blood and Black Lace. See *Sei Donne per l'Assassino.*
Blood and Roses. See *Et Mourir de Plaisir.*
Blood Feast, 154; cast and credits, 179
Blood of Dracula, 140; cast and credits, 179
Bloom, Claire, 153
Bodeen, DeWitt, 112
Body Snatcher, The, 114, 152; cast and credits, 179
Boehm, Carl, 145
Borland, Carol, 71
Boyer, Charles, 36
Bradbury, Ray, 118, 131, 166
Brahm, John, 102
Brasseur, Pierre, 154
Brecht, Bertolt, 164
Bride of Frankenstein, 67–69, 72, 98, 128; cast and credits, 179–80
Brides of Dracula, 142–43; cast and credits, 180
British Lion-Columbia, 144
Broekman, David, 68
Brontë, Charlotte, 113, 157
Brooks, Jean, 114
Brophy, Edward, 74
Brown, John Mason, 82
Browning, Ricou, 138
Browning, Tod, 38, 41, 50–51, 60, 61, 62, 65, 69–72, 90
Buchowetzki, Dimitri, 54
Buck Rogers, 120; cast and credits, 180
Bucket of Blood, 148; cast and credits, 180
Buñuel, Luis, 149
Burke, Kathleen, 84
Burn Witch Burn. See *Night of the Eagle, The.*
Burroughs, Edgar Rice, 118
Byron, George Lord, 9

Cabinet of Dr. Caligari, The. See *Kabinett des Dr. Caligari, Das.*
Cable, George Washington, 37
Cabot, Bruce, 94
Cagney, James, 51, 83
Calling Dr. Death, 101; cast and credits, 180
Caltiki, Il Mostro Immortale, 156, 157; cast and credits, 181
Campbell, John W., Jr., 123
Canary Murder Case, The, 60
Capek, Karel, 119
Capote, Truman, 146, 147
Captive Wild Woman, 102; cast and credits, 181
Carew, Arthur Edmund, 50, 79
Carey, Macdonald, 163
Carmen, 39
Carnival of Sinners. See *Main du Diable, La.*
Carradine, John, 62, 103
Carter, Ann, 114
Castle, William, 139
Castle of Doom. See *Vampyr.*

Cat and the Canary, The (1927), 44, 55, 57; cast and credits, 181
Cat and the Canary, The (1939), 56, 99; cast and credits, 181
Cat Creeps, The, 56; cast and credits, 181
Cat People, The, 110, 111, 112–113; cast and credits, 182
Cawthorn, Joseph, 89
Cézanne, Paul, 13
Chaney, Lon, 38, 46–48, 50–52, 58, 60, 61, 62, 69, 78, 101, 102
Chaney, Lon, Jr., 64, 78, 100–01
Chaplin, Charlie, 8, 51
Chavannes, Puvis de, 41
Chikyu Boeigun, 122, 124, 132; cast and credits, 182
Chinese Parrot, The, 56; cast and credits, 182
Christensen, Benjamin, 57–58
Christie, Julie, 167
Christopher, John, 119
Chronicle of the Gray House, The. See *Chronik von Grieshuus.*
Chronik von Grieshuus, 24, 27; cast and credits, 182
Churchill, Marguerite, 76
Cibrián, José, 158
Cinderella, 4
CinemaScope, 96, 119, 138, 150, 152
Cinématographe Lumière, 1, 2, 3
Císařuv Pekař, Pekařuv Císař, 21; cast and credits, 182
City Streets, 81
Civilization Through the Ages, 7
Clair, René, 8
Clarke, Arthur C., 119
Clarke, Betty Ross, 73
Clayton, Jack, 146, 147
Climax, The, 102; cast and credits, 183
Clive, Colin, 63, 73
Cocteau, Jean, 8, 50, 86, 155
Cohen, Herbert, 140
Collins, Wilkie, 9, 39, 82, 157
Columbia Pictures, 76, 99, 102, 103
Connell, Richard, 97
Conquering Power, The, 53; cast and credits, 183
Conquest of Space, 122; cast and credits, 183
Conquest of the Pole. See *À la Conquête du Pôle.*
Conrad, Joseph, 47
Constantine, Eddie, 169
Conway, Gary, 140
Conway, Jack, 60
Conway, Moncure D., 112
Conway, Tom, 112, 113
Coogan, Jackie, 47
Cook, Donald, 79
Coolidge, Philip, 139
Cooper, Gary, 87
Cooper, Merian C., 91–92, 95, 96
Cooper, Violet Kemble, 75
Corelli, Marie, 44, 46
Corman, Roger, 81, 147–51, 157
Cornthwaite, Robert, 124
Crawford, Joan, 69, 70
Creation, 92, 95
Creation of the Humanoids, 137; cast and credits, 183
Creature from the Black Lagoon, The, 138; cast and credits, 183
Creelman, James, 92, 97
Creeping Unknown, The. See *Quatermass Experiment, The.*
Crosby, Floyd, 148
Crowley, Aleister, 53, 54, 83
Cruze, James, 41
Curse of Frankenstein, The, 141, 143; cast and credits, 184
Curse of the Cat People, The, 114, 152; cast and credits, 184
Curse of the Demon. See *Night of the Demon, The.*
Curse of the Fly, The, 152; cast and credits, 184
Curse of the Mummy's Tomb, The, 142; cast and credits, 184
Curse of the Werewolf, The, 143; cast and credits, 184
Curtiz, Michael, 54, 80
Cusack, Cyril, 167
Cushing, Peter, 141

Dade, Frances, 61
Dagover, Lil, 15
Damned, The, 163–65; cast and credits, 185
Dante's Inferno, 185
Dark Eyes of London, 76; cast and credits, 185
David Copperfield, 82
Davies, Marion, 46
Day Mars Invaded the Earth, The, 136–37; cast and credits, 185
Day of Wrath. See *Vredens Dag.*
Day the Earth Stood Still, The, 122, 125–27, 128, 152; cast and credits, 186
Dead Man's Eyes, 101; cast and credits, 186
Dead of Night, 116–17; cast and credits, 186
Deadly Mantis, The, 132; cast and credits, 186
Dead Secret, The, 39
Dean, Julia, 114
Deane, Hamilton, 61
Death Kiss, The, 76, 87; cast and credits, 186–87
Death Takes a Holiday, 86–87; cast and credits, 187

Debussy, Claude, 18
Decima Vittima, La, 163, 167; cast and credits, 187
Decla Film Company, 14, 15, 26
Dee, Frances, 113
Deluge, 95; cast and credits, 187
De Mille, Cecil B., 44
Dempster, Carol, 44
Destination Moon, 120–21; cast and credits, 187
Destiny. See *Müde Tod, Der.*
Devil, The, 7
Devil Commands, The, 187–88
Devil Doll, The, 188
Devil's Assistant, The, 38; cast and credits, 188
Devil's Circus, 58
Devil's Commandment, The. See *Vampiri, I.*
Devil's Darling, The, 38
Devil's Manor, The, 4
Diamond Ship, The, 26
Die, Monster, Die, 99, 151; cast and credits, 188
Die Die My Darling. See *Fanatic.*
Dieterle, William, 56
Dinosaur and the Missing Link, The, 52; cast and credits, 188
Disney, Walt, 92, 129
Doctor and the Devils, The, 114
Dr. Cyclops, 81; cast and credits, 188
Dr. Jekyll and Mr. Hyde (1908), 7, 40; cast and credits, 188
Dr. Jekyll and Mr. Hyde (1910), 40; cast and credits, 189
Dr. Jekyll and Mr. Hyde (1912), 40; cast and credits, 189
Dr. Jekyll and Mr. Hyde (1913), 40; cast and credits, 189
Dr. Jekyll and Mr. Hyde (1920), 40–41; cast and credits, 189
Dr. Jekyll and Mr. Hyde (1932), 81–83; cast and credits, 189
Dr. Jekyll and Mr. Hyde (1941), 83–84, 103; cast and credits, 189
Doctor Mabuse, 25, 27–28, 29; cast and credits, 190
Dr. Renault's Secret, 102; cast and credits, 190
Dr. Terror's House of Horrors, 109, 144; cast and credits, 190
Dr. X, 80; cast and credits, 190
Domergue, Faith, 128
Donlevy, Brian, 133
Donne, John, 114
Donovan, King, 135
Donovan Affair, The, 60
Doré, Gustave, xiii
Dostoyevsky, Fëdor, 18
Douglas, Melvyn, 87
Doyle, Arthur Conan, 29, 37, 52, 118
Dracula (1927), 61–62
Dracula (1931), 79, 90, 98, 128; cast and credits, 191
Dracula (1958), 141–42; cast and credits, 191
Dracula Prince of Darkness, 142; cast and credits, 191
Dracula's Daughter, 75–76, 98; cast and credits, 191
Drake, Frances, 73
Dream Woman, The, 39
Dreyer, Carl Theodor, 44, 57, 76, 105, 107–10, 145
Dreyfus Case, The, 4, 7
Drums of Jeopardy, 191
Dudgeon, John, 65
Du Maurier, George, 42, 79, 87
Dumke, Ralph, 135
Dupont, André Edwald, 54, 55
Duvivier, Julian, 21, 109

Earles, Harry, 70
Eck, Johnny, 70
Edeson, Arthur, 64
Edison Company, 7, 38, 39, 52
Edison Kinetoscope, 1, 3
Edwards, Bill, 133
Electric Man, The, 101
Eleventh Hour, The, xv
Emergo, 138
Emery, Katherine, 115
Emperor and the Golem, The. See *Císařuv Pekař, Pekařuv Císař.*
Endore, Guy, 143
Ernst, Max, xii, 71
Essanay, 39
Et Mourir de Plaisir, 76; cast and credits, 192
Evelyn, Judith, 139
Evil of Frankenstein, The, 142; cast and credits, 192
Ewers, Hanns Heinz, 10, 24
Expressionism, 13–14, 25, 27, 31

Face of Fu Manchu, The, 144; cast and credits, 192
Fahrenheit 451, 163, 165, 166–67; cast and credits, 192–93
Famous Players, 40
Fanatic, 144; cast and credits, 193
Fantasia, 92
Fantastic Voyage, 162; cast and credits, 193
Faust, 23; cast and credits, 193
Faust and Marguerite, 4
Fazenda, Louise, 60
Feher, Friedrich, 18
Ferber, Edna, 69
Feuillade, Louis, 42, 49
Field, Shirley Ann, 163
Finney, Jack, 119

First Man into Space, The, 133; cast and credits, 193
First Men in the Moon, The, 125, 162; cast and credits, 194
First National, 57
Fisher, Terence, 142, 143, 159
Flash Gordon, xiv, 54, 120; cast and credits, 194
Fleming, Victor, 83
Flight to Mars, 121; cast and credits, 194
Florey, Robert, 62, 63, 72–73, 104
Fly, The, 151–52; cast and credits, 194
Flying Saucer, The, 121; cast and credits, 194
Folie du Docteur Tube, La, 17; cast and credits, 195
Fønss, Olaf, 13
Forbidden Planet, The, 129, 153; cast and credits, 195
Ford, Grace, 72
Ford, John, 25
For the Crown of Asia, 26
Foster, Preston, 80
Four Feathers, The, 91
Four Horsemen of the Apocalypse, The, 53
Four-Sided Triangle, The, 141; cast and credits, 195
Francis, Arlene, 72
Franco, Jesús, 156
Franju, Georges, 154, 155
Frankenstein (1910), 38–39; cast and credits, 195
Frankenstein (1931), 62–64, 67, 73, 79, 98, 128, 141; cast and credits, 195
Frankenstein Meets the Wolf Man, 78, 102; cast and credits, 195
Frau im Mond, 34–35, 120; cast and credits, 196
Frazer, Robert, 88
Freaks, 70–71, 85; cast and credits, 196
Freda, Riccardo, 155–57, 160
Freud, Sigmund, 39
Freund, Karl, 25, 73–74, 100, 159
Fric, Mac, 21
Froehlich, Gustav, 31
Frozen Ghost, The, 101; cast and credits, 196
Frusta e il Corpo, La, 158; cast and credits, 196
Frye, Dwight, 64, 87
Fulton, John P., 66, 78, 100
Funeral of President Faure, The, 4
Fury, 33

Gabo, Naum, 19
Galeen, Henrik, 21, 22, 24
Game of Death, A, 97, 152; cast and credits, 196
Gance, Abel, 17, 25
Garbo, Greta, 41, 51, 70
Garden of Allah, The, 54
Gaunt, Valerie, 142
Genuine, 18; cast and credits, 197
Gerlack, Arthur von, 24
Germany (1913–1932), 9–36
Ghost, The. See *Spettro, Lo.*
Ghost Breakers, The, 100; cast and credits, 197
Ghost of Frankenstein, The, 98, 101; cast and credits, 197
Ghost of Slumber Mountain, The, 53; cast and credits, 197
Ghost Talks, The, 197
Ghoul, The, 76; cast and credits, 197
Giant Behemoth, The, 96, 132; cast and credits, 198
Gide, André, 21
Gillette, William, 39
Glory of Love, The. See *While Paris Sleeps.*
Godard, Jean-Luc, 169, 170, 171
Goddard, Paulette, 100
Godzilla, King of the Monsters, 132; cast and credits, 198
Godzilla versus the Thing, 132
Goebbels, Paul, 35
Goethe, Johann Wolfgang von, 23
Goetzke, Bernhard, 28
Gogol, Nikolai, 157
Gold, 134; cast and credits, 198
Golden Lake, The, 26
Goldwyn, Sam, 46
Golem, Der (1915), 11–12
Golem, Der (1920), 20–21, 24, 25; cast and credits, 198
Golem, Le (1936), 109; cast and credits, 199
Golem und die Tänzerin, Der, 12, cast and credits, 199
Gordon, Christine, 113
Gordon, Gavin, 67
Gorgon, The, 143; cast and credits, 199
Gorilla, The (1927), 199
Gorilla, The (1931), 56; cast and credits, 199
Gorilla, The (1939), 99; cast and credits, 199
Graft, 63
Granach, Alexander, 22, 23
Graves, Peter, 127
Gray, Billie, 126
Gray, Nan, 76
Great Northern Company, 40
Great Train Robbery, The, 7
Greene, Graham, 34
Griffies, Ethel, 78, 169
Griffith, D. W., 8, 27, 39, 42–45, 100
Grimm, Jacob and Wilhelm, 37
Grinde, Nick, 99

Gunzburg, Baron Nicolas de, 105, 109
Gwangi, 95

Haggard, Rider, 4, 119
Hale, Creighton, 55, 56
Hall, Charles, D., 128
Haller, Daniel, 148, 151
Halperin, Victor, 90–91
Halperin Brothers, 88
Hameister, Willie, 18
Hammer Studios, 81, 141–47, 154, 164
Hands of Orlac, The. See *Orlacs Haende*.
Hangmen Also Die, 25
Harbou, Thea von, 24, 26, 27, 31, 32, 36
Harding, Ann, 87
Harrigan, William, 66
Harris, Julie, 153
Harron, John, 88
Harryhausen, Ray, 96, 131
Hart, William S., 46
Hathaway, Henry, 87
Hatton, Rondo, 103
Haunted Castle, The. See *Schloss Vogelöd.*
Haunted Cave, The, 4
Haunted House, The, 200
Haunted Palace, The, 148; cast and credits, 200
Haunting, The, 152–54; cast and credits, 200
Hawks, Howard, 123, 124
Hawthorne, Nathaniel, 37, 45
Häxan, 57–58; cast and credits, 200
Hayers, Sidney, 145
Hedison, Al, 151
Hedron, Tippi, 168
Heine, Heinrich, 30
Heinlein, Robert, 119
Hellman, Monte, 150
Helm, Brigitte, 31
Helm, Fay, 103
Herodotus, 76
Herrera, Victor, 159
Hillyer, Lambert, 75–76
Hilton, Daisy and Violet, 70
Hinds, Anthony, 143
Hitchcock, Alfred, 26, 34, 167, 168, 169
Hitler, Adolf, 31, 35, 36
Hobart, Rose, 83
Hobson, Valerie, 77
Hodkinson Company, 42
Hoffmann, E. T. A., xi, 10
Hohl, Arthur, 72
Holden, Gloria, 76
Homunculus, 12–13; cast and credits, 200
Hope, Bob, 56, 100
Hopkins, Mitiam, 83
Hopwood, Avery, 38
Horn, Camilla, 54
Horner, Harry, 128
Horrible Dr. Hichcock, The, See *Raptus.*
Horror Chamber of Dr. Faustus, The. See *Yeux sans Visage, Les.*
Horror of Dracula. See *Dracula* (1958).
Horrors of the Black Museum, 138–39, 140; cast and credits, 201
Houdin, Robert, 2
Hound of the Baskervilles, The (1939), 99; cast and credits, 201
Hound of the Baskervilles, The (1959), 142; cast and credits, 201
House of Dracula, 78, 103; cast and credits, 201
House of Frankenstein, 78, 103; cast and credits, 201–02
House of Fright. See *Two Faces of Dr. Jekyll, The.*
House of Horror, 58; cast and credits, 202
House of Rothschild, The, 76
House of Usher, The, 148, 150; cast and credits, 202
House of Wax, 80–81, 138; cast and credits, 202
House on Haunted Hill, The, 138–39; cast and credits, 202
Howe, James Wong, 71
Howes, Sally Ann, 117
How to Make a Monster, 140; cast and credits, 202–03
Hoyt, Harry, 52
Hubbard, L. Ron, 119
Hugo, Victor, 39, 40, 47, 56
Hull, Henry, 77, 78
Human Wreckage, 19
Hume, Cyril, 129
Hunchback of Notre Dame (1923), 47; cast and credits, 203
Hunchback of Notre Dame (1939), 47, 99; cast and credits, 203
Hunchback of Notre Dame (1957), 203
Hunt, Martita, 143
Hunter, Glenn, 45
Hurlbut, William, 67
Hussey, Ruth, 116
Huxley, Aldous, 118
Hypnovista, 138

Ikaria XB1, 130–31; cast and credits, 204
Impossible Deshabillé, An, 4
Impossible Voyage, The, 6
Impressionism, 13
Ince, George, 17, 42
Incredible Shrinking Man, The, 132–33; cast and credits, 204
Ingram, Rex, 38, 41, 53–54
Innocents, The, 146–47; cast and credits, 204–05
Intolerance, 27

Invaders from Mars, The, 124; cast and credits, 205
Invasion of the Body Snatchers, 134–35, 136; cast and credits, 205
Invisible Man, The, 65–67; cast and credits, 205
Invisible Man Returns, The, 100; cast and credits, 205
Invisible Ray, The, 62, 75, 101, cast and credits, 205–06
Irving, Henry, 63
I Saw What You Did, 139
Island of Lost Souls, 84–86; cast and credits, 206
Isle-Adam, Villiers de l', 119
Isle of the Dead, 110, 115; cast and credits, 206
Italy, 155–57
It Came from Beneath the Sea, 132; cast and credits, 206
It Came from Outer Space, 124; cast and credits, 206
It's a Mad, Mad, Mad, Mad World, 96
I Walked with a Zombie, 111, 113; cast and credits, 203–04
I Was a Teenage Frankenstein, 140; cast and credits, 204
I Was a Teenage Werewolf, 140; cast and credits, 204

Jackson, Shirley, 152
Jacques, Norbert, 27
James, Henry, 146, 147
James, Montague R., 144
Jannings, Emil, 54, 56
Janowitz, Hans, 14, 15, 18, 19
Januskopf, Der, 19, 21, 40; cast and credits, 206–07
Jarre, Maurice, 155
Jason and the Argonauts, 96; cast and credits, 207
Jazz Singer, The, 57, 59
Jetée, La, 163, 165–66; cast and credits, 207
Johann, Zita, 73
Johnson, Noble, 100
Johnson, Richard, 153
Jolson, Al, 59
Jones, Carolyn, 135
Jonson, Ben, 42
Journey to the Seventh Planet, 130; cast and credits, 207
Judex, 49
Jul, Christen, 105
Julian, Rupert, 48
Jung, Carl, 39
Jungle Captive, 102; cast and credits, 207
Jungle Woman, 102; cast and credits, 207
Just Imagine, 33; cast and credits, 208

Kabinett des Dr. Caligari, Das, 15–19, 24, 57; cast and credits, 208
Kafka, Franz, 14
Karina, Anna, 170
Karloff, Boris, 63–64, 65, 68, 73, 74, 75, 76, 78, 80, 98, 99–100, 101, 102, 115, 141, 149
Kenton, Erle C., 85
Kern, Jerome, 69
Kerr, Deborah, 147
Kerr, Frederick, 67
Kerry, Norman, 50
Killers from Space, 124; cast and credits, 208
King, Andrea, 127
King Kong, 53, 69, 81, 91–95, 96, 131, 132; cast and credits, 208
King Kong versus Godzilla, 132
Kipling, Rudyard, 85
Klein, Cesar, 18
Klein-Rogge, Rudolf, 26, 28–29, 32, 33
Kneale, Nigel, 119
Knoll, Hans, 121
Knox, Alexander, 164
Kokoschka, Oskar, 18
Konga, 140; cast and credits, 208
Korda, Alexander, 54
Kosleck, Martin, 103
Krafft-Ebing, Richard von, 156
Kramer, Stanley, 96
Krampf, Günther, 24
Krauss, Werner, 15, 25, 56, 57

Lackaye, Wilton, 79
Ladrón de Cadáberes, 159; cast and credits, 209
Laemmle, Carl, 54, 56, 73
LaMarr, Barbara, 53
Lanchester, Elsa, 67, 68
Landers, Lew, 75
Lang, Fritz, xiv, 15, 24, 25–36, 86, 120
La Plante, Laura, 54, 55
Last Days of Pompeii, The, 95
Last Laugh, The, 23
Last Warning, The, 57; cast and credits, 209
Laughton, Charles, 65, 84, 85
Lavista, Raúl, 159
Leakey, Phil, 141
Leaves from Satan's Book. See *Blade am Satans Bog.*
Lee, Anna, 115
Lee, Christopher, 62, 141, 142
Lee, Rowland V., 98, 99
Le Fanu, Sheridan, 10, 105
Leiber, Fritz, 145
Leni, Paul, 25, 55–57
Leonov, Aleksei A., 121
Leopard Man, The, 113; cast and credits, 209
Leroux, Gaston, 42, 47, 48, 57

Lewin, Albert, 102
Lewis, Jerry, 84
Lewis, Matthew Gregory, 9
Lewis, Ralph, 43
Lewis, Sheldon, 41
Lewton, Val, 110, 111–16, 141, 152
Ley, Willy, 34, 35
Life of an American Fireman, The, 6
Life Without Soul, 39; cast and credits, 209
Lights of New York, The, 59
Light Within, The. See *Müde Tod, Der.*
Liliom (1930), 36; cast and credits, 209
Liliom (1933), 210
Lindfors, Viveca, 163, 165
Lindsay, Vachel, 43
Little Women, 82
Lodger, The, 146; cast and credits, 210
Loewy, Raymond, 121
Lombard, Carole, 90
London After Midnight, 51, 61, 71; cast and credits, 210
Lorre, Peter, 35, 73, 149
Losey, Joseph, 164
Lost Patrol, The, 76
Lost World, The (1925), 52, 53, 96; cast and credits, 210
Lost World, The (1960), 96; cast and credits, 210
Love, Bessie, 52
Lovecraft, H. P., 148, 151
Love in Morocco, 54
Love Me and the World Is Mine, 54
Low Ben Bezalel, Rabbi Judah, 11
Lubitsch, Ernst, 54
Ludwig of Bavaria, 31
Lugosi, Bela, 23, 60, 61, 62–63, 64, 71, 72, 74, 75, 76, 85, 87, 88, 89, 90, 98, 101, 102, 103, 109
Lumière, Louis and Auguste, 2
Lunatics, The, 42
Lunatics in Power, 7

M, 35
Macardle, Dorothy, 116
MacKaye, Percy, 45
Mad Genius, The, 79–80; cast and credits, 211
Mad Love, 73–74; cast and credits, 211
Maeterlinck, Maurice, 86, 163
Magician, The, 53–54; cast and credits, 211
Magnetic Monster, The, 133–34; cast and credits, 211
Main du Diable, La, 42; cast and credits, 211
Malleson, Miles, 117
Mamoulian, Rouben, 81–83
Maniac, 143
Man from Planet X, The, 119, 124, 128; cast and credits, 211–12
Manikin Films, 52
Man in the Iron Mask, The, 69
Mankowitz, Wolf, 84
Mansfield, Martha, 40
Mansfield, Richard, 7, 40
Man They Could Not Hang, The, 99; cast and credits, 212
Man Who Changed His Mind, The, 76; cast and credits, 212
Man Who Could Work Miracles, The, 85, 150
Man Who Laughs, The, 40, 56–57; cast and credits, 212
Man with Four Heads, The, 4
Man with Nine Lives, The, 99; cast and credits, 212
Man-Made Monster, The, 101; cast and credits, 212–13
March, Fredric, 81, 82, 86, 87
Mare Nostrum, 54
Margheriti, Antonio, 156
Marker, Chris, 166
Mark of the Vampire, The, 71; cast and credits, 213
Marriage of Figero, The, xii
Marsh, Carol, 142
Marsh, Marian, 79
Marshall, Herbert, 152
Martha the Armless Wonder, 70
Maschera del Demonio, La, 157–58; cast and credits, 213
Masciocchi, Raffaele, 156
Mask, The, 138; cast and credits, 213
Mask of Fu Manchu, The, 76; cast and credits, 213
Masque of the Red Death, 148, 149; cast and credits, 213–14
Massey, Raymond, 65
Massie, Paul, 84
Maté, Rudolf, 107
Matheson, Richard, 119, 132, 145, 148, 149
Matisse, Henri, 13
Maugham, Somerset, 53
Maurus, Gerda, 35
Maxwell, Lois, 153
May, Joe, 26
Mayer, Carl, 14, 15, 18
Mayer, Louis B., 41
Maze, The, 138; cast and credits, 214
McAvoy, May, 60
McCarthy, Kevin, 134
McKee, Raymond, 46
Megowan, Don, 137
Méliès, Georges, 2–8, 11, 17, 19, 66
Melville, Herman, 40
Mendes, Lothar, 54
Méndez, Fernando, 158, 159
Menjou, Adolphe, 44
Merrill, Judith, 119
Merritt, A. A., (Abraham), 57, 72

Merritt, Abraham, 57
Merry Go Round, 48
Mescall, John D., 68, 74
Metro-Goldwyn-Mayer, 42, 50, 51, 60, 65, 70, 71, 73, 76, 83, 102, 129
Metropolis, 25, 31–34, 36, 57, 134; cast and credits, 214
Mexico, 158–60
Meyrink, Gustav, 11
Midnight Sun, The, 54
Mighty Joe Young, 95, 96; cast and credits, 214
Milland, Ray, 116, 150
Ministry of Fear, 34
Miracle Man, The, 47
Miracles for Sale, 72; cast and credits, 214
Misérables, Les, 39
Misraki, Paul, 170
Moby Dick, 40
Mockery, 58
Molnar, Ferenc, 36
Monk, The, 9
Monlaur, Yvonne, 142
Monolith Monsters, The, 124; cast and credits, 214
Monster, The, 45, 50
Monster of Fate, The. See *Golem, Der* (1915).
Monster That Challenged the World, The, 132; cast and credits, 215
Monster Walks, The, 87; cast and credits, 215
Montana, Bull, 52
Moonstone, The, 39
Moore, Eva, 65
Moore, Terry, 95
Moreau, Gustave, xiii
Morgan, Ralph, 103
Morrow, Jeff, 128
Most Dangerous Game, The, 29, 96–98; cast and credits, 215
Mothra, 215
Motion Picture Daily, 52
Moussorgsky, Modest P., 18
Movin, Lisbeth, 110
Müde Tod, Der, 25, 26–28; cast and credits, 215
Mummy, The (1932), 73; cast and credits, 215–16
Mummy, The (1959), 142; cast and credits, 216
Mummy's Curse, The, 101; cast and credits, 216
Mummy's Ghost, The, 101; cast and credits, 216
Mummy's Hand, The, 100; cast and credits, 216
Mummy's Tomb, The, 101; cast and credits, 216
Munch, Edvard, 18
Murders in the Rue Morgue, 7, 19, 63, 72–73, 138; cast and credits, 217
Murnau, Friedrich Wilhelm, 19, 21–22, 23, 25, 54
Mutual, 39
Mysterians, The. See *Chikyu Boeigun.*
Mysterious Island, 42, 96; cast and credits, 217
Mystery of the Marie Celeste, The, 76
Mystery of the Wax Museum, 80–81, 138, 148; cast and credits, 217
Mystic, The, 69
My World Dies Screaming, 138; cast and credits, 217

Nagel, Conrad, 59
Naish, J. Carrol, 103
Naldi, Nita, 41
Nanny, The, 144; cast and credits, 218
Napier, Alan, 115
Naturalism, 13
Neal, Patricia, 126
Negri, Pola, 54
Neumann, Kurt, 121, 152
Neuss, Alwin, 41
New Statesman, The, 118
New York Times, The, 118
Niblungen, Der, 24, 25, 29–31; cast and credits, 218
Night Is the Phantom. See *Frusta e il Corpo, La.*
Night of Terror, 218
Night of the Demon, The, 115, 144–45; cast and credits, 218
Night of the Eagle, The, 115, 145; cast and credits, 218–19
Nosferatu, Eine Symphonie des Grauens, 21–23, 25, 38; cast and credits, 219
Novarro, Ramon, 53
Nutty Professor, The, 84
Nyby, Christian, 123, 124

Oberth, Hermann, 34, 120
O'Brien, Willis H., 52–53, 92, 93, 95, 96
Ocean Film Company, 39
O'Connor, Una, 64
Of Mice and Men, 100
Ogle, Charles, 39
Oland, Warner, 77
Old Dark House, 56, 65; cast and credits, 219
Oliver Twist, 47
On Borrowed Time, 86; cast and credits, 219
One Exciting Night, 43–44; cast and credits, 219
One Man Band, The, 4
One Million B.C., 52, 100–101; cast and credits, 219–20
Oppenheim, E. Phillips, 38
Orla, Ressel, 26

Orlacs Haende, 24, 73; cast and credits, 220
Orphée, 86; cast and credits, 220
Orpheus. See *Orphée.*
Orwell, George, 118
Osborne, Vivienne, 90
Oswald, Richard, 109
Ouspenskaya, Maria, 103
Outer Limits, The, xv
Owens, Patricia, 152

Padgett, Lewis, 119
Pain, Barry, 46
Pal, George, 120, 121, 122, 124
Paramount, 56, 60, 81, 84, 85, 86, 87, 90, 116, 121
Paranoia, 143
Parker, Eddie, 103
Passion of Joan of Arc, The, 105, 107, 110
Pathé, 7
Pausanias, 76
Peel, David, 143
Peeping Tom, 145–46, 157; cast and credits, 220
Perkins, Osgood, 45
Perrault, Pierre, 37
Peter Ibbetson, 86, 87; cast and credits, 220
Petronius, 77
Phantom from Space, The, 124; cast and credits, 221
Phantom of the Opera, The (1925), 47–50, 69; cast and credits, 221
Phantom of the Opera, The (1943), 81, 102; cast and credits, 221
Phantom of the Opera, The (1962), 142; cast and credits, 221
Phantom of the Rue Morgue, 138; cast and credits, 221–22
Philbin, Mary, 56
Pichel, Irving, 96
Pickford, Mary, 41
Picture of Dorian Gray, The, 40, 102; cast and credits, 222
Pied Piper of Hamelin, The, 11, 12
Pierce, Jack, 63, 78, 101, 103, 141
Pillow of Death, 101; cast and credits, 222
Pit and the Pendulum, The, 148, 150; cast and credits, 222
Plague of the Zombies, 144; cast and credits, 222
Planet Bura, 131; cast and credits, 222–23
Planet of the Vampires. See *Terrore nello Spazio.*
Plato, 76
Pleshette, Suzanne, 168
Poe, Edgar Allan, xi, 7, 10, 39, 42, 43, 72, 74, 75, 148, 149, 151
Poelzig, Hans, 20, 24
Pohl, Klaus, 34
Pommer, Erich, 14, 15, 16, 26, 29, 31, 36
Porter, Edwin S., 6
Powell, Michael, 145, 146
Powell, William, 60
Premature Burial, The, 148; cast and credits, 223
Price, Vincent, 139, 149, 150, 151, 152
Priestley, J. B., 65
Prisoner of Zenda, The, 82
Protozanov, Jacob, 19
Prunella, The Blue Bird, 42
Psycho, 145, 157; cast and credits, 223
Psychorama, 138
Puppetoons, 120
Puritan Passions, 45; cast and credits, 223
Putti, Lya de, 44, 54
Pygmalion and Galatea, 4

Quatermass Experiment, The, 133, 156; cast and credits, 223

Radcliffe, Ann, 9
Radford, Basil, 117
Rains, Claude, 65, 102
Randian the Living Torso, 70
Randolph, Jane, 112
Raptus, 156, 157; cast and credits, 223–24
Raskolnikov, 18
Rasp, Fritz, 35
Rasputin the Mad Monk, 143
Rathbone, Basil, 60, 98, 99, 103
Raven, The (1935), 75; cast and credits, 224
Raven, The (1963), 149; cast and credits, 224
Reason, Rex, 128
Redgrave, Michael, 117
Redon, Odilon, xiii
Red Planet Mars, 127–28, 131; cast and credits, 224
Red Shoes, The, 146
Reed, Oliver, 143
Reeve, Clara, 9
Reinhardt, Max, 11, 15, 20, 108
Reimann, Walter, 15, 18
Renard, Maurice, 24
Rennie, Michael, 125
Reptile, The, 144; cast and credits, 224
Repulsion, 157; cast and credits, 224–25
Return of Chandu, The, 109
Return of Dr. X, The, 99; cast and credits, 225
Return of Godzilla, The, 132
Return of Peter Grimm, The, 116
Return of the Fly, The, 152; cast and credits, 225

Return of the Vampire, The, 103; cast and credits, 225
Revenge of Frankenstein, The, 142, 145; cast and credits, 225
Revolt of the Zombies, The, 91; cast and credits, 225
Richter, Hans, 7
Riddle Gawne, 46
Rilke, Rainer Maria, 14
Rinehart, Mary Roberts, 38
Rippert, Otto, 13, 26
RKO Radio, 92, 95, 111, 115
Roach, Hal, 100
Road to Mandalay, The, 51
Robbins, Tod, 70
Robertson, John S., 41
Robinson, Ann, 125
Robinson Crusoe on Mars, 122; cast and credits, 226
Robles, Germán, 159
Robson, Mark, 113
Rocket Ship XM, 121; cast and credits, 226
Rodin, François Auguste René, 41
Roeg, Nicholas, 167
Rohmer, Sax, 38
Röhrig, Walter, 15, 18, 24
Roose, Thorkild, 109–10
Rose, Ruth, 92
Run for the Sun, 97; cast and credits, 226
Rural Delivery, 52
Russell, Elizabeth, 114
Russell, Gail, 116
Russell, Ray, 148
Rye, Stellan, 10

Sabu, 100
Sade, Marquis de, 9, 146
Salmonova, Lyda, 20
Sanders, George, 136
San Francisco, 95
Sangster, Jimmy, 142, 143
Santo contra las Mujeres Vampiro, 159; cast and credits, 226
Scaramouche, 53
Schayer, Richard, 62
Schloss Vogelöd, 21; cast and credits, 226
Schmitz, Sybille, 108–09
Schoedsack, Ernest, 91, 92, 95, 96
Schoenberg, Arnold, 18
Schreck, Max, 23
Schroeder, Greta, 22
Schutz, Maurice, 109
Science fiction films, 118–37, 161–71
Scob, Edith, 154
Seabrook, William B., 88
Secrets of the Sphinx, 26
Sedgwick, Edward, 48
Sei Donne per l'Assassino, 158; cast and credits, 226
Selig Polyscope Company, 7, 40
Selznick, David O., 92, 111
Seven Footprints to Satan, 57, 58; cast and credits, 227
Seventh Victim, The, 113–14; cast and credits, 227
Seventh Voyage of Sinbad, The, 96; cast and credits, 227
Shape of Things to Come, 32, 85, 122, 165; cast and credits, 227
She, 4
Shearer, Norma, 70
Shelley, Barbara, 136
Shelley, Mary, 12, 38, 62, 63, 141
Sheridan, Margaret, 123
Sherlock Holmes and the Great Murder Mystery, 7
Sherriff, R. C., 64, 65
"Shock Theatre," 140
Show, The, 69
Showboat, 69
Shuftan, Eugen, 31, 155
Sibelius, Jan, 86
Siegel, Don, 134
Simon, Simone, 112
Siodmak, Curt, 113
Siodmak, Robert, 101
Skull, The, 144; cast and credits, 227–28
Sloan, Edward Van, 61, 76
Sniper, The, 146; cast and credits, 228
Sondergaard, Gale, 103
Son of Dracula, 101; cast and credits, 228
Son of Frankenstein, 98–99; cast and credits, 228
Son of Kong, 95, 96; cast and credits, 228
Sorrows of Satan, The, 44; cast and credits, 228–29
Sound Era, 59
Space Children, The, 119; cast and credits, 229
Spaceways, 141; cast and credits, 229
Spettro, Lo, 156, 157; cast and credits, 229
Sphinx, The, 87; cast and credits, 229
Spiders, The. See *Spinnen, Die.*
Spinnen, Die, 15, 25, 26; cast and credits, 229–30
Spione, 34; cast and credits, 230
Standing, Percy Darrell, 39
Star Films, 5, 6, 7
Stark-Gesettenbaur, Gustl, 35
Steele, Barbara, 157
Steinbeck, John, 100
Steiner, Max, 93
Steinerne Reiter, Der, 24, 27; cast and credits, 230
Steinrück, Albert, 20
Stendhal, 14
Stephens, Martin, 147
Stern, Seymour, 43

Sternberg, Josef von, 44
Stevenson, Robert Louis, xiii, 7, 9, 19, 37, 81, 82, 83, 114
Stoker, Bram, 21, 22, 61, 141
Stone, Lewis, 52
Stone Rider. See *Steinerne Reiter, Der.*
Storm, Theodor, 24
Storm Planet. See *Planet Bura.*
Straight-Jacket, 139
Strange, Glenn, 64
Strange Confession, 101; cast and credits, 230
Stranglers of Bombay, 143
Strauss, Richard, 18
Stroheim, Erich von, 48, 72
Struss, Karl, 85
Stuart, Gloria, 66
Stuart, Ian, 119
Student von Prag (1913), 10–11, 24; cast and credits, 230
Student von Prag (1926), 24–25; cast and credits, 230–31
Stumar, Charles, 73, 159
Sturm, Der, 15
Sue, Eugène, 26
Sullivan, T. R., 39
Sunrise, 23
Supernatural, 90; cast and credits, 231
Svengali, 11, 79; cast and credits, 231
Svierkier, Anna, 109
Swift, Jonathan, 119
Swiss Family Robinson, The, 120
System of Dr. Tarr and Professor Fether, 7

Tales of Hoffmann, 146
Tales of Terror, 148; cast and credits, 231
Tandy, Jessica, 168
Tarantula, 132; cast and credits, 231
Taylor, Kent, 136
Taylor, Rod, 168
Technicolor, 80, 148, 156
Tell It to the Marines, 47
Tenth Victim. See *Decima Vittima, La.*
Terror, The (1928), 59–60, 150; cast and credits, 232
Terror, The (1963), 232
Terror from the Year 5000, The, 119; cast and credits, 232
Terrore nello Spazio, 158; cast and credits, 232
Terror of the Tongs, 143
Terry, Alice, 53, 54
Testament des Dr. Mabuse, Das, 35; cast and credits, 232
Testament du Dr. Cordelier, Le, 84; cast and credits, 232
Them!, 131–32; cast and credits, 232
Thesiger, Ernest, 65, 67
Thief of Bagdad, The, 100, 146; cast and credits, 233
Thing, The, 122–24, 125; cast and credits, 233
Things to Come. See *Shape of Things to Come.*
Thirteen Ghosts, 138; cast and credits, 233
Thirteenth Chair, The, 60; cast and credits, 233
Thirty-Nine Steps, The, 34
This Island Earth, 128–29, 132; cast and credits, 233
Thomas, Dylan, 114
Thomas l'Imposteur, 155
Three Chapters from Hamburg, 14
Three-dimensional films, 138
Three Wax Men. See *Wachsfigurenkabinett.*
Three Worlds of Gulliver, The, 96; cast and credits, 234
Thunder, 47
Tichenor, Edna, 51
Tilbury, Zeffie, 78
Tingler, The, 139; cast and credits, 234
Tobey, Kenneth, 123
Tomb of Ligeia, The, 151; cast and credits, 234
Topper, 116
Tourneur, Jacques, 112, 115, 144, 145
Tourneur, Maurice, 38, 41–42, 47, 79
Tower of London, 99; cast and credits, 234
Tracy, Spencer, 83
Transatlantic Tunnel, 122; cast and credits, 234–35
Travers, Henry, 66
Treasure Island, 42, 47
Tre Volti della Paura, I, 158; cast and credits, 235
Trick photography, discovery of, 3–6
Trifling Women, 53; cast and credits, 235
Trilby (1915), 42; cast and credits, 235
Trilby (1923), 79; cast and credits, 235
Trip to the Moon. See *Voyage dans la Lune, Le.*
Trois Lumières, Les. See *Müde Tod, Der.*
Truffaut, François, 167
Tsuburuya, Eiji, 132
Tunneling the English Channel, 6
Turhan Bey, 103
Turn of the Screw, The, 114, 116, 146, 147
Tuttle, Frank, 45
TV programs, 161–62
20th Century-Fox, 102, 151
Twenty Million Miles to Earth, 96; cast and credits, 235

Twenty-Seventh Day, The, 122; cast and credits, 235–36
Twenty Thousand Leagues Under the Sea, 162
Twilight Zone, The, xv
Two Faces of Dr. Jekyll, The, 84, 142; cast and credits, 236
Tyler, Tom, 100

UFA Studios, 19, 29, 33, 36
Ulmer, Edgar G., 74
Underwater City, The, 119; cast and credits, 236
Undying Monster, The, 102; cast and credits, 236
Unearthly Stranger, The, 136; cast and credits, 236
Unheimliche Geschichten, 109
Unholy Night, The, 60; cast and credits, 236–37
Unholy Three, The, 51, 60, 69, 70, 72; cast and credits, 237
Uninvited, The, 115, 116; cast and credits, 237
United Artists, 44
Universal, 47, 48, 50, 51, 57, 61, 62, 64, 67, 68, 73, 74, 75, 76, 77, 78, 79, 80, 81, 98, 99, 100, 101, 102, 103, 140, 141, 143, 145
Unknown, The, 51, 69; cast and credits, 237
Urban, Joseph, 46
Urueta, Chano, 158

Vadim, Roger, 76
Valentino, Rudolph, 53
Valli, Alida, 154
Vampire Bat, The, 87–88; cast and credits, 237
Vampires, Les, xiv, 26, 49
Vampiri, I, 99, 155–56, 157; cast and credits, 238
Vampiro, El, 159; cast and credits, 238
Vampyr, 76, 105–09, 110, 145; cast and credits, 238
Van Dine, S. S., 38
Van Doren, Carl, 147
Van Eyssen, John, 142
Van Gogh, Vincent, 13
Veidt, Conrad, 15, 19, 24, 54, 56, 57, 100
Venable, Evelyn, 86
Verne, Jules, 5, 42, 118, 162
Victor, Henry, 70
Victoria, Queen, 44
Victory, 47
Village of the Damned, The, 135–36; cast and credits, 238
Volpone, 42
Voyage dans la Lune, Le, 4–5; cast and credits, 238
Voyage to the End of the Universe. See *Ikaria XB1.*
Vredens Dag, 109–10; cast and credits, 239

Wachsfigurenkabinett, 55, 56; cast and credits, 239
Wagner, Richard, 31
Walbrook, Anton, 25
Walker, Stuart, 77
Walking Dead, The, 76, 99; cast and credits, 239
Wallace, Edgar, 38, 59, 92
Walsh, Raoul, 25
Walthall, Henry B., 43
Walton, Douglas, 67
Wangenheim, Gustav von, 22, 35
Warm, Hermann, 15, 18
Warner Brothers, 59, 76, 79, 80, 96, 99, 103
Warning, The, 38
War of the Satellites, 119; cast and credits, 239
War of the Worlds, The, 122, 124–25, 132; cast and credits, 239
Waterloo Bridge, 63
Waxman, Franz, 68, 83
Wayne, Naunton, 117
Wegener, Paul, 11–12, 20, 21, 54, 79
Weird Woman, 101, 145; cast and credits, 240
Weiss, Erich (Houdini), 2
Wells, Brember, 65
Wells, H. G., 5, 32, 46, 65, 84, 85, 119, 124, 125, 150, 162, 165
Wendhausen, Fritz, 24
Werewolf of London, The, 77–78; cast and credits, 240
West, Julian, 109
West of Zanzibar, 51, 69
Whale, James, 63–64, 67, 68–69, 73, 100, 141
What Ever Happened to Baby Jane?, 144; cast and credits, 240
When Worlds Collide, 121; cast and credits, 240
While Paris Sleeps, 42, 47; cast and credits, 240
White Zombie, 76, 88–90, 91, 109, 141; cast and credits, 240–41
Wieck, Dorothea, 25
Wiene, Robert, 15, 18, 24
Wilde, Oscar, 40, 102
Wilhelm II, Kaiser, 31
Willard, John, 55
Williams, Grant, 132
Willis, Matt, 103
Windsor, Marie, 136
Wise, Robert, 126, 152, 153
Witchcraft Through the Ages. See *Häxan.*

Without Warning, 146
Wizard, The, 57; cast and credits, 241
Wizard of Oz, The, xiv
Wolf Man, The, 78, 101; cast and credits, 241
Woman in the Moon. See *Frau im Mond.*
Woman in White, The, 39
Woolrich, Cornell, 113
Wordsworth, Richard, 133
Worsley, Wallace, 47
Wozzeck, xii
Wray, Ardel, 113
Wray, Fay, 80, 81, 87, 93, 103
Wycherly, Margaret, 60
Wylie, Philip, 65, 85, 121
Wyndham, John, 119, 135
Wynter, Dana, 135

X, The Man with the X-ray Eyes, 150; cast and credits, 241
Yeux sans Visage, Les, 154–55; cast and credits, 241
Young Diana, 241

Zeller, Wolfgang, 109
Zucco, George, 103

GHOSTS

Ralph Lewis is haunted by the specter of greed in *The Conquering Power* (1922).

Ray Milland, Ruth Hussey, and Gail Russell in *The Uninvited* (1944).

Deborah Kerr and Peter Wyngarde in *The Innocents,* a 1961 adaptation of Henry James' *The Turn of the Screw.*

THE LABORATORY

Pedro de Cordoba and Marion Davies in *Young Diana* (1922).

Paul Wegener in *The Magician* (1926).

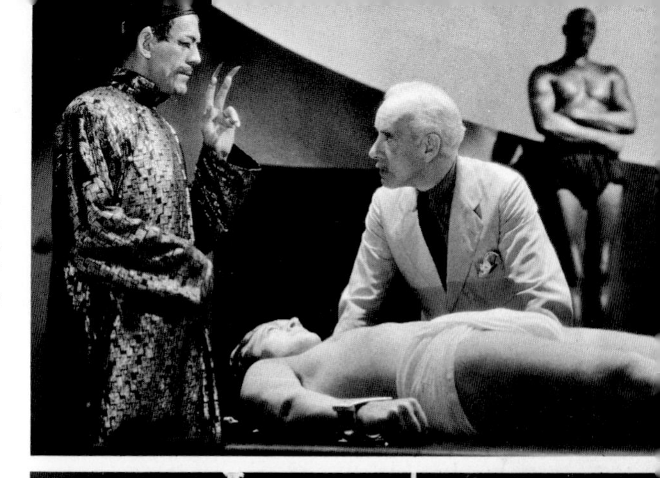

Boris Karloff, Charles Starrett, and Lewis Stone in *The Mask of Fu Manchu* (1932).

Lionel Atwill and Fay Wray in *The Vampire Bat* (1933).

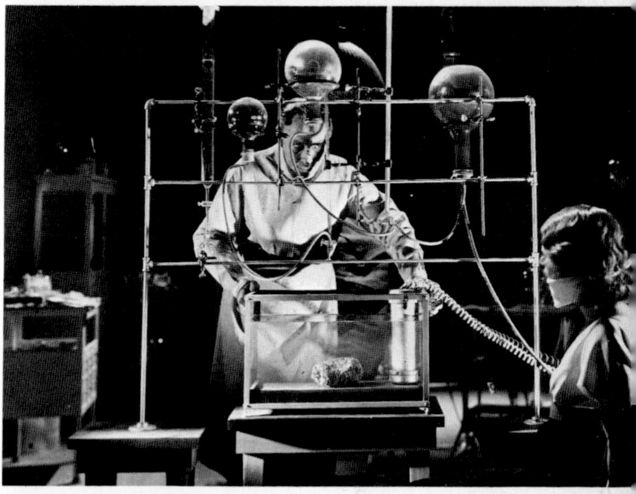

Oscar Quitak in *The Revenge of Frankenstein* (1958).

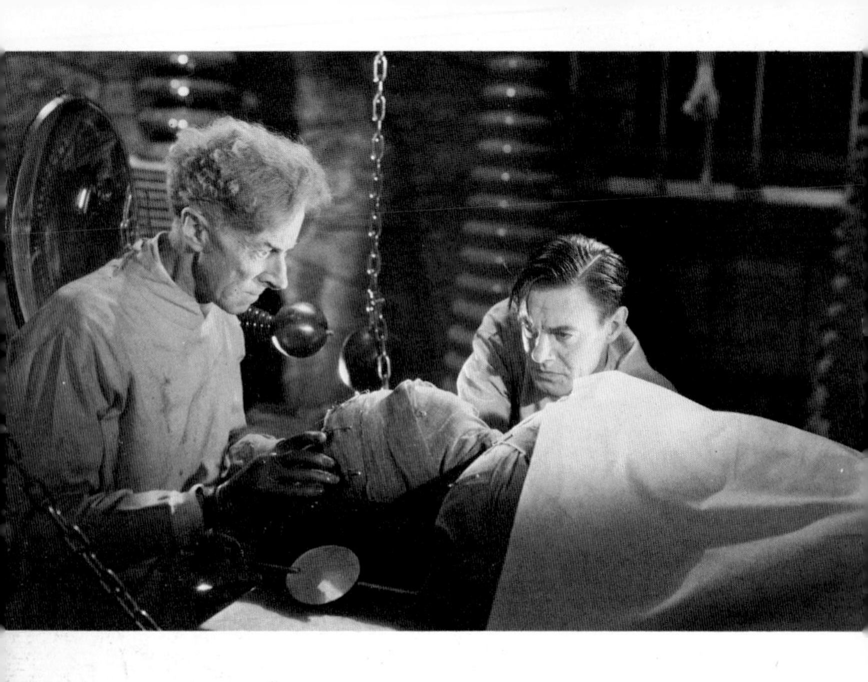

HOW TO MAKE A MONSTER

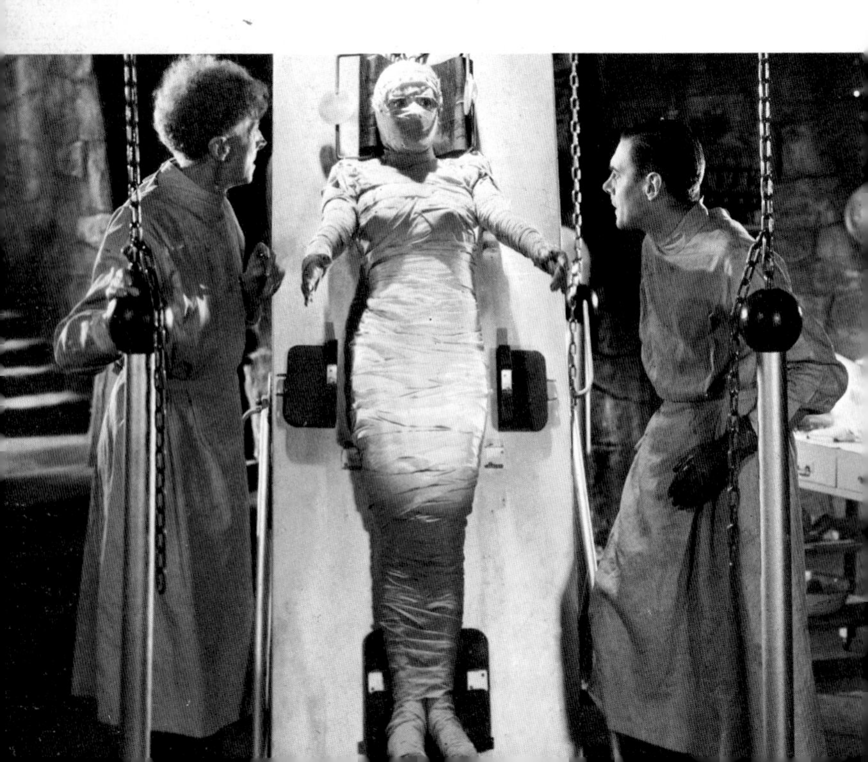

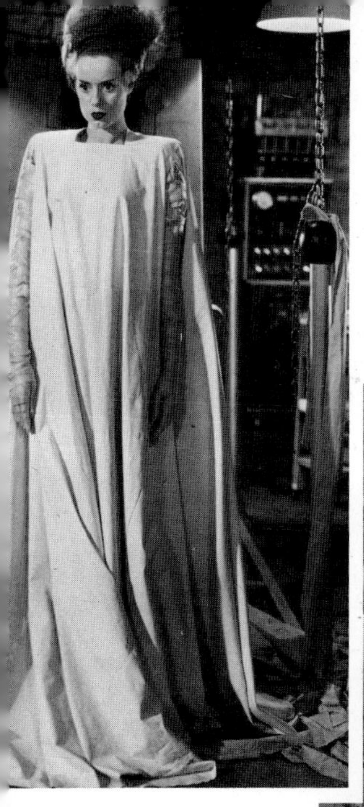

An artificial woman (Elsa Lanchester) is created by Dr. Clive) and Dr. Frankenstein (Colin Pretorius (Ernest Thesiger) as a mate for the Monster (Boris Karloff). The most famous sequence from *The Bride of Frankenstein* (1935).

VAMPIRES

Max Schreck as Count Orlock in *Nosferatu* (1922), an unauthorized adaptation of Bram Stoker's novel *Dracula*, made in Germany by F. W. Murnau.

Lon Chaney and Edna Tichenor as the vampire couple of *London After Midnight* (1927).

Bela Lugosi and Carol Borland in the 1935 remake retitled *The Mark of the Vampire.*

Gloria Holden as *Dracula's Daughter* (1936).

Louise Allbritton and Lon Chaney, Jr., in *Son of Dracula* (1943).

HOW TO DESTROY

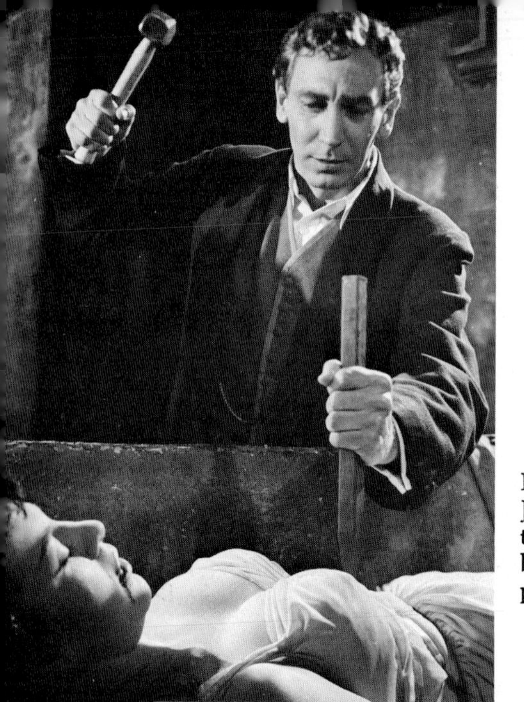

In the British *Dracula* (1958), John Van Eyssen drives a stake through the heart of young, buxom Valerie Gaunt with surprising results.

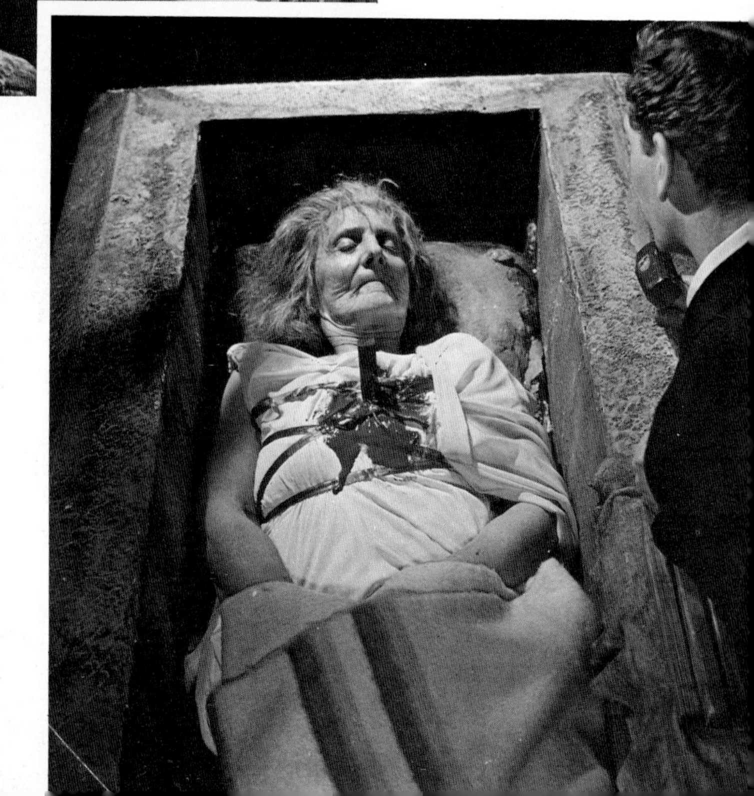

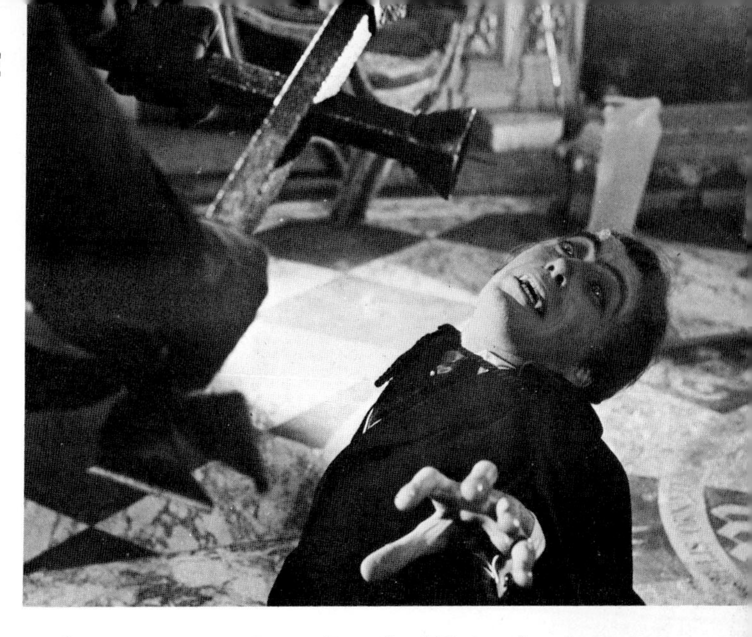

In the same movie, Count Dracula (Christopher Lee) is destroyed by a makeshift cross and the light of day.

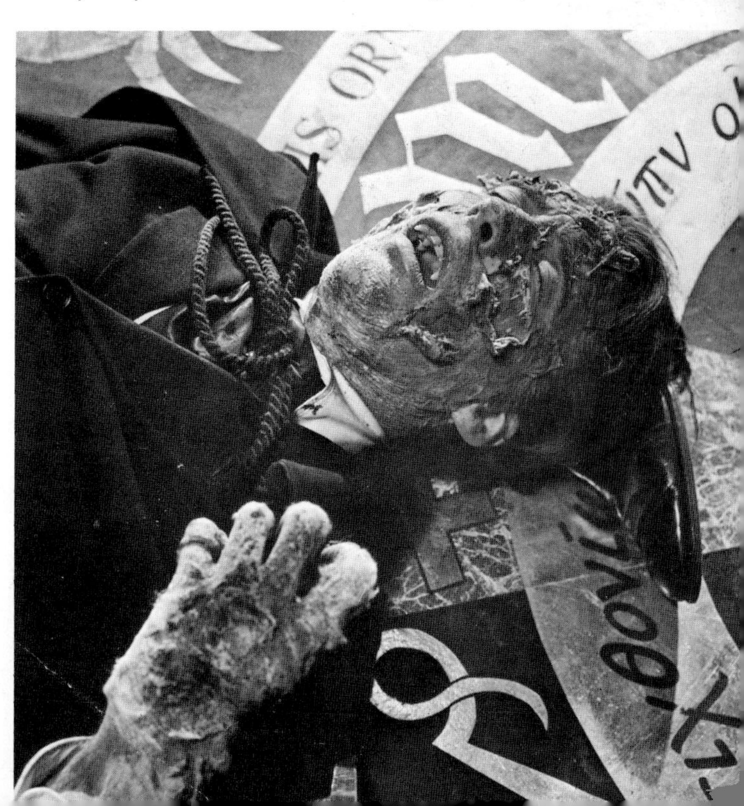

KARLOFF

As a mesmerist patterned after Dr. Caligari in *The Bells* (1926).

Being made up as *The Mummy* (1932).

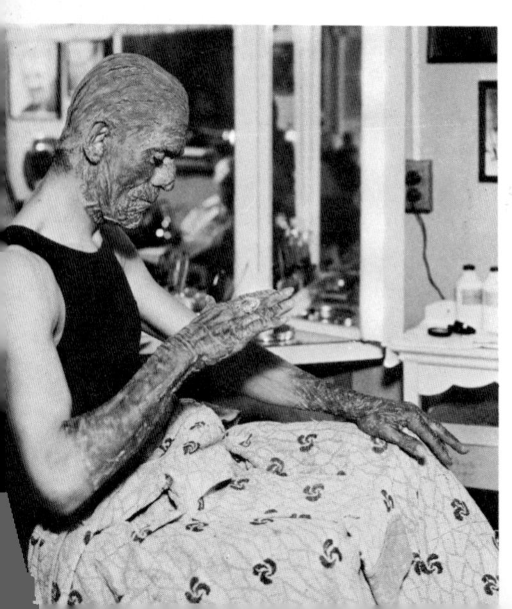

In the British-made *The Gh* (1933).

In *Old Dark House* (1932).

LUGOSI

In *Dracula* (1931).

In *Murders in the Rue Morgue* (1932).

In *White Zombie* (1932).

Ricardo Cortez in *The Sorrows of Satan* (1925).

Carrie Daumery in *The Last Warning* (1929).

THE FACE OF TERROR

Patricia Owens in *The Fly* (1958).

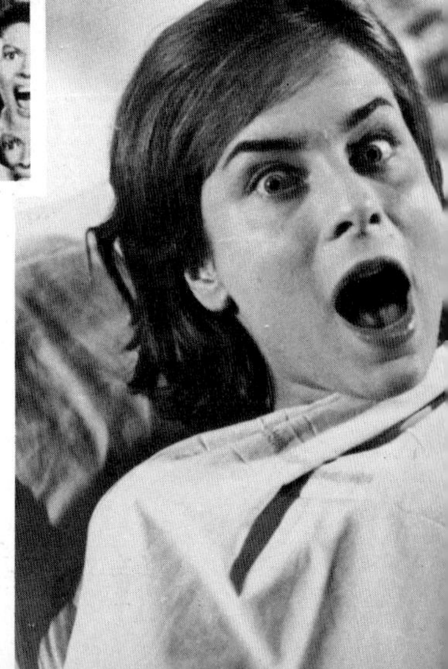

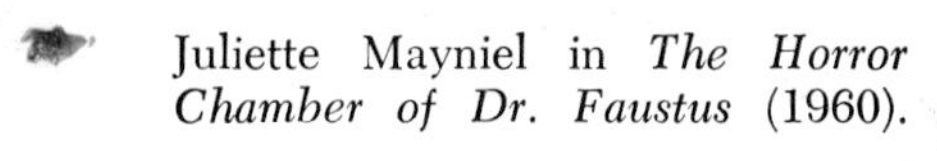

Juliette Mayniel in *The Horror Chamber of Dr. Faustus* (1960).

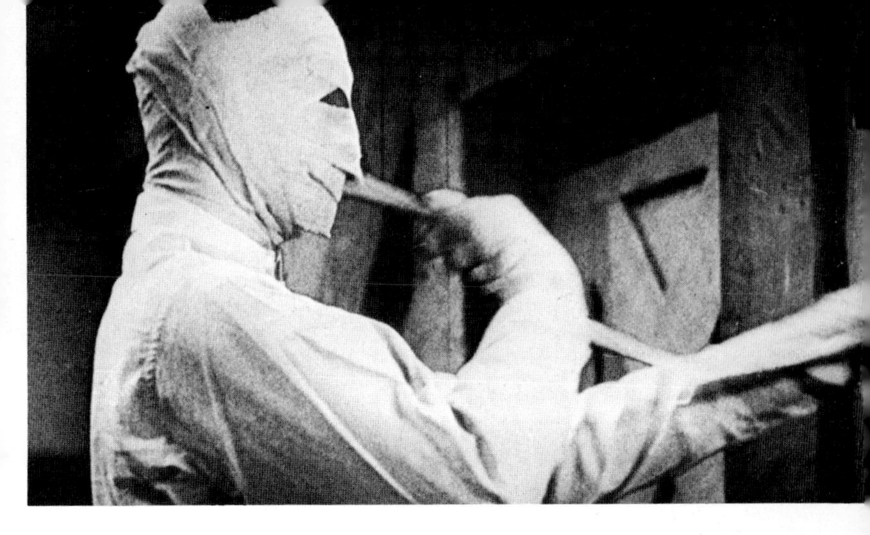

The Invisible Man (Vincent Price) removes his bandages to reveal . . . nothing. A superb example of John P. Fulton's special effects for *The Invisible Man Returns* (1940).

SUSPENSION OF DISBELIEF

Sinbad (Kerwin Mathews) fights a duel with a skeleton in *The Seventh Voyage of Sinbad* (1958), the work of animator Ray Harryhausen.

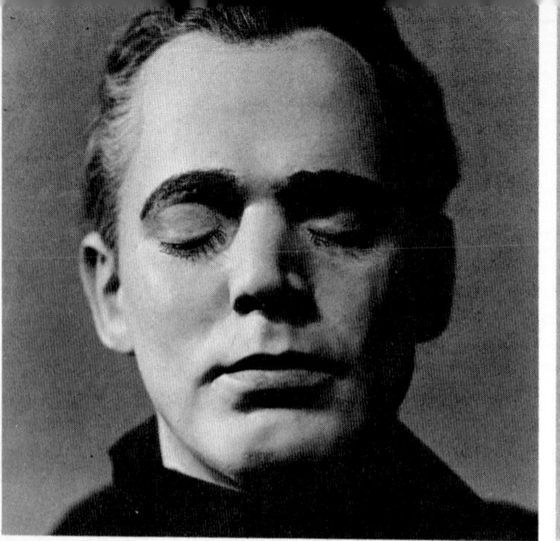

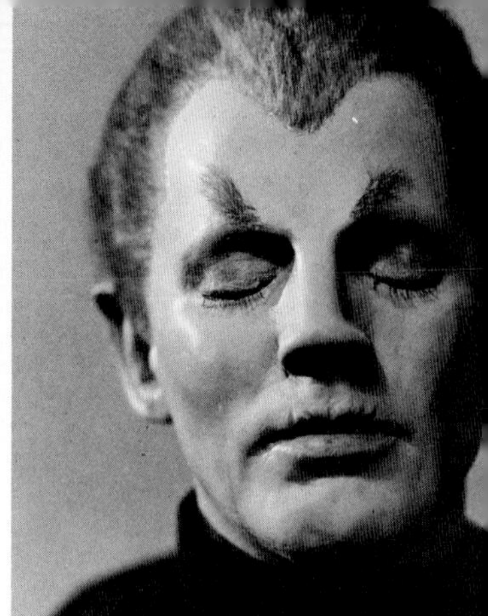

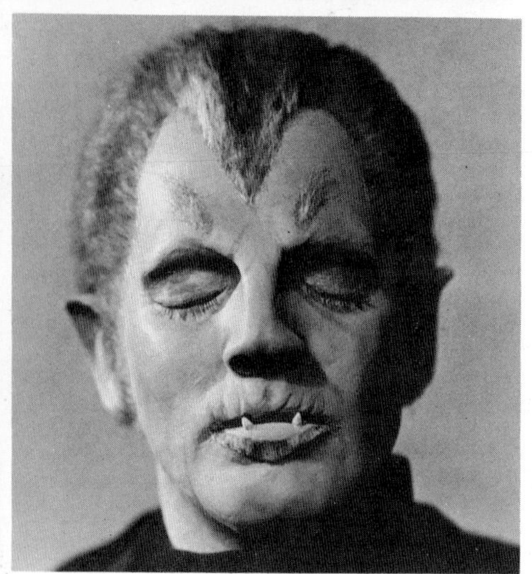

Henry Hull in *The Werewolf of London* (1935). Makeup created by Jack Pierce.

MAN INTO WOLF

Nina Foch and Matt Willis in *The Return of the Vampire* (1944).

Lou Costello and Lon Chaney, Jr., in *Abbott and Costello Meet Frankenstein* (1948).

Oliver Reed in *The Curse of the Werewolf* (1961). Makeup created by Roy Ashton.

THE BESTIARY

Lon Chaney as an ape-man in *A Blind Bargain* (1922). The gorilla-man on the right has proven unidentifiable.

Gustav Von Seyffertitz and George Kotsonaros in *The Wizard* (1927).

Charles Laughton as Wells' Dr. Moreau in *Island of Lost Souls* (1933). The hirsute hybrid in the center is Bela Lugosi.

Lawyer Crosby (Tully Marshall) about to be clutched by the Cat in *The Cat and the Canary* (1927).

THE CLUTCHING HAND

More than a decade later the same hand threatens Paulette Goddard in the 1939 remake of the successful play.

Alice Day in *The Gorilla* (1927).

Thelma Todd and Sheldon Lewis in *Seven Footprints to Satan* (1929).

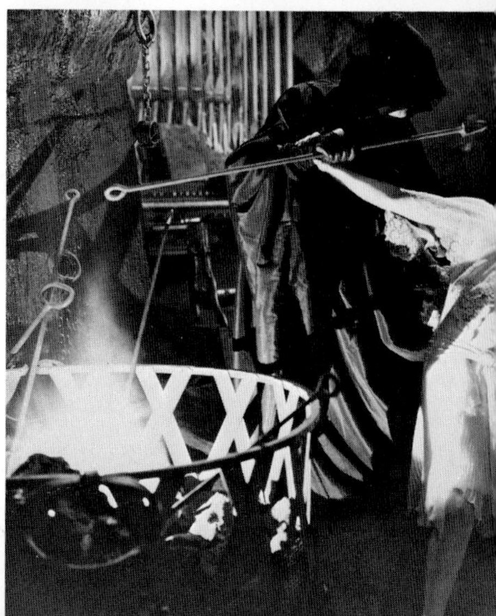

May McAvoy in the first all-talking horror movie, *The Terror* (1928).

Jean Marais and Josette Day in Jean Cocteau's straight version of Madame LePrince de Beaumont's fairy tale, *Beauty and the Beast* (1946).

Julia Adams and Ricou Browning in *Creature from the Black Lagoon* (1954).

In 1925, Willis J. O'Brien animated some excellent miniature models for *The Lost World,* based on Conan Doyle's "scientific romance."

The peak of O'Brien's art: *King Kong* (1933).

COLOSSAL

The Beast from 20,000 Fathoms invades lower Manhattan. Ray Harryhausen was responsible for the special effects of this 1953 thriller.

Above, Ernest Thesiger as Dr. Pretorius displays his menagerie of homunculi in *The Bride of Frankenstein* (1935).

Grace Ford as a deadly, living doll in *The Devil Doll* (1936).

Albert Dekker and Charles Halton in *Dr. Cyclops* (1940). The shot is a superb combination of back-screen projection and an outsized hand.

MINUSCULE

The Incredible Shrinking Man (Grant Williams) fights off the attack of his own cat in this 1957 classic.

Conrad Veidt as Gwynplaine in the 1928 adaptation of Victor Hugo's *The Man Who Laughs*.

Leslie Banks as Count Zaroff in *The Most Dangerous Game* (1932).

Lionel Atwill as the scarred proprietor of a waxworks in *Mystery of the Wax Museum* (1933).

Peter Lorre as the maniacal scientist of *Mad Love* (1935).

Olga Baclanova, the once-beautiful trapeze artist maimed by the circus freaks in *Freaks* (1932).

Jacqueline Pearce as the Snake Woman attacks Jennifer Daniel in *The Reptile* (1966).

Acquanetta as Paula the Ape Woman in *Captive Wild Woman* (1943).

VAMPYR

Scenes from Carl Dreyer's 1932 masterpiece. Sybille Schmitz as Leone, the Vampire's victim.

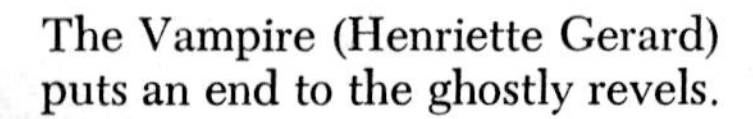

The Vampire (Henriette Gerard) puts an end to the ghostly revels.

The Vampire peeks through the transom of David Gray's coffin.

David (Julian West) sees himself in the coffin.

PSYCHOLOGICAL TERROR

These stills almost succeed in capturing some of the eerie, elusive moods of the Val Lewton films.

Frances Dee and Christine Gordon in *I Walked with a Zombie* (1943).

Katherine Emery and Jason Robards in *Isle of the Dead* (1945).

Jean Brooks is condemned to death by poison by her fellow devil-worshipers in *The Seventh Victim* (1943).

Metropolis (1926).

THE WORLD OF TOMORROW

Just Imagine (1930).

Shape of Things to Come (1936)

AND OTHER WORLDS

An American expedition lands on the Moon in George Pal's *Destination Moon* (1950).

The Czechoslovakian *Ikaria XB1* (1963) was set aboard a gigantic spaceship headed for a distant star.

An uneasy mixture of old and new themes was *Planet of the Vampires* (1965).

Scientists and the military discuss what to do with a visitor from outer space imprisoned in a block of ice in *The Thing* (1951).

THINGS FROM OUTER SPACE

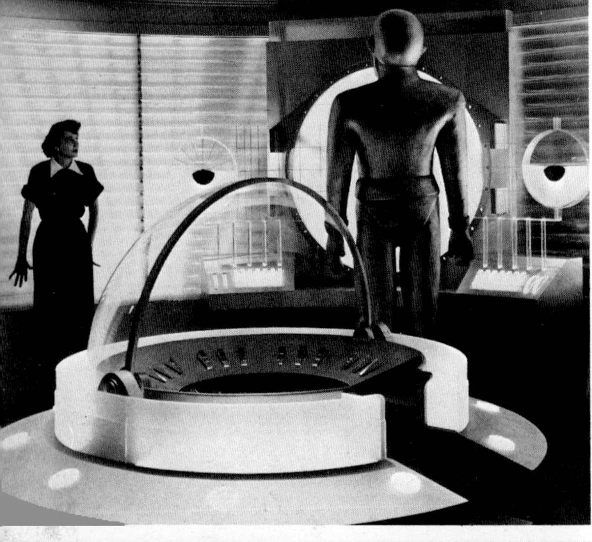

Patricia Neal saves the world in *The Day the Earth Stood Still* (1951).

A spaceship has buried itself in a crater hole in the Arizona Desert in *It Came from Outer Space* (1953).

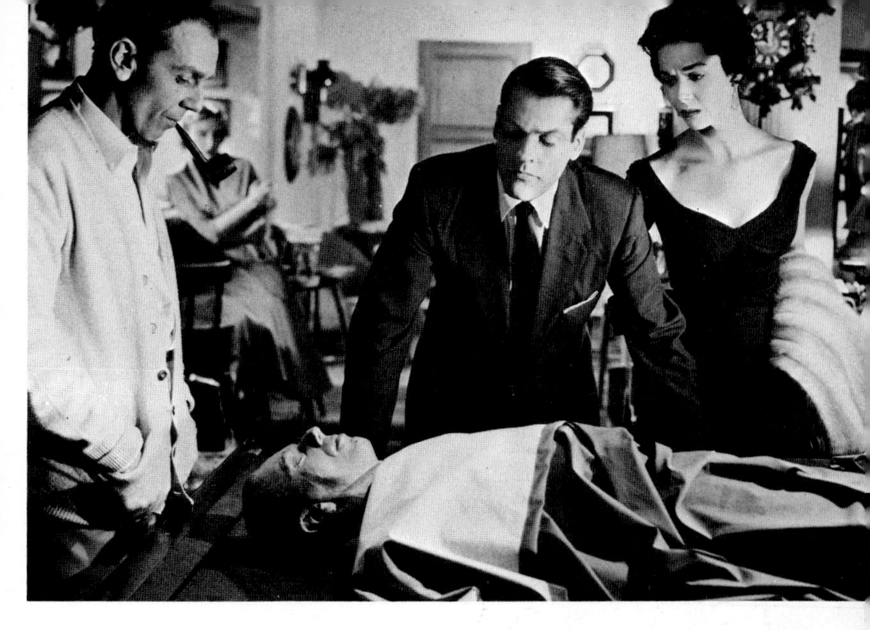

A perfect human counterfeit seems to shape up before the eyes of King Donovan, Carolyn Jones, Kevin McCarthy, and Dana Wynter in *Invasion of the Body Snatchers* (1956).

Martin Stephens is the leader of some unearthly children in *The Village of the Damned* (1960).

END OF THE WORLD

New York is destroyed by a tidal wave in George Pal's *When Worlds Collide* (1951). This and other such sequences won the film an Academy Award for Special Effects.

The world ends not with a bang but with a chirp in Alfred Hitchcock's *The Birds* (1963).

Macdonald Carey and Shirley Ann Field are inspected by a group of "ice-cold" children conditioned to survive atomic warfare, in *The Damned* (1961).

Lemmy Caution (Eddie Constantine) arrives in Alphaville to destroy the omniscient Alpha-60 in Jean-Luc Godard's *Alphaville* (1965).

SCIENCE FICTION IN THE AGE OF ANXIETY

The book-burning brigade in François Truffaut's *Fahrenheit 451* (1966), adapted from the novel by Ray Bradbury.

3

-6038-